MYRTLEFIELD
HOUSE

FINDING ULTIMATE REALITY

THE QUEST FOR REALITY AND SIGNIFICANCE

BOOK 2

FINDING ULTIMATE REALITY

IN SEARCH OF THE BEST ANSWERS TO THE BIGGEST QUESTIONS

DAVID GOODING
JOHN LENNOX

Myrtlefield House
Belfast, Northern Ireland

Cover design: Frank Gutbrod.
Interior design and composition: Sharon VanLoozenoord.

Published by The Myrtlefield Trust
PO Box 2216
Belfast, N Ireland, BT1 9YR
w: www.myrtlefieldhouse.com
e: info@myrtlefieldhouse.com

ISBN: 978-1-912721-05-4 (hbk.)
ISBN: 978-1-912721-06-1 (pbk.)
ISBN: 978-1-912721-07-8 (PDF)
ISBN: 978-1-912721-08-5 (Kindle)
ISBN: 978-1-912721-09-2 (EPUB without DRM)
ISBN: 978-1-912721-30-6 (box set)

23 22 21 20 19   10 9 8 7 6 5 4 3

DEDICATED TO OUR YOUNGER FELLOW STUDENTS,

REMEMBERING THAT WE WERE ONCE STUDENTS—AND STILL ARE

CONTENTS

BOOK 2: FINDING ULTIMATE REALITY

IN SEARCH OF THE BEST ANSWERS TO THE BIGGEST QUESTIONS

ILLUSTRATIONS

SERIES PREFACE

The average student has a problem—many problems in fact, but one in particular. No longer a child, he or she is entering adult life and facing the torrent of change that adult independence brings. It can be exhilarating but sometimes also frightening to have to stand on one's own feet, to decide for oneself how to live, what career to follow, what goals to aim at and what values and principles to adopt.

How are such decisions to be made? Clearly much thought is needed and increasing knowledge and experience will help. But leave these basic decisions too long and there is a danger of simply drifting through life and missing out on the character-forming process of thinking through one's own worldview. For that is what is needed: a coherent framework that will give to life a true perspective and satisfying values and goals. To form such a worldview for oneself, particularly at a time when society's traditional ideas and values are being radically questioned, can be a very daunting task for anyone, not least university students. After all, worldviews are normally composed of many elements drawn from, among other sources, science, philosophy, literature, history and religion; and a student cannot be expected to be an expert in any one of them, let alone in all of them (indeed, is any one of us?).

Nevertheless we do not have to wait for the accumulated wisdom of life's later years to see what life's major issues are; and once we grasp what they are, it is that much easier to make informed and wise decisions of every kind. It is as a contribution to that end that the authors offer this series of books to their younger fellow students. We intend that each book will stand on its own while also contributing to the fuller picture provided by the whole series.

So we begin by laying out the issues at stake in an extended introduction that overviews the fundamental questions to be asked, key voices to be listened to, and why the meaning and nature of ultimate reality matter to each one of us. For it is inevitable that each one of us will, at some time and at some level, have to wrestle with the fundamental questions of our existence. Are we meant to be here, or is it really by accident that we are? In what sense, if any, do we matter, or are we simply rather insignificant specks inhabiting an insubstantial corner of our galaxy? Is there a purpose in it all? And if indeed it does matter, where would we find reliable answers to these questions?

In Book 1, *Being Truly Human*, we consider questions surrounding the value of humans. Besides thinking about human freedom and the dangerous way it is often devalued, we consider the nature and basis of morality and how other moralities compare with one another. For any discussion of the freedom humans have to choose raises the question of the power we wield over other humans and also over nature, sometimes with disastrous consequences. What should guide our use of power? What, if anything, should limit our choices, and to what extent can our choices keep us from fulfilling our full potential and destiny?

The realities of these issues bring before us another problem. It is not the case that, having developed a worldview, life will unfold before us automatically and with no new choices. Quite the opposite. All of us from childhood onward are increasingly faced with the practical necessity of making ethical decisions about right and wrong, fairness and injustice, truth and falsity. Such decisions not only affect our individual relationships with people in our immediate circle: eventually they play their part in developing the social and moral tone of each nation and, indeed, of the world. We need, therefore, all the help we can get in learning how to make truly ethical decisions.

But ethical theory inevitably makes us ask what is the ultimate authority behind ethics. Who or what has the authority to tell us: you ought to do this, or you ought not to do that? If we cannot answer that question satisfactorily, the ethical theory we are following lacks a sufficiently solid and effective base. Ultimately, the answer to this question unavoidably leads us to the wider philosophical question: how are we related to the universe of which we form a part? What is the nature of ultimate reality? Is there a creator who made us and built into us our moral awareness, and requires us to live according to his laws? Or, are human beings the product of mindless, amoral forces that care nothing about ethics, so that as a human race we are left to make up our own ethical rules as best we can, and try to get as much general agreement to them as we can manage, either by persuasion or even, regretfully, by force?

For this reason, we have devoted Book 2, *Finding Ultimate Reality*, to a discussion of Ultimate Reality; and for comparison we have selected views and beliefs drawn from various parts of the world and from different centuries: the Indian philosophy of Shankara; the natural and moral philosophies of the ancient Greeks, with one example of Greek mysticism; modern atheism and naturalism; and finally, Christian theism.

The perusal of such widely differing views, however, naturally provokes further questions: how can we know which of them, if any, is true? And what is truth anyway? Is there such a thing as absolute truth? And how should we recognise it, even if we encountered it? That, of course, raises the fundamental question that affects not only scientific and philosophical theories, but our day-to-day experience as well: how do we know anything?

The part of philosophy that deals with these questions is known as epistemology, and to it we devote Book 3, *Questioning Our Knowledge*. Here we pay special attention to a theory that has found wide popularity in recent times, namely, postmodernism. We pay close attention to it, because if it were true (and we think it isn't) it would seriously affect not only ethics, but science and the interpretation of literature.

When it comes to deciding what are the basic ethical principles that all should universally follow we should observe that we are not the first generation on earth to have thought about this question. Book 4, *Doing What's Right*, therefore, presents a selection of notable but diverse ethical theories, so that we may profit from their insights that are of permanent value; and, at the same time, discern what, if any, are their weaknesses, or even fallacies.

But any serious consideration of humankind's ethical behaviour will eventually raise another practical problem. As Aristotle observed long ago, ethics can tell us what we ought to do; but by itself it gives us no adequate power to do it. It is the indisputable fact that, even when we know that something is ethically right and that it is our duty to do it, we fail to do it; and contrariwise, when we know something is wrong and should not be done, we nonetheless go and do it. Why is that? Unless we can find an answer to this problem, ethical theory—of whatever kind—will prove ultimately ineffective, because it is impractical.

Therefore, it seemed to us that it would be seriously deficient to deal with ethics simply as a philosophy that tells us what ethical standards we ought to attain to in life. Our human plight is that, even when we know that something is wrong, we go and do it anyway. How can we overcome this universal weakness?

Jesus Christ, whose emphasis on ethical teaching is unmistakable, and in some respects unparalleled, nevertheless insisted that ethical teaching is ineffective unless it is preceded by a spiritual rebirth (see Gospel of John 3). But this brings us into the area of religion, and many people find that difficult. What right has religion to talk about ethics, they say, when religion has been the cause of so many wars, and still leads to much violence? But the same is true of political philosophies—and it does not stop us thinking about politics.

Then there are many religions, and they all claim to offer their adherents help to fulfil their ethical duties. How can we know if they are true, and that they offer real hope? It seems to us that, in order to know whether the help a religion offers is real or not, one would have to practise that religion and discover it by experience. We, the authors of this book, are Christians, and we would regard it as impertinent of us to try to describe what other religions mean to their adherents. Therefore, in Book 5, *Claiming to Answer,* we confine ourselves to stating why we think the claims of the Christian gospel are valid, and the help it offers real.

However, talk of God raises an obvious and very poignant problem: how can there be a God who cares for justice, when, apparently, he makes no attempt to put a stop to the injustices that ravage our world? And how can it be thought that there is an all-loving, all-powerful, and all-wise creator when so many people suffer such bad things, inflicted on them not just by man's cruelty but by natural disasters and disease? These are certainly difficult questions. It is the purpose of Book 6, *Suffering Life's Pain,* to discuss these difficulties and to consider possible solutions.

It only remains to point out that every section and subsection of the book is provided with questions, both to help understanding of the subject matter and to encourage the widest possible discussion and debate.

DAVID GOODING
JOHN LENNOX

ANALYTICAL OUTLINE

FINDING
ULTIMATE REALITY

SERIES INTRODUCTION

Our worldview . . . includes our views,
however ill or well thought out, right or
wrong, about the hard yet fascinating
questions of existence and life: What am I
to make of the universe? Where did it come
from? Who am I? Where did I come from?
How do I know things? Do I have any
significance? Do I have any duty?

THE SHAPING OF A WORLDVIEW
FOR A LIFE FULL OF CHOICES

In this introductory section we are going to consider the need for each one of us to construct his or her own worldview. We shall discuss what a worldview is and why it is necessary to form one; and we shall enquire as to what voices we must listen to as we construct our worldview. As we set out to examine how we understand the world, we are also trying to discover whether we can know the ultimate truth about reality. So each of the subjects in this series will bring us back to the twin questions of what is real and why it matters whether we know what is real. We will, therefore, need to ask as we conclude this introductory section what we mean by 'reality' and then to ask: what is the nature of ultimate reality?[1]

WHY WE NEED A WORLDVIEW

There is a tendency in our modern world for education to become a matter of increasing specialisation. The vast increase of knowledge during the past century means that unless we specialise in this or that topic it is very difficult to keep up with, and grasp the significance of, the ever-increasing flood of new discoveries. In one sense this is to be welcomed because it is the result of something that in itself is one of the marvels of our modern world, namely, the fantastic progress of science and technology.

But while that is so, it is good to remind ourselves that true education has a much wider objective than this. If, for instance, we are to understand the progress of our modern world, we must see it against

---

[1] Please note this Introduction is the same for each book in the series, except for the final section—Our Aim.

the background of the traditions we have inherited from the past and that will mean that we need to have a good grasp of history.

Sometimes we forget that ancient philosophers faced and thought deeply about the basic philosophical principles that underlie all science and came up with answers from which we can still profit. If we forget this, we might spend a lot of time and effort thinking through the same problems and not coming up with as good answers as they did.

Moreover, the role of education is surely to try and understand how all the various fields of knowledge and experience in life fit together. To understand a grand painting one needs to see the picture as a whole and understand the interrelationship of all its details and not simply concentrate on one of its features.

Moreover, while we rightly insist on the objectivity of science we must not forget that it is we who are doing the science. And therefore, sooner or later, we must come to ask how we ourselves fit into the universe that we are studying. We must not allow ourselves to become so engrossed in our material world and its related technologies that we neglect our fellow human beings; for they, as we shall later see, are more important than the rest of the universe put together.[2] The study of ourselves and our fellow human beings will, of course, take more than a knowledge of science. It will involve the worlds of philosophy, sociology, literature, art, music, history and much more besides.

Educationally, therefore, it is an important thing to remember—and a thrilling thing to discover—the interrelation and the unity of all knowledge. Take, for example, what it means to know what a rose is: *What is the truth about a rose?*

To answer the question adequately, we shall have to consult a whole array of people. First the scientists. We begin with the *botanists*, who are constantly compiling and revising lists of all the known plants and flowers in the world and then classifying them in terms of families and groups. They help us to appreciate our rose by telling us what family it belongs to and what are its distinctive features.

Next, the *plant breeders* and *gardeners* will inform us of the history of our particular rose, how it was bred from other kinds, and the conditions under which its sort can best be cultivated.

---

2   Especially in Book 1 of this series, *Being Truly Human.*

FIGURE I.1. A Rose.

In William Shakespeare's play *Romeo and Juliet*, the beloved dismisses the fact that her lover is from the rival house of Montague, invoking the beauty of one of the best known and most favourite flowers in the world: 'What's in a name? that which we call a rose / By any other name would smell as sweet'.

Reproduced with permission of ©iStock/OGphoto.

Then, the *chemists, biochemists, biologists* and *geneticists* will tell us about the chemical and biochemical constituents of our rose and the bewildering complexities of its cells, those micro-miniaturised factories which embody mechanisms more complicated than any built by human beings, and yet so tiny that we need highly specialised equipment to see them. They will tell us about the vast coded database of genetic information which the cell factories use in order to produce the building blocks of the rose. They will describe, among a host of other things, the processes by which the rose lives: how it photosynthesises sunlight into sugar-borne energy and the mechanisms by which it is pollinated and propagated.

After that, the *physicists* and *cosmologists* will tell us that the chemicals of which our rose is composed are made up of atoms which themselves are built from various particles like electrons, protons and neutrons. They will give us their account of where the basic material in the universe comes from and how it was formed. If we ask how such knowledge helps us to understand roses, the cosmologists may well point out that our earth is the only planet in our solar system that is able to grow roses! In that respect, as in a multitude of other respects, our planet is very special—and that is surely something to be wondered at.

But when the botanists, plant breeders, gardeners, chemists, biochemists, physicists and cosmologists have told us all they can, and it is a great deal which would fill many volumes, even then many of us will feel that they will scarcely have begun to tell us the truth about roses. Indeed, they have not explained what perhaps most of us would think is the most important thing about roses: the beauty of their form, colour and fragrance.

Now here is a very significant thing: scientists can explain the astonishing complexity of the mechanisms which lie behind our senses of vision and smell that enable us to see roses and detect their scent. But we don't need to ask the scientists whether we ought to consider roses beautiful or not: we can see and smell that for ourselves! We perceive this by *intuition*. We just look at the rose and we can at once see that it is beautiful. We do not need anyone to tell us that it is beautiful. If anyone were so foolish as to suggest that because science cannot measure beauty, therefore beauty does not exist, we should simply say: 'Don't be silly.'

But the perception of beauty does not rest on our own intuition alone. We could also consult the *artists*. With their highly developed sense of colour, light and form, they will help us to perceive a depth and intensity of beauty in a rose that otherwise we might miss. They can educate our eyes.

Likewise, there are the *poets*. They, with their finely honed ability as word artists, will use imagery, metaphor, allusion, rhythm and rhyme to help us formulate and articulate the feelings we experience when we look at roses, feelings that otherwise might remain vague and difficult to express.

Finally, if we wanted to pursue this matter of the beauty of a rose deeper still, we could talk to the *philosophers*, especially experts in aesthetics. For each of us, perceiving that a rose is beautiful is a highly subjective experience, something that we see and feel at a deep level inside ourselves. Nevertheless, when we show a rose to other people, we expect them too to agree that it is beautiful. They usually have no difficulty in doing so.

From this it would seem that, though the appreciation of beauty is a highly subjective experience, yet we observe:

1. there are some objective criteria for deciding what is beautiful and what is not;
2. there is in each person an inbuilt aesthetic sense, a capacity for perceiving beauty; and
3. where some people cannot, or will not, see beauty, in, say,

a rose, or will even prefer ugliness, it must be that their internal capacity for seeing beauty is defective or damaged in some way, as, for instance, by colour blindness or defective shape recognition, or through some psychological disorder (like, for instance, people who revel in cruelty, rather than in kindness).

Now by this time we may think that we have exhausted the truth about roses; but of course we haven't. We have thought about the scientific explanation of roses. We have then considered the value we place on them, their beauty and what they mean to us. But precisely because they have meaning and value, they raise another group of questions about the moral, ethical and eventually spiritual significance of what we do with them. Consider, for instance, the following situations:

First, a woman has used what little spare money she had to buy some roses. She likes roses intensely and wants to keep them as long as she can. But a poor neighbour of hers is sick, and she gets a strong feeling that she ought to give at least some of these roses to her sick neighbour. So now she has two conflicting instincts within her:

1. an instinct of self-interest: a strong desire to keep the roses for herself, and
2. an instinctive sense of duty: she ought to love her neighbour as herself, and therefore give her roses to her neighbour.

Questions arise. Where do these instincts come from? And how shall she decide between them? Some might argue that her selfish desire to keep the roses is simply the expression of the blind, but powerful, basic driving force of evolution: self-propagation. But the altruistic sense of duty to help her neighbour at the expense of loss to herself—where does that come from? Why ought she to obey it? She has a further problem: she must decide one way or the other. She cannot wait for scientists or philosophers, or indeed anyone else, to help her. She has to commit herself to some course of action. How and on what grounds should she decide between the two competing urges?

Second, a man likes roses, but he has no money to buy them. He sees that he could steal roses from someone else's garden in such a way that he could be certain that he would never be found out. Would it be wrong to steal them? If neither the owner of the roses, nor the police, nor the courts would ever find out that he stole them, why shouldn't he steal them? Who has the right to say that it is wrong to steal?

Third, a man repeatedly gives bunches of roses to a woman whose husband is abroad on business. The suspicion is that he is giving her roses in order to tempt her to be disloyal to her husband. That would be adultery. Is adultery wrong? Always wrong? Who has the right to say so?

Now to answer questions like these in the first, second, and third situations thoroughly and adequately we must ask and answer the most fundamental questions that we can ask about roses (and indeed about anything else).

Where do roses come from? We human beings did not create them (and are still far from being able to create anything like them). Is there a God who designed and created them? Is he their ultimate owner, who has the right to lay down the rules as to how we should use them?

Or did roses simply evolve out of eternally existing inorganic matter, without any plan or purpose behind them, and without any ultimate owner to lay down the rules as to how they ought to be used? And if so, is the individual himself free to do what he likes, so long as no one finds out?

So far, then, we have been answering the simple question 'What is the truth about a rose?' and we have found that to answer it adequately we have had to draw on, not one source of knowledge, like science or literature, but on many. Even the consideration of roses has led to deep and fundamental questions about the world beyond the roses.

It is our answers to these questions which combine to shape the framework into which we fit all of our knowledge of other things. That framework, which consists of those ideas, conscious or unconscious, which all of us have about the basic nature of the world and of ourselves and of society, is called our worldview. It includes our views, however ill or well thought out, right or wrong, about the hard yet fascinating questions of existence and life: What am I to make of the universe? Where did it come from? Who am I? Where did I come from? How do I know things? Do I have any significance? Do I have any duty? Our worldview is the big picture into which we fit everything else. It is the lens through which we look to try to make sense of the world.

> Our worldview is the big picture into which we fit everything else. It is the lens through which we look to try to make sense of the world.

ASKING THE FUNDAMENTAL QUESTIONS

'He who will succeed', said Aristotle, 'must ask the right questions'; and so, when it comes to forming a worldview, must we.

It is at least comforting to know that we are not the first people to have asked such questions. Many others have done so in the past (and continue to do so in the present). That means they have done some of the work for us! In order to profit from their thinking and experience, it will be helpful for us to collect some of those fundamental questions which have been and are on practically everybody's list. We shall then ask why these particular questions have been thought to be important. After that we shall briefly survey some of the varied answers that have been given, before we tackle the task of forming our own answers. So let's get down to compiling a list of 'worldview questions'. First of all there are questions about the universe in general and about our home planet Earth in particular.

The Greeks were the first people in Europe to ask scientific questions about what the earth and the universe are made of, and how they work. It would appear that they asked their questions for no other reason than sheer intellectual curiosity. Their research was, as we would nowadays describe it, disinterested. They were not at first concerned with any technology that might result from it. Theirs was pure, not applied, science. We pause to point out that it is still a very healthy thing for any educational system to maintain a place for pure science in its curriculum and to foster an attitude of intellectual curiosity for its own sake.

But we cannot afford to limit ourselves to pure science (and even less to technology, marvellous though it is). Centuries ago Socrates perceived that. He was initially curious about the universe, but gradually came to feel that studying how human beings ought to behave

FIGURE I.2. *The School of Athens* by Raphael.

Italian Renaissance artist Raphael likely painted the fresco *Scuola di Atene* (The School of Athens), representing Philosophy, between 1509 and 1511 for the Vatican. Many interpreters believe the hand gestures of the central figures, Plato and Aristotle, and the books each is holding respectively, *Timaeus* and *Nicomachean Ethics*, indicate two approaches to metaphysics. A number of other great ancient Greek philosophers are featured by Raphael in this painting, including Socrates (eighth figure to the left of Plato).

Reproduced from Wikimedia Commons.

was far more important than finding out what the moon was made of. He therefore abandoned physics and immersed himself in moral philosophy.

On the other hand, the leaders of the major philosophical schools in ancient Greece came to see that you could not form an adequate doctrine of human moral behaviour without understanding how human beings are related both to their cosmic environment and to the powers and principles that control the universe. In this they were surely right, which brings us to what was and still is the first fundamental question.[3]

First fundamental worldview question

What lies behind the observable universe? Physics has taught us that things are not quite what they seem to be. A wooden table, which looks solid, turns out to be composed of atoms bound together by powerful forces which operate in the otherwise empty space between them. Each atom turns out also to be mostly empty space and can be modelled from one point of view as a nucleus surrounded by orbiting electrons. The nucleus only occupies about one billionth of the space of the atom. Split the nucleus and we find protons and neutrons. They turn out to be composed of even stranger quarks and gluons. Are these the basic building blocks of matter, or are there other even more mysterious elementary building blocks to be found? That is one of the exciting quests of modern physics. And even as the search goes on, another question keeps nagging: what lies behind basic matter anyway?

The answers that are given to this question fall roughly into two groups: those that suggest that there is nothing 'behind' the basic matter of the universe, and those that maintain that there certainly is something.

Group A. There is nothing but matter. It is the prime reality, being self-existent and eternal. It is not dependent on anything or on anyone. It is blind and purposeless; nevertheless it has within it the power to develop and organise itself—

---

[3] See Book 4: *Doing What's Right.*

still blindly and purposelessly—into all the variety of matter and life that we see in the universe today. This is the philosophy of materialism.

Group B. Behind matter, which had a beginning, stands some uncreated self-existent, creative Intelligence; or, as Jews and Muslims would say, God; and Christians, the God and Father of the Lord Jesus Christ. This God upholds the universe, interacts with it, but is not part of it. He is spirit, not matter. The universe exists as an expression of his mind and for the purpose of fulfilling his will. This is the philosophy of theism.

Second fundamental worldview question

This leads us to our second fundamental worldview question, which is in three parts: *how did our world come into existence, how has it developed, and how has it come to be populated with such an amazing variety of life?*

Again, answers to these questions tend to fall into two groups:

Group A. Inanimate matter itself, without any antecedent design or purpose, formed into that conglomerate which became the earth and then in some way (not yet observed or understood) as a result of its own inherent properties and powers by spontaneous generation spawned life. The initial lowly life forms then gradually evolved into the present vast variety of life through the natural processes of mutation and natural selection, mechanisms likewise without any design or purpose. There is, therefore, no ultimate rational purpose behind either the existence of the universe, or of earth and its inhabitants.

Group B. The universe, the solar system and planet Earth have been designed and precision engineered to make it possible for life to exist on earth. The astonishing complexity of living systems, and the awesome sophistication of their mechanisms, point in the same direction.

It is not difficult to see what different implications the two radically different views have for human significance and behaviour.

Third fundamental worldview question

The third fundamental worldview question comes, again, as a set of related questions with the answers commonly given to central ideas falling into two groups: *What are human beings? Where do their rationality and moral sense come from? What are their hopes for the future, and what, if anything, happens to them after death?*

Group A.   *Human nature.* Human beings are nothing but matter. They have no spirit and their powers of rational thought have arisen out of mindless matter by non-rational processes.

Morality. Man's sense of morality and duty arise solely out of social interactions between him and his fellow humans.

Human rights. Human beings have no inherent, natural rights, but only those that are granted by society or the government of the day.

Purpose in life. Man makes his own purpose.

The future. The utopia dreamed of and longed for will be brought about, either by the irresistible outworking of the forces inherent in matter and/or history; or, alternatively, as human beings learn to direct and control the biological processes of evolution itself.

Death and beyond. Death for each individual means total extinction. Nothing survives.

Group B.   *Human nature.* Human beings are created by God, indeed in the image of God (according, at least, to Judaism, Christianity and Islam). Human beings' powers of rationality are derived from the divine 'Logos' through whom they were created.

Morality. Their moral sense arises from certain 'laws of God' implanted in them by their Creator.

Human rights. They have certain inalienable rights which all other human beings and governments must respect, simply because they are creatures of God, created in God's image.

Purpose in life. Their main purpose in life is to enjoy fellowship with God and to serve God, and likewise to serve their fellow creatures for their Creator's sake.

The future. The utopia they long for is not a dream, but a sure hope based on the Creator's plan for the redemption of humankind and of the world.

Death and beyond. Death does not mean extinction. Human beings, after death, will be held accountable to God. Their ultimate state will eventually be, either to be with God in total fellowship in heaven; or to be excluded from his presence.

These, very broadly speaking, are the questions that people have asked through the whole of recorded history, and a brief survey of some of the answers that have been, and still are, given to them.

The fundamental difference between the two groups of answers

Now it is obvious that the two groups of answers given above are diametrically opposed; but we ought to pause here to make sure that we have understood what exactly the nature and cause of the opposition is. If we were not thinking carefully, we might jump to the conclusion that the answers in the A-groups are those given by science, while the answers in the B-groups are those given by religion. But that would be a fundamental misunderstanding of the situation. It is true that the majority of scientists today would agree with the answers given in the A-groups; but there is a growing number of scientists who would agree with the answers given in the B-groups. It is not therefore a conflict between science and religion. It is a difference in the basic philosophies which determine the interpretation of the evidence which science provides. Atheists will interpret that evidence in one way; theists (or pantheists) will interpret it in another.

This is understandable. No scientist comes to the task of doing research with a mind completely free of presuppositions. The atheist does research on the presupposition that there is no God. That is his basic philosophy, his worldview. He claims that he can explain everything without God. He will sometimes say that he cannot imagine what kind of scientific evidence there could possibly be for the existence of God; and not surprisingly he tends not to find any.

The theist, on the other hand, starts by believing in God and finds in his scientific discoveries abundant—overwhelming, he would say—evidence of God's hand in the sophisticated design and mechanisms of the universe.

It all comes down, then, to the importance of recognising what worldview we start with. Some of us, who have never yet thought deeply about these things, may feel that we have no worldview, and that we come to life's questions in general, and science in particular, with a completely open mind. But that is unlikely to be so. We pick up ideas, beliefs and attitudes from our family and society, often without realising that we have done so, and without recognising how these largely unconscious influences and presuppositions control our reactions to the questions with which life faces us. Hence the importance of consciously thinking through our worldview and of adjusting it where necessary to take account of the evidence available.

> We pick up ideas, beliefs and attitudes from our family and society, often without realising that we have done so, and without recognising how these largely unconscious influences and presuppositions control our reactions to the questions with which life faces us.

In that process, then, we certainly must listen to science and allow it to critique where necessary and to amend our presuppositions. But to form an adequate worldview we shall need to listen to many other voices as well.

VOICES TO BE LISTENED TO

So far, then, we have been surveying some worldview questions and various answers that have been, and still are, given to them. Now we must face these questions ourselves, and begin to come to our own decisions about them.

Our worldview must be our own, in the sense that we have personally thought it through and adopted it of our own free will. No one has the right to impose his or her worldview on us by force. The days are rightly gone when the church could force Galileo to deny what science had plainly taught him. Gone, too, for the most part, are the days when the State could force an atheistic worldview on people on pain of prison and even death. Human rights demand that people should be free to hold and to propagate by reasoned argument whatever worldview they believe in—so long, of course, that their view does not injure other people. We, the authors of this book, hold a theistic worldview. But we shall not attempt to force our view down anybody's throat. We come from a tradition whose basic principle is 'Let everyone be persuaded in his own mind.'

So we must all make up our own minds and form our own worldview. In the process of doing so there are a number of voices that we must listen to.

The voice of intuition

The first voice we must listen to is intuition. There are things in life that we see and know, not as the result of lengthy philosophical reasoning, nor as a result of rigorous scientific experimentation, but by direct, instinctive intuition. We 'see' that a rose is beautiful. We instinctively 'know' that child abuse is wrong. A scientist can sometimes 'see' what the solution to a problem is going to be even before he has worked out the scientific technique that will eventually provide formal proof of it.

A few scientists and philosophers still try to persuade us that the laws of cause and effect operating in the human brain are completely deterministic so that our decisions are predetermined: real choice is not possible. But, say what they will, we ourselves intuitively know that we do have the ability to make a free choice, whether, say, to read a book, or to go for a walk, whether to tell the truth or to tell a lie. We know we are free to take either course of action, and everyone else knows it too, and acts accordingly. This freedom is such a part of our innate concept of human dignity and value that we (for the most part) insist on being treated as responsible human beings and on treating others as such. For that reason, if we commit a crime, the magistrate will first enquire (*a*) if, when we committed the crime, we knew we were doing wrong; and (*b*) whether or not we were acting under duress. The answer to these questions will determine the verdict.

We must, therefore, give due attention to intuition, and not allow ourselves to be persuaded by pseudo-intellectual arguments to deny (or affirm) what we intuitively know to be true (or false).

On the other hand, intuition has its limits. It can be mistaken. When ancient scientists first suggested that the world was a sphere, even some otherwise great thinkers rejected the idea. They intuitively felt that it was absurd to think that there were human beings on the opposite side of the earth to us, walking 'upside-down', their feet pointed towards our feet (hence the term 'antipodean') and their heads hanging perilously down into empty space! But intuition had misled them. The scientists who believed in a spherical earth were right, intuition was wrong.

The lesson is that we need both intuition and science, acting as checks and balances, the one on the other.

The voice of science

Science speaks to our modern world with a very powerful and authoritative voice. It can proudly point to a string of scintillating theoretical breakthroughs which have spawned an almost endless array of technological spin-offs: from the invention of the light bulb to virtual-reality environments; from the wheel to the moon-landing vehicle; from the discovery of aspirin and antibiotics to the cracking of the genetic code; from the vacuum cleaner to the smartphone; from the abacus to the parallel computer; from the bicycle to the self-driving car. The benefits that come from these achievements of science are self-evident, and they both excite our admiration and give to science an immense credibility.

Yet for many people the voice of science has a certain ambivalence about it, for the achievements of science are not invariably used for the good of humanity. Indeed, in the past century science has produced the most hideously efficient weapons of destruction that the world has ever seen. The laser that is used to restore vision to the eye can be used to guide missiles with deadly efficiency. This development has led in recent times to a strong anti-scientific reaction.

This is understandable; but we need to guard against the obvious fallacy of blaming science for the misuse made of its discoveries. The blame for the devastation caused by the atomic bomb, for instance, does not chiefly lie with the scientists who discovered the possibility of atomic fission and fusion, but with the politicians who for reasons of global conquest insisted on the discoveries being used for the making of weapons of mass destruction.

Science, in itself, is morally neutral. Indeed, as scientists who are Christians would say, it is a form of the worship of God through the reverent study of his handiwork and is by all means to be encouraged. It is for that reason that James Clerk Maxwell, the nineteenth-century Scottish physicist who discovered the famous equations governing electromagnetic waves which are now called after him, put the following quotation from the Hebrew Psalms above the door of the Cavendish Laboratory in Cambridge where it still stands: 'The works of the LORD are great, sought out of all them that have pleasure therein' (Ps 111:2).

We must distinguish, of course, between science as a method of investigation and individual scientists who actually do the investigation. We must also distinguish between the facts which they establish beyond (reasonable) doubt and the tentative hypotheses and theories which they construct on the basis of their initial observations and experiments, and which they use to guide their subsequent research.

These distinctions are important because scientists sometimes mistake their tentative theories for proven fact, and in their teaching of students and in their public lectures promulgate as established fact what has never actually been proved. It can also happen that scientists advance a tentative theory which catches the attention of the media who then put it across to the public with so much hype that the impression is given that the theory has been established beyond question.

> Scientists sometimes mistake their tentative theories for proven fact, and in their teaching of students and in their public lectures promulgate as established fact what has never actually been proved.

Then again, we need to remember the proper limits of science. As we discovered when talking about the beauty of roses, there are things which science, strictly so called, cannot and should not be expected to explain.

Sometimes some scientists forget this, and damage the reputation of science by making wildly exaggerated claims for it. The famous mathematician and philosopher Bertrand Russell, for instance, once wrote: 'Whatever knowledge is attainable, must be attained by scientific methods; and what science cannot discover, mankind cannot know.'[4] Nobel laureate Sir Peter Medawar had a saner and more realistic view of science. He wrote:

> There is no quicker way for a scientist to bring discredit upon himself and on his profession than roundly to declare—particularly when no declaration of any kind is called for—that science knows or soon will know the answers to all questions worth asking, and that the questions that do not admit a scientific answer are in some way nonquestions or 'pseudoquestions' that only simpletons ask and only the gullible profess to be able to answer.[5]

Medawar says elsewhere: 'The existence of a limit to science is, however, made clear by its inability to answer childlike elementary questions having to do with first and last things—questions such as "How did everything begin?"; "What are we all here for?"; "What is the point of living?"' He adds that it is to imaginative literature and religion that we must turn for answers to such questions.[6]

However, when we have said all that should be said about the limits of science, the voice of science is still one of the most important voices to which we must listen in forming our worldview. We cannot, of course, all be experts in science. But when the experts report their findings to students in other disciplines or to the general public, as they increasingly do, we all must listen to them; listen as critically as we listen to experts in other fields. But we must listen.[7]

The voice of philosophy

The next voice we must listen to is the voice of philosophy. To some people the very thought of philosophy is daunting; but actually any-

---

4 Russell, *Religion and Science*, 243.
5 Medawar, *Advice to a Young Scientist*, 31.
6 Medawar, *Limits of Science*, 59–60.
7 Those who wish to study the topic further are directed to the Appendix in this book: 'The Scientific Endeavour', and to the books by John Lennox noted there.

one who seriously attempts to investigate the truth of any statement is already thinking philosophically. Eminent philosopher Anthony Kenny writes:

> Philosophy is exciting because it is the broadest of all disciplines, exploring the basic concepts which run through all our talking and thinking on any topic whatever. Moreover, it can be undertaken without any special preliminary training or instruction; anyone can do philosophy who is willing to think hard and follow a line of reasoning.[8]

Whether we realise it or not, the way we think and reason owes a great deal to philosophy—we have already listened to its voice!

Philosophy has a number of very positive benefits to confer on us. First and foremost is the shining example of men and women who have refused to go through life unthinkingly adopting whatever happened to be the majority view at the time. Socrates said that the unexamined life is not worth living. These men and women were determined to use all their intellectual powers to try to understand what the universe was made of, how it worked, what man's place in it was, what the essence of human nature was, why we human beings so frequently do wrong and so damage ourselves and society; what could help us to avoid doing wrong; and what our chief goal in life should be, our *summum bonum* (Latin for 'chief good'). Their zeal to discover the truth and then to live by it should encourage—perhaps even shame—us to follow their example.

Secondly, it was in their search for the truth that philosophers from Socrates, Plato, and Aristotle onwards discovered the need for, and the rules of, rigorous logical thinking. The benefit of this to humanity is incalculable, in that it enables us to learn to think straight, to expose the presuppositions that lie sometimes unnoticed behind even our scientific experiments and theories, to unpick the assumptions that lurk in the formulation and expressions of our opinions, to point to fallacies in our argumentation, to detect instances of circular reasoning, and so on.

However, philosophy, just like science, has its proper limits. It cannot tell us what axioms or fundamental assumptions we should

---

[8] Kenny, *Brief History of Western Philosophy*, xi.

adopt; but it can and will help us to see if the belief system which we build on those axioms is logically consistent.

There is yet a third benefit to be gained from philosophy. The history of philosophy shows that, of all the many different philosophical systems, or worldviews, that have been built up by rigorous philosophers on the basis of human reasoning alone, none has proved convincing to all other philosophers, let alone to the general public. None has achieved permanence, a fact which can seem very frustrating. But perhaps the frustration is not altogether bad in that it might lead us to ask whether there could just be another source of information without which human reason alone is by definition inadequate. And if our very frustration with philosophy for having seemed at first to promise so much satisfaction, and then in the end to have delivered so little, disposes us to look around for that other source of information, even our frustration could turn out to be a supreme benefit.

The voice of history

Yet another voice to which we must listen is the voice of history. We are fortunate indeed to be living so far on in the course of human history as we do. Already in the first century AD a simple form of jet propulsion was described by Hero of Alexandria. But technology at that time knew no means of harnessing that discovery to any worthwhile practical purpose. Eighteen hundred years were to pass before scientists discovered a way of making jet engines powerful enough to be fitted to aircraft.

When in the 1950s and 1960s scientists, working on the basis of a discovery of Albert Einstein's, argued that it would be possible to make laser beams, and then actually made them, many people mockingly said that lasers were a solution to a non-existent problem, because no one could think of a practical use to which they could be put. History has proved the critics wrong and justified the pure scientists (if pure science needs any justification!).

In other cases history has taught the opposite lesson. At one point the phlogiston theory of combustion came to be almost universally accepted. History eventually proved it wrong.

Fanatical religious sects (in spite, be it said, of the explicit prohibition of the Bible) have from time to time predicted that the end of the world would take place at such-and-such a time in such-and-such a place. History has invariably proved them wrong.

In the last century, the philosophical system known as logical positivism arose like a meteor and seemed set to dominate the philosophical landscape, superseding all other systems. But history discovered its fatal flaw, namely that it was based on a verification principle which allowed only two kinds of meaningful statement: *analytic* (a statement which is true by definition, that is a tautology like 'a vixen is a female fox'), or *synthetic* (a statement which is capable of verification by experiment, like 'water is composed of hydrogen and oxygen'). Thus all metaphysical statements were dismissed as meaningless! But, as philosopher Karl Popper famously pointed out, the Verification Principle itself is neither analytic nor synthetic and so is meaningless! Logical positivism is therefore self-refuting. Professor Nicholas Fotion, in his article on the topic in *The Oxford Companion to Philosophy*, says: 'By the late 1960s it became obvious that the movement had pretty much run its course.'[9]

Earlier still, Marx, basing himself on Hegel, applied his dialectical materialism first to matter and then to history. He claimed to have discovered a law in the workings of social and political history that would irresistibly lead to the establishment of a utopia on earth; and millions gave their lives to help forward this process. The verdict has been that history seems not to know any such irresistible law.

History has also delivered a devastating verdict on the Nazi theory of the supremacy of the Aryan races, which, it was promised, would lead to a new world order.

History, then, is a very valuable, if sometimes very disconcerting, adjudicator of our ideas and systems of thought. We should certainly pay serious heed to its lessons and be grateful for them.

But there is another reason why we should listen to history. It introduces us to the men and women who have proved to be world leaders of thought and whose influence is still a live force among us today. Among them, of course, is Jesus Christ. He was rejected, as we know, by his contemporaries and executed. But, then, so was Socrates. Socrates' influence has lived on; but Christ's influence has been and still is infinitely greater than that of Socrates, or of any other world leader.

---

[9] Fotion, 'Logical Positivism'.

It would be very strange if we listened, as we do, to Socrates, Plato, Aristotle, Hume, Kant, Marx and Einstein, and neglected or refused to listen to Christ. The numerous (and some very early) manuscripts of the New Testament make available to us an authentic record of his teaching. Only extreme prejudice would dismiss him without first listening to what he says.

History introduces us to the men and women who have proved to be world leaders of thought and whose influence is still a live force among us today. . . . It would be very strange if we listened, as we do, to Socrates, Plato, Aristotle, Hume, Kant, Marx and Einstein, and neglected or refused to listen to Christ.

The voice of divine self-revelation

The final voice that claims the right to be heard is a voice which runs persistently through history and refuses to be silenced in claiming that there is another source of information beyond that which intuition, scientific research and philosophical reasoning can provide. That voice is the voice of divine self-revelation. The claim is that the Creator, whose existence and power can be intuitively perceived through his created works, has not otherwise remained silent and aloof. In the course of the centuries he has spoken into our world through his prophets and supremely through Jesus Christ.

Of course, atheists will say that for them this claim seems to be the stuff of fairy tales; and atheistic scientists will object that there is no scientific evidence for the existence of a creator (indeed, they may well claim that assuming the existence of a creator destroys the foundation of true scientific methodology—for more of that see this book's Appendix); and that, therefore, the idea that we could have direct information from the creator himself is conceptually absurd. This reaction is, of course, perfectly consistent with the basic assumption of atheism.

However, apparent conceptual absurdity is not proof positive that something is not possible, or even true. Remember what we noticed earlier, that many leading thinkers, when they first encountered the suggestion that the earth was not flat but spherical, rejected it out of hand because of the conceptual absurdities to which they imagined it led.

In the second century AD a certain Lucian of Samosata decided to debunk what he thought to be fanciful speculations of the early scientists and the grotesque traveller's tales of so-called explorers. He wrote a book which, with his tongue in his cheek, he called *Vera historia* (A True Story). In it he told how he had travelled through space to the moon. He discovered that the moon-dwellers had a special kind of mirror by means of which they could see what people were doing on earth. They also possessed something like a well shaft by means of which they could even hear what people on earth were saying. His prose was sober enough, as if he were writing factual history. But he expected his readers to see that the very conceptual absurdity of what he claimed to have seen meant that these things were impossible and would forever remain so.

Unknown to him, however, the forces and materials already existed in nature, which, when mankind learned to harness them, would send some astronauts into orbit round the moon, land others on the moon, and make possible radio and television communication between the moon and the earth!

We should remember, too, that atomic radiation and radio frequency emissions from distant galaxies were not invented by scientists in recent decades. They were there all the time, though invisible and undetected and not believed in nor even thought of for centuries; but they were not discovered until comparatively recent times, when brilliant scientists conceived the possibility that, against all popular expectation, such phenomena might exist. They looked for them, and found them.

Is it then, after all, so conceptually absurd to think that our human intellect and rationality come not from mindless matter through the agency of impersonal unthinking forces, but from a higher personal intellect and reason?

An old, but still valid, analogy will help us at this point. If we ask about a particular motor car: 'Where did this motor car begin?' one answer would be: 'It began on the production lines of such-and-such a factory and was put together by humans and robots.'

Another, deeper-level, answer would be: 'It had its beginning in the mineral from which its constituent parts were made.'

But in the prime sense of beginning, the motor car, of which this particular motor car is a specimen, had its beginning, not in the factory, nor in its basic materials, but in something altogether different: in the intelligent mind of a person, that is, of its inventor. We know this, of course, by history and by experience; but we also know it intuitively: it is self-evidently true.

Millions of people likewise have felt, and still do feel, that what Christ and his prophets say about the 'beginning' of our human rationality is similarly self-evidently true: 'In the beginning was the Logos, and the Logos was with God, and the Logos was God. . . . All things were made by him . . .' (John 1:1–2, our trans.). That is, at any rate, a far more likely story than that our human intelligence and rationality sprang originally out of mindless matter, by accidental permutations, selected by unthinking nature.

Now the term 'Logos' means both rationality and the expression of that rationality through intelligible communication. If that rational intelligence is God and personal, and we humans are endowed by him with personhood and intelligence, then it is far from being absurd to think that the divine Logos, whose very nature and function it is to be the expression and communicator of that intelligence, should communicate with us. On the contrary, to deny a priori the possibility of divine revelation and to shut one's ears in advance to what Jesus Christ has to say, before listening to his teaching to see if it is, or is not, self-evidently true, is not the true scientific attitude, which is to keep an open mind and explore any reasonable avenue to truth.[10]

Moreover, the fear that to assume the existence of a creator God would undermine true scientific methodology is contradicted by the sheer facts of history. Sir Francis Bacon (1561–1626), widely regarded as the father of the modern scientific method, believed that God had revealed himself in two great Books, the Book of Nature and the Book of God's Word, the Bible. In his famous *Advancement of Learning* (1605), Bacon wrote: 'Let no man . . . think or maintain, that a man can search too far, or be too well studied in the book of God's word, or in the book of God's works; divinity or philosophy; but rather let men endeavour an endless progress or proficience in both.'[11] It is this quotation which Charles Darwin chose to put at the front of *On the Origin of Species* (1859).

---

[10] For the fuller treatment of these questions and related topics, see Book 5 in this series, *Claiming to Answer*.

[11] Bacon, *Advancement of Learning*, 8.

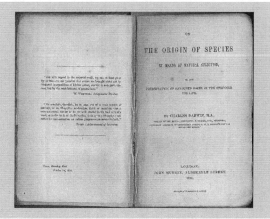

FIGURE I.3.
On the Origin of Species (1859) **by Charles Darwin.**

One of the book epigraphs Charles Darwin selected for his magnum opus is from Francis Bacon's *Advancement of Learning* (1605).

Reproduced from Dennis O'Neil.

Historians of science point out that it was this theistic 'Two-Book' view which was largely responsible for the meteoric rise of science beginning in the sixteenth century. C. S. Lewis refers to a statement by one of the most eminent historians of all time, Sir Alfred North Whitehead, and says: 'Professor Whitehead points out that centuries of belief in a God who combined "the personal energy of Jehovah" with "the rationality of a Greek philosopher" first produced that firm expectation of systematic order which rendered possible the birth of modern science. Men became scientific because they expected Law in Nature and they expected Law in Nature because they believed in a Legislator.'[12] In other words, theism was the cradle of science. Indeed, far from thinking that the idea of a creator was conceptually absurd, most of the great leaders of science in that period did believe in a creator.

Johannes Kepler	1571–1630	Celestial mechanics
Blaise Pascal	1623–62	Hydrostatics
Robert Boyle	1627–91	Chemistry, Gas dynamics
Isaac Newton	1642–1727	Mathematics, Optics, Dynamics
Michael Faraday	1791–1867	Magnetism
Charles Babbage	1791–1871	Computer science
Gregor Mendel	1822–84	Genetics
Louis Pasteur	1822–95	Bacteriology
Lord Kelvin	1824–1907	Thermodynamics
James Clerk Maxwell	1831–79	Electrodynamics, Thermodynamics

---

12 Lewis, *Miracles*, 110.

All of these famous men would have agreed with Einstein: 'Science without religion is lame, religion without science is blind.'[13] History shows us very clearly, then, that far from belief in God being a hindrance to science, it has provided one of the main impulses for its development.

Still today there are many first-rate scientists who are believers in God. For example, Professor William D. Phillips, Nobel laureate for Physics 1997, is an active Christian, as is the world-famous botanist and former Director of the Royal Botanic Gardens, Kew in London, Sir Ghillean Prance, and so is the geneticist Francis S. Collins, who was the Director of the National Institutes of Health in the United States who gained recognition for his leadership of the international Human Genome Project which culminated in 2003 with the completion of a finished sequence of human DNA.[14]

But with many people another objection arises: if one is not sure that God even exists, would it not be unscientific to go looking for evidence for God's existence? Surely not. Take the late Professor Carl Sagan and the Search for Extra Terrestrial Intelligence (the SETI project), which he promoted. Sagan was a famous astronomer, but when he began this search he had no hard-and-fast proven facts to go on. He proceeded simply on the basis of a hypothesis. If intelligent life has evolved on earth, then it would be possible, perhaps even likely, that it would have developed on other suitable planets elsewhere in the universe. He had no guarantee that it was so, or that he would find it, even if it existed. But even so both he and NASA (the National Aeronautics and Space Administration) thought it worth spending great effort, time and considerable sums of money to employ radio telescopes to listen to remote galaxies for evidence of intelligent life elsewhere in the universe.

Why, then, should it be thought any less scientific to look for an intelligent creator, especially when there is evidence that the universe bears the imprint of his mind? The only valid excuse for not seeking for God would be the possession of convincing evidence that God does not, and could not, exist. No one has such proof.

But for many people divine revelation seems, nonetheless, an utter

---

13 Einstein, 'Science and Religion'.
14 The list could go on, as any Internet search for 'Christians in science' will show.

impossibility, for they have the impression that science has outgrown the cradle in which it was born and somehow proved that there is no God after all. For that reason, we examine in greater detail in the Appendix to this book what science is, what it means to be truly scientific in outlook, what science has and has not proved, and some of the fallacious ways in which science is commonly misunderstood. Here we must consider even larger questions about reality.

> The only valid excuse for not seeking for God would be the possession of convincing evidence that God does not, and could not, exist. No one has such proof.

THE MEANING OF REALITY

One of the central questions we are setting out to examine is: can we know the ultimate truth about reality? Before we consider different aspects of reality, we need to determine what we mean by 'reality'. For that purpose let's start with the way we use the term in ordinary, everyday language. After that we can move on to consider its use at higher levels.

In everyday language the noun 'reality', the adjective 'real', and the adverb 'really' have several different connotations according to the contexts in which they are used. Let's think about some examples.

First, in some situations the opposite of 'real' is 'imaginary' or 'illusory'. So, for instance, a thirsty traveller in the Sahara may see in the distance what looks to him like an oasis with water and palm trees, when in fact there is no oasis there at all. What he thinks he sees is a mirage, an optical illusion. The oasis is not real, we say; it does not actually exist.[15] Similarly a patient, having been injected with powerful drugs in the course of a serious operation, may upon waking up from the anaesthetic suffer hallucinations, and imagine she sees all kinds of weird creatures stalking round her room. But if we say, as we do, that these things which she imagines she sees, are not real, we

---

[15] Mirages occur 'when sharp differences in temperature and therefore in density develop between thin layers of air at and immediately above the ground. This causes light to be bent, or refracted, as it travels through one layer to the next. . . . During the day, when a warm layer occurs next to the ground, objects near the horizon often appear to be reflected in flat surfaces, such as beaches, deserts, roads and water. This produces the shimmering, floating images which are commonly observed on very hot days.' *Oxford Reference Encyclopaedia*, 913.

mean that they do not in actual fact exist. We could argue, of course, that something is going on in the patient's brain, and she is experiencing impressions similar to those she would have received if the weird creatures had been real. Her impressions, then, are real in the sense that they exist in her brain; but they do not correspond with the external reality that the patient supposes is creating these sense impressions. The mechanisms of her brain are presenting her with a false picture: the weird creatures do not exist. She is not seeing *them*. They are not real. On the basis of examples like this (the traveller and the patient) some philosophers have argued that none of us can ever be sure that the sense impressions which we think we receive from the external world are true representations of the external world, and not illusions. We consider their arguments in detail in Book 3 in this series, *Questioning Our Knowledge*, dealing with epistemology and related matters.

To sum up so far, then: neither the traveller nor the patient was perceiving external reality as it really was. But the reasons for their failure were different: with the traveller it was an external illusion (possibly reinforced by his thirst) that made him misread reality and imagine there was a real oasis there, when there wasn't. With the patient there was nothing unusual in the appearance of her room to cause her disordered perception. The difficulty was altogether internal to her. The drugs had distorted the perception mechanisms of her brain.

From these two examples we can learn some practical lessons:

1. It is important for us all to question from time to time whether what we unthinkingly take to be reality is in fact reality.
2. In cases like these it is external reality that has to be the standard by which we judge whether our sense perceptions are true or not.
3. Setting people free from their internal subjective misperceptions will depend on getting them, by some means or other, to face and perceive the external, objective reality.

Second, in other situations the opposite of 'real', in everyday language, is 'counterfeit', 'spurious', 'fraudulent'. So if we describe a piece of metal as being 'real gold', we mean that it is genuine gold, and not something such as brass that looks like gold, but isn't. The practical importance of being able to discern the difference between what is real in this sense and what is spurious or counterfeit, can easily be illustrated.

Take coinage, for instance. In past centuries, when coins were made (or supposed to be made) of real gold, or real silver, fraudsters would often adulterate the coinage by mixing inferior metal with gold or silver. Buyers or sellers, if they had no means of testing whether the coins they were offered were genuine, and of full value, or not, could easily be cheated.

Similarly, in our modern world counterfeiters print false bank notes and surreptitiously get them into circulation. Eventually, when the fraud is discovered, banks and traders refuse the spurious bank notes, with the result that innocent people are left with worthless pieces of paper.

Or, again, a dishonest jeweller might show a rich woman a necklace made, according to him, of valuable gems; and the rich, but unsuspecting, woman might pay a large price for it, only to discover later on that the gems were not real: they were imitations, made of a kind of glass called paste, or strass.

Conversely, an elderly woman might take her necklace, made of real gems, to a jeweller and offer to sell it to him in order to get some money to maintain herself in her old age. But the unscrupulous jeweller might make out that the gems were not as valuable as she thought: they were imitations, made of paste; and by this deceit he would persuade the reluctant woman to sell him the necklace for a much lesser price than it was worth.

Once more it will be instructive to study the underlying principles at work in these examples, because later on, when we come to study reality at a higher level, they could provide us with helpful analogies and thought models.[16]

Notice, then, that these last three examples involve significantly different principles from those that were operating in the two which we studied earlier. The oasis and the weird creatures were not real, because they did not actually exist in the external world. But the spurious coins, the fraudulent bank notes, and the genuine and the

---

[16] See especially in Book 2: *Finding Ultimate Reality.*

imitation gems, all existed in the external world. In that sense, therefore, they were all real, part of the external reality, actual pieces of matter.

What, then, was the trouble with them? It was that the fraudsters had claimed for the coins and the bank notes a value and a buying power that they did not actually possess; and in the case of the two necklaces the unscrupulous jewellers had on both occasions misrepresented the nature of the matter of which the gems were composed.

The question arises: how can people avoid being taken in by such spurious claims and misrepresentations of matter? It is not difficult to see how questions like this will become important when we come to consider the matter of the universe and its properties.

In modern, as in ancient, times, to test whether an object is made of pure gold or not, use is made of a black, fine-grained, siliceous stone, called a touchstone. When pure gold is rubbed on this touchstone, it leaves behind on the stone streaks of a certain character; whereas objects made of adulterated gold, or of some baser metal, will leave behind streaks of a different character.

FIGURE I.4. A Touchstone.

First mentioned by Theophrastus (c.372–c.287 BC) in his treatise *On Stone,* touchstones are tablets of finely grained black stones used to assay or estimate the proportion of gold or silver in a sample of metal. Traces of gold can be seen on the stone.

Reproduced from Mauro Cateb/Flickr.

In the ancient world merchants would always carry a touchstone with them; but even so it would require considerable knowledge and expertise to interpret the test correctly. When it comes to bank notes and gems, the imitations may be so cleverly made that only an expert could tell the difference between the real thing and the false. In that case non-experts, like ourselves, would have to depend on the judgments of experts.

But what are we to do when the experts disagree? How do we decide which experts to trust? Is there any kind of touchstone that ordinary people can use on the experts themselves, or at least on their interpretations?

There is one more situation worth investigating at this point before we begin our main study.

Third, when we are confronted with what purports to be an account of something that happened in the past and of the causes that led to its happening, we rightly ask questions: 'Did this event really take place? Did it take place in the way that this account says it did? Was the alleged cause the real cause?' The difficulty with things that happened in the past is that we cannot get them to repeat themselves in the present, and watch them happening all over again in our laboratories. We have therefore to search out and study what evidence is available and then decide which interpretation of the evidence best explains what actually happened.

This, of course, is no unusual situation to be in. Detectives, seeking to solve a murder mystery and to discover the real criminal, are constantly in this situation; and this is what historians and archaeologists and palaeontologists do all the time. But mistakes can be made in handling and interpreting the evidence. For instance, in 1980 a man and his wife were camping in the Australian outback, when a dingo (an Australian wild dog) suddenly attacked and killed their little child. When, however, the police investigated the matter, they did not believe the parents' story; they alleged that the woman herself had actually killed the child. The courts found her guilty and she was duly sentenced. But new evidence was discovered that corroborated the parents' story, and proved that it really was a dingo that killed the infant. The couple was not fully and finally exonerated until 2012.

Does this kind of case mean, then, that we cannot ever be certain that any historical event really happened? Or that we can never be sure as to its real causes? Of course not! It is beyond all doubt that, for instance, Napoleon invaded Russia, and that Genghis Khan besieged Beijing (then called Zhongdu). The question is, as we considered earlier: what kind of evidence must we have in order to be sure that a historical event really happened?

But enough of these preliminary exercises. It is time now to take our first step towards answering the question: can we know the ultimate truth about reality?

WHAT IS THE NATURE OF ULTIMATE REALITY?

We have thought about the meaning of reality in various practical situations in daily life. Now we must begin to consider reality at the higher levels of our own individual existence, and that of our fellow human beings, and eventually that of the whole universe.

Ourselves as individuals

Let's start with ourselves as individuals. We know we exist. We do not have to engage in lengthy philosophical discussion before we can be certain that we exist. We know it intuitively. Indeed, we cannot logically deny it. If I were to claim 'I do not exist', I would, by stating my claim, refute it. A non-existent person cannot make any claim. If I didn't exist, I couldn't even say 'I do not exist', since I have to exist in order to make the claim. I cannot, therefore, logically affirm my own non-existence.[17]

There are other things too which we know about ourselves by intuition.

First, we are self-conscious, that is, we are aware of ourselves as separate individuals. I know I am not my brother, or my sister, or my next-door neighbour. I was born of my parents; but I am not just an extension of my father and mother. I am a separate individual, a human being in my own right. My will is not a continuation of their will, such that, if they will something, I automatically will the same thing. My will is my own.

My will may be conditioned by many past experiences, most of which have now passed into my subconscious memory. My will may well be pressurised by many internal desires or fears, and by external circumstances. But whatever philosophers of the determinist school may say, we know in our heart of hearts that we have the power of choice. Our wills, in that sense, are free. If they weren't, no one could ever be held to be guilty for doing wrong, or praised for doing right.

Second, we are also intuitively aware of ourselves as persons, intrinsically different from, and superior to, non-personal things. It is

---

[17] We call this law of logic the law of non-affirmability.

not a question of size, but of mind and personality. A mountain may be large, but it is mindless and impersonal. It is composed of non-rational matter. We are aware of the mountain; it is not aware of us. It is not aware of itself. It neither loves nor hates, neither anticipates nor reflects, has no hopes nor fears. Non-rational though it is, if it became a volcano, it might well destroy us, though we are rational beings. Yet we should not conclude from the fact that simply because such impersonal, non-rational matter is larger and more powerful that it is therefore a higher form of existence than personal, rational human beings. But it poignantly raises the question: what, then, is the status of our human existence in this material world and universe?

Our status in the world

We know that we did not always exist. We can remember being little children. We have watched ourselves growing up to full manhood and womanhood. We have also observed that sooner or later people die, and the unthinking earth, unknowingly, becomes their grave. What then is the significance of the individual human person, and of his or her comparatively short life on earth?

Some think that it is Mankind, the human race as a whole, that is the significant phenomenon: the individual counts for very little. On this view, the human race is like a great fruit tree. Each year it produces a large crop of apples. All of them are more or less alike. None is of any particular significance as an individual. Everyone is

FIGURE I.5. An Apple.

Apple trees take four to five years to produce their first fruit, and it takes the energy from 50 leaves to produce one apple. Archaeologists have found evidence that humans have been enjoying apples since before recorded history.

Reproduced with permission of ©iStock/ChrisBoswell.

destined for a very short life before, like the rest of the crop, it is consumed and forgotten; and so makes room for next year's crop. The tree itself lives on, producing crops year after year, in a seemingly endless cycle of birth, growth and disappearance. On this view then, the tree is the permanent, significant phenomenon; any one individual apple is of comparatively little value.

Our origin

But this view of the individual in relation to the race does not get us to the root of our question; for the human race too did not always exist, but had a beginning, and so did the universe itself. This, therefore, only pushes the question one stage further back: to what ultimately do the human race as a whole and the universe itself owe their existence? What is the Great Reality behind the non-rational matter of the universe, and behind us rational, personal, individual members of the human race?

Before we begin to survey the answers that have been given to this question over the centuries, we should notice that though science can point towards an answer, it cannot finally give us a complete answer. That is not because there is something wrong with science; the difficulty lies in the nature of things. The most widely accepted scientific theory nowadays (but not the only one) is that the universe came into being at the so-called Big Bang. But the theory tells us that here we encounter a singularity, that is, a point at which the laws of physics all break down. If that is true, it follows that science by itself cannot give a scientific account of what lay before, and led to, the Big Bang, and thus to the universe, and eventually to ourselves as individual human beings.

Our purpose

The fact that science cannot answer these questions does not mean, of course, that they are pseudo-questions and not worth asking. Adam Schaff, the Polish Marxist philosopher, long ago observed:

> What is the meaning of life? What is man's place in the universe? It seems difficult to express oneself scientifically on such

hazy topics. And yet if one should assert ten times over that these are typical pseudo-problems, *problems would remain.*[18]

Yes, surely problems would remain; and they are life's most important questions. Suppose by the help of science we could come to know everything about every atom, every molecule, every cell, every electrical current, every mechanism in our body and brain. How much further forward should we be? We should now know what we are made of, and how we work. But we should still not know what we are made for.

Suppose for analogy's sake we woke up one morning to find a new, empty jeep parked outside our house, with our name written on it, by some anonymous donor, specifying that it was for our use. Scientists could describe every atom and molecule it was made of. Engineers could explain how it worked, and that it was designed for transporting people. It was obviously intended, therefore, to go places. But where? Neither science as such, nor engineering as such, could tell us where we were meant to drive the jeep to. Should we not then need to discover who the anonymous donor was, and whether the jeep was ours to do what we liked with, answerable to nobody: or whether the jeep had been given to us on permanent loan by its maker and owner with the expectation that we should consult the donor's intentions, follow the rules in the driver's handbook, and in the end be answerable to the donor for how we had used it?

That surely is the situation we find ourselves in as human beings. We are equipped with a magnificent piece of physical and biological engineering, that is, our body and brain; and we are in the driver's seat, behind the steering wheel. But we did not make ourselves, nor the 'machine' we are in charge of. Must we not ask what our relationship is to whatever we owe our existence to? After all, what if it turned out to be that we owe our existence not to an impersonal what but to a personal who?

To some the latter possibility is instinctively unattractive if not frightening; they would prefer

> Must we not ask what our relationship is to whatever we owe our existence to? After all, what if it turned out to be that we owe our existence not to an impersonal what but to a personal who?

---

[18] Schaff, *Philosophy of Man*, 34 (emphasis added).

to think that they owe their existence to impersonal material, forces and processes. But then that view induces in some who hold it its own peculiar *angst*. Scientist Jacob Bronowski (1908–74) confessed to a deep instinctive longing, not simply to exist, but to be a recognisably distinct individual, and not just one among millions of otherwise undifferentiated human beings:

> When I say that I want to be myself, I mean as the existentialist does that I want to be free to be myself. This implies that I want to be rid of constraints (inner as well as outward constraints) in order to act in unexpected ways. Yet I do not mean that I want to act either at random or unpredictably. It is not in these senses that I want to be free, but in the sense that I want to be allowed to be different from others. I want to follow my own way—but I want it to be a way recognisably my own, and not zig-zag. And I want people to recognise it: I want them to say, 'How characteristic!'[19]

Yet at the same time he confessed that certain interpretations of science roused in him a fear that undermined his confidence:

> This is where the fulcrum of our fears lies: that man as a species and we as thinking men, will be shown to be no more than a machinery of atoms. We pay lip service to the vital life of the amoeba and the cheese mite; but what we are defending is the human claim to have a complex of will and thoughts and emotions—to have a mind. . . .
>
> The crisis of confidence . . . springs from each man's wish to be a mind and a person, in face of the nagging fear that he is a mechanism. The central question I ask is this: Can man be both a machine and a self?[20]

Our search

And so we come back to our original question; but now we clearly notice that it is a double question: not merely to what or to whom

---

[19] Bronowski, *Identity of Man*, 14–5.
[20] Bronowski, *Identity of Man*, 7–9.

does humanity as a whole owe its existence, but what is the status of the individual human being in relation to the race as a whole and to the uncountable myriads of individual phenomena that go to make up the universe? Or, we might ask it another way: what is our significance within the reality in which we find ourselves? This is the ultimate question hanging over every one of our lives, whether we seek answers or we don't. The answers we have for it will affect our thinking in every significant area of life.

These, then, are not merely academic questions irrelevant to practical living. They lie at the heart of life itself; and naturally in the course of the centuries notable answers to them have been given, many of which are held still today around the world.

If we are to try to understand something of the seriously held views of our fellow human beings, we must try to understand their views and the reasons for which they hold them. But just here we must sound a warning that will be necessary to repeat again in the course of these books: those who start out seriously enquiring for truth will find that at however lowly a level they start, they will not be logically able to resist asking what the Ultimate Truth about everything is!

In the spirit of truthfulness and honesty, then, let us say directly that we, the authors of this book, are Christians. We do not pretend to be indifferent guides; we commend to you wholeheartedly the answers we have discovered and will tell you why we think the claims of the Christian gospel are valid, and the help it offers real. This does not, however, preclude the possibility of our approaching other views in a spirit of honesty and fairness. We hope that those who do not share our views will approach them in the same spirit. We can ask nothing more as we set out together on this quest—in search of reality and significance.

OUR AIM

Our small contribution to this quest is set out in the 6 volumes of this series. In this, the second book in the series, we propose to select four broadly representative answers to the big questions about the reality in which we find ourselves. They are representative in the sense that each answer is, in part or whole, held in common by a number of different philosophies and/or religions, and has been, and still is, believed by millions of people. Having considered the answers, we can then ask which, if any of them, strikes us as likely to be true.

So let us state precisely the questions that we shall want to put to these four representative philosophies/religions:

1. What is the Ultimate Reality?

(*a*) Is it one, as many philosophies and religions have maintained, or many?

(*b*) Is it personal or impersonal?

(*c*) Is it the Creator of the universe, or is the creation of the universe the work of some lower power or process?

(*d*) Does it exist independently of the universe or is it part of the stuff of the universe?

(*e*) Or is the universe itself the self-existent, self-contained, self-sufficient Ultimate Reality?

2. How, and on what terms, are we related to the Ultimate Reality?

If we owe our existence to the Ultimate Reality, we must in some sense be its products. But in what sense?

(*a*) Are we, body, soul and spirit, created by the Ultimate Reality, in the sense that the human race did not always exist, but began to exist when the Ultimate Reality deliberately created the first human pair?

(*b*) Are we emanations from Ultimate Reality, like sunbeams that continuously emanate from the sun, so that while we ourselves are not the Ultimate Reality, we are of the same stuff as the Ultimate Reality?

(*c*) Is the Ultimate Reality blind, mindless matter from which we have, all unintended, evolved?

(*d*) Was there some vital force, or impersonal intelligence, inherent in original matter, that has right from the start driven and guided matter to evolve into us human beings?

3. Have we any moral responsibility to Ultimate Reality?

4. Has Ultimate Reality taken the initiative to disclose itself to us, or are we left to ourselves to discover it?

These then are the questions; and as we survey the various answers that are given, we shall naturally be looking to see on what authority they are based. The answers will be given by:

(*a*) Indian pantheistic monism
(*b*) Greek philosophy and mysticism
(*c*) Naturalism and atheistic materialism
(*d*) Christian theism

And now let's begin.

CHAPTER 1

INDIAN PANTHEISTIC MONISM
AN INDIAN SEARCH FOR ULTIMATE REALITY

Believe me, my son, an invisible and subtle
essence is the Spirit of the whole universe.
That is Reality. That is Atman. THOU ART
THAT.

—The Chandogya Upanishad

HISTORICAL INTRODUCTION

We are about to study Indian pantheistic monism as interpreted by the famous Indian philosopher Shankara,[1] but first some necessary, preliminary observations. In some languages the term 'Hinduism' is used as if it were an adequate label to denote the religion believed and practised by the people of India. But in this sense it is a misleading label. In the first place there are other religions native to India: Buddhism, Sikhism and Jainism.

In the second place, if we do use the term 'Hinduism' to refer to Indian religion, then we should be aware that Hinduism is not one homogeneous religion with a central creed laid down by some religious authority, like the Magisterium in Roman Catholicism or the Ecumenical Councils acknowledged by the Orthodox Churches. There are many forms of Hindu religion, each concentrated on the worship of its favoured god, gods or goddesses (there are traditionally said to be 330 million gods, or 300 or 30—in other words it does not matter how many), though some gods, like Krishna, are more widely recognised than others.

In the nineteenth century, European scholars thought, and so do many Indians still, that Indian civilisation began with the arrival in India (c.1500 BC) of the Aryan tribes whose language, Sanskrit, is a member of the Indo-European family of languages. It is also the language in which the sacred books of Indian religion were originally written.

However, in the early period of the twentieth century, British and Indian archaeologists discovered the remains of several early cities in what was then North India (now Pakistan), which have been dated to around 2500–1800 BC. This culture, known now as the Indus or Harappan Civilisation, had a developed religious system, elements of

---

[1] Alternative spellings: Śangkara, Shangkara. In Sanskrit his system of philosophy is called *advaita*, meaning 'non-dualistic'.

which may well have intermingled with the later Aryan systems.[2] In addition it must be realised that Hinduism is an umbrella term covering not only a non-unified religion but also a whole way of life, a richly variegated national culture built up of many elements.

Its sacred books fall into two groups:

1. The Vedas and the Upanishads. These are referred to as *Shruti* ('what is heard') and are said to contain truths divinely revealed to the early sages and later written down between 1500 and 300 BC.
2. A collection of texts, said to be based upon revealed truth, but of human composition. They are referred to as *Smriti*, meaning 'remembered' or 'handed' down, i.e. they are regarded as tradition rather than revelation.

According to Kim Knott 'Most Hindus accept the status and authority of the Veda', though he adds: 'but very few have read it'.[3] V. P. (Hemant) Kanitkar (a Hindu priest) and W. Owen Cole in their book[4] state that 'When questioned about the beliefs which an orthodox Hindu should hold, the reply tends to include:

- belief in one ultimate reality;
- belief in the authority of the *Vedas* (which includes the *Upanishads*);
- belief in the principles of karma and samsara, and the eventual attainment of moksha; to these might often be added the performance of *dharma*, right conduct, and the observance of caste duties.'[5]

In the course of the centuries, however, in addition to the cultic side of Hindu religion, a more philosophical approach was developed; and the result has been the formation of six orthodox schools of philosophy based on the Vedas.[6] The six philosophical systems are:

---

[2] See Knott, *Hinduism*, 5–9.

[3] *Hinduism*, 15.

[4] *Hinduism*, 183.

[5] The technical terms used here will be explained in a moment.

[6] Kanitkar and Cole (*Hinduism*, 184–5) state that all these systems can be traced back to times BC. The unorthodox schools are the Carvakas, Buddhism and Jainism; they reject the authority of the Vedas.

- Nyaya
- Vaisheshika
- Samkhya
- Yoga
- Mimamsa
- Vedanta

Of these six, the Vedanta system (Vedanta means the end of the Vedas) is the one that particularly interests us in this chapter, because it is concerned with expounding what the Vedic texts have to say on the topic of Ultimate Reality.

Within this system three scholars stand out, each with his own different interpretation: Shankara[7] (trad. AD 788–820), Ramanuja (trad. AD 1017–1137) and Madhva (thirteenth century AD). We shall be studying Shankara's philosophy. Until comparatively recently he was thought to be the most influential of the Indian philosophers, and still is by many. One of his modern admirers claims that he was 'a towering mystic of the ninth century AD whose word carries the authority of Augustine, Eckhart and Aquinas all in one'.[8] *The Encyclopaedia Britannica* reads:

> One of Shankara's modern admirers claims that he was 'a towering mystic of the ninth century AD whose word carries the authority of Augustine, Eckhart and Aquinas all in one'.

> The most renowned philosopher of this school, and, indeed, of all Hinduism was Śangkara. . . . The Śangkaran system has sounded the keynote of intellectual Hinduism down to the present, but later teachers founded sub-schools of Vedanta, which are perhaps equally important. . . . Śangkara is also said to have founded the four monasteries (*maṭha*) at the four corners of India: Sringeri in Karnataka, Badrīnāth in the Himalayas, Dwārkā in Gujarat, and Puri in Orissa. The abbots of these monasteries control the spiritual lives of many millions of devout Śaiva laymen throughout India, and their establishments strive to maintain the philosophical Hinduism of the strict Vedānta.[9]

Shankara's philosophical system is known as 'Advaita Vedantism': 'vedantism' because it is based on (his interpretation of) the Veda; and 'advaita', which means 'non-dualistic', because he teaches

---

[7] Also spelt Śaṅkara, or Śangkara.

[8] Easwaran, *Bhagavad Gita*, 18.

[9] 15th edn, 1989, 603.

that the human soul, or self, and the Ultimate Reality, Brahman, are one and the same thing—not two entities, but one.[10]

Here is a short glossary[11] giving the meaning of other Indian technical terms that we shall encounter:

1. BRAHMAN [*Brahman*, from *bṛh* 'grow, expand': that which expands, bursts into growth]. The Supreme Godhead, beyond all distinctions or forms; Ultimate Reality.

2. BRAHMA [*Brahmā*]. The Creator; in the Upanishads, a secondary deity of the Vedic pantheon. Not to be confused with Brahman.

3. ATMAN [*ātman*, 'self']. Self; the innermost soul in every creature, which is divine.

4. SAMSARA [*saṃsāra*] 'That which is constantly changing'; the phenomenal world; the cycle of birth, death, and rebirth.

5. MOKSHA [*mokṣa*]. Liberation (from *samsara*, the cycle of birth, death and rebirth).

6. KARMA [*karma*, 'something done']. Action, work, behaviour; also the consequences of action, spiritually and mentally, as well as physically.

The difference between Brahman and Brahmā

To understand Hindu thought, it is of fundamental importance to distinguish between the terms Brahman and Brahmā. In non-Sanskrit orthographies they often look almost the same; but in Sanskrit orthography they are totally different.

Brahman is a neuter noun and carries the connotation that the godhead, the Supreme Reality underlying all life, the divine ground of existence, is impersonal. But this Supreme Reality is not the Creator. The Creator is Brahmā (this noun is masculine), one of the Hindu triad of major gods that proceeded from, but are less than, Brahman. The other two are Vishnu, the Preserver, and Shiva, the Destroyer, called 'the auspicious one'. Vishnu is thought to have incarnated himself from time to time, in animal form, in half animal and half

---

[10] For Shankara's work see Bādarāyana et al., *The Vedānta Sūtras of Bādarāyana*.

[11] This glossary is taken from Easwaran, *Upanishads*, 337–44.

human form, and in human form, as in Rama and Krishna. All three gods of the Triad are frequently spoken of as performing more or less the same functions.

This idea that the Supreme Godhead is not the Creator, but that the Creator is some lesser god, is not exclusive to Hinduism. It occurs also in Greek thought. To see its significance, we should perhaps contrast it with the very different Hebrew, Christian and Islamic doctrine of creation in which the one and only God is himself the Creator and there are no other gods: cf. 'I am the LORD, and there is no other, besides me there is no God . . . I made the earth and created man on it; it was my hands that stretched out the heavens . . . For thus says the LORD, who created the heavens . . . "I am the LORD, and there is no other"' (Isa 45:5, 12, 18).

> This idea that the Supreme Godhead is not the Creator, but that the Creator is some lesser god, is not exclusive to Hinduism.

SHANKARA'S ADVAITA VEDANTA PHILOSOPHY

We come, then, to Shankara's philosophy, looking for its answers to our questions: What is the nature of the Ultimate Reality to which the human race and we as individual men and women owe our existence? And how are we related to that Ultimate Reality?

Put succinctly its answers are:

1. The inner Self of each individual human being, the Atman, is essentially the same as Brahman, the Supreme Reality, in the sense that they are not two different entities but one. Atman *is* Brahman. The true inner Self in each person *is* God. Each person can say 'I am God'.

2. The myriad apparent individual phenomena in the universe, whether human, animal, vegetable, or mineral are illusions. The only reality is Atman = Brahman.

3. The aim of every individual person is to realise his or her true identity with the divine Self, which is Brahman. This realisation can be achieved only by meditation (a form of sophisticated psychological activity), if need be assisted by the constant recitation of a mantra.

4. Those who manage to achieve this realisation of the identity of the inner Self with Brahman, will, upon death, find their sense of Self dissolved by complete immersion in the infinite sea of pure consciousness that is Brahman.

5. Those who do not in this life achieve the realisation of the identity of their inner Self with Brahman, or having achieved it, do not live as they should, will have to undergo reincarnation (or a series of reincarnations) in a material body, to work off their *karma*, i.e. the ongoing effects of their wrong behaviour, until at length they achieve *moksha*, that is, liberation from the otherwise inevitable cycle of birth, death and rebirth.[12]

An explanation

In saying that the Self, the Atman, in each individual person is Brahman, Shankara is not claiming that this Self in the individual person is the sum total of Brahman. On the other hand, since Brahman is believed to be non-complex, and indivisible, one cannot speak of a part of Brahman being present in one individual. Rather one must say that the Self of the individual is like a drop of water in the Atlantic Ocean, of the same essence as the ocean, and only logically, but not actually, distinct from the undivided waters of the ocean itself.

One of the *Upanishads* contains a number of parables told by a father to his son, Svetaketu, in order to teach him that Atman, the Self, is Brahman. In one of them the father says to his son:

'Bring me a fruit from this banyan tree.'
'Here it is, father.'
'Break it.'
'It is broken, Sir.'
'What do you see in it?'
'Very small seeds, Sir.'
'Break one of them, my son.'
'It is broken, Sir.'
'What do you see in it?'
'Nothing at all, Sir.'

12 See Shvetashvatara Upanishad, 5.11–12, Easawaran (tr.), *Upanishads*, 131–2.

Then his father spoke to him: 'My son, from the very essence in the seed which you cannot see comes in truth this vast banyan tree. 'Believe me, my son, an invisible and subtle essence is the Spirit of the whole universe. That is Reality. That is Atman. THOU ART THAT.'[13]

Shankara himself says:

In the same way as those parts of ethereal space which are limited by jars and water pots are not really different from the universal ethereal space . . . so this manifold world with its objects of enjoyment, enjoyers and so on has no existence apart from Brahman.[14]

What he means by the phrase 'has no existence apart from Brahman' he further illustrates by an analogy. Take a number of objects made of clay, a pot, say, or a jar or a dish. We differentiate them and use different words to denote these things that to us at first sight appear to be different. But in reality, he claims, they are not different: they are all made of exactly the same substance, namely clay. In this way the objects in this world, and the persons, are not different from Brahman:

The individual soul and the highest Self differ in name only, it being a settled matter that perfect knowledge has for its object the absolute oneness of the two.[15]

Brahman, then, *is* Atman, the Self of every human being; and therefore every human being is God.

Question 1 – Knowing this to be true

The question naturally arises, *how can anyone know for certain that all this is in fact so?* The answer given is 'by meditation'.[16] But it is a very special kind of meditation. We are told that it is not intellectual study, nor intuition, nor imagination. It is not concentration on a

---

[13] Chandogya Upanishad, 6.12, Mascaró (tr.), *Upanishads*, 117.

[14] Shankara, *Vedānta Sūtras*, 2.1.14, Thibaut (tr.), 1:321.

[15] Shankara, *Vedānta Sūtras*, 1.4.22, Thibaut (tr.), 282; cf. 2.3.43, Thibaut (tr.), 441.

[16] Easwaran, *Upanishads*, 16–17.

topic, not even on the mind itself, for in the process the 'I' deliberately withdraws awareness from the mind that it regards as a mere, constantly changing, mechanism. It is said to be a concentration on consciousness, as Easwaran explains:

> When awareness has been consolidated even beyond the mind, little remains except the awareness of the 'I'. Concentration is so profound that the mind-process has almost come to a standstill. . . . gradually you become aware of the presence of something vast, intimately your own but not at all the finite, limited self you had been calling 'I'. All that divides us from the sea of infinite consciousness at this point is a thin envelope of personal identity. That envelope cannot be removed by any amount of will; the 'I' cannot erase itself. Yet, abruptly, it does vanish. . . . the barrier of individuality disappears, dissolving in a sea of pure, undifferentiated awareness. . . . What remains when every trace of individuality is removed? We call it pure being . . . The sages called it Brahman . . . the irreducible ground of existence, the essence of every thing—of the earth and sun and all creatures, of gods and human beings, of every power of life. . . . this unitary awareness is also the ground of one's own being, the core of personality. This divine ground the Upanishads call simply *Atman*, 'the Self'—spelled with a capital to distinguish it from the individual personality. . . . In all persons, all creatures, the Self is the innermost essence. And it is identical with Brahman: our real Self is not different from the ultimate Reality called God. This tremendous equation—'the Self is Brahman'—is the central discovery of the Upanishads. Its most famous formulation is . . . : *Tat tvam asi* 'You are That'. 'That' is . . . a Reality that cannot be described; and 'you', of course, is not the petty, finite personality, but that pure consciousness . . . the Self. . . . there is no time, no space, no causality. These are forms imposed by the mind, and the mind is still. Nor is there awareness of any object; even the thought of 'I' has dissolved. Yet awareness remains.[17]

---

[17] Easwaran, *Upanishads*, 37–9.

A difficulty with Shankara's non-dualistic philosophy

First, we must underline the warning that Easwaran himself gives, that meditation of this kind is 'dangerous territory. We know what forces can buffet us in the dream world, and that is only the foothills of the dark ranges of the mind.'[18] His advice is that such meditation should never be attempted without the guidance of an expert.

This very warning raises an immediate question. If there is a God who created us and wants us to know him, how likely is it that he would have made the process of getting to know him so difficult and so dangerous, as to be beyond the abilities of most of his creatures?

If those who practise this kind of meditation must first withdraw their awareness from all around them, from their minds, and ultimately from their own identity, what guarantee have they that the awareness they achieve by this process is an awareness of God, and not just the effect of probing the physical state of the deep brain? How do they know that it is God that they are aware of, if they did not have some intellectual idea, before they started, of what the God they were seeking might be like? And how can they assure us that what they have become aware of is God, since, according to them, God is beyond all description?

> If there is a God who created us and wants us to know him, how likely is it that he would have made the process of getting to know him so difficult and so dangerous, as to be beyond the abilities of most of his creatures?

They tell us that in the process of meditation they become aware of the presence of something vast . . . the sea of infinite consciousness, which they eventually discover is The Self. So at this point they appear to be aware of an object; but when the 'I' dissolves in this sea of undifferentiated awareness, they report that they are no longer aware of any object. Even the thought of 'I' has dissolved. Then who or what is it that becomes aware that this not only is 'The Self' but is the core of *their* personality as it is of the personality of every creature? How could they be aware of the existence of other creatures, let alone of the core of their personalities, if at the time they were not aware of any object?

---

[18] *Upanishads*, 31.

If 'The Self' is pure being, pure consciousness, and 'The Self' is Brahman, then Brahman likewise is pure consciousness and aware of no object. And if in this state The Self has lost all awareness of 'I', then so must Brahman, the Supreme Reality, the godhead, be unaware of himself, and of all his creatures! But how can there be a pure consciousness that is not conscious of anything?

They report that in this state of undifferentiated consciousness they experience *sat*, Absolute Reality, and *ananda*, pure, limitless, unconditioned joy.[19] But once again, we have to ask who or what is it that experiences these things, in the total absence of self-consciousness? Is the godhead no better than a baby of two months old that is not yet self-conscious, but whose smile suggests it is having pleasant sensations?

There appears to be, then, a very serious logical difficulty with Shankara's non-dualistic philosophy. R. C. Zaehner expresses it thus:

> If the Absolute is conscious, it must also be conscious either of itself or of something other than itself. But by definition nothing but the Absolute truly exists. Therefore the Absolute must be self-conscious. But if it is self-conscious, it must in some sense have personality, which it is said to transcend. Moreover self-consciousness is hardly conceivable without consciousness of that which is not self.[20]

And, of course, if the Absolute is conscious of itself, there is here a logical duality, and Shankara's non-dualism contradicts itself.

Question 2 – Explaining the particulars

If the real Self in everyone and everything is one and the same Brahman, how do we explain the myriad, individual, distinct, particular phenomena in the universe? (And how do normal people have such strong conviction that we are different from one another and from God?)

Shankara's answer to the question is that all this apparent individuality is an illusion (*maya*). What he means by illusion is something like the impressions created by a skilful magician. Or take

---

[19] Easwaran, *Upanishads*, 40.
[20] *Concise Encyclopedia of Living Faiths*, 234.

another, often quoted, analogy: at a distance someone might think he sees a snake; but on close inspection it turns out to be not a snake but a rope. The rope itself exists; it is not an illusion, but its seeming to be a snake was an illusion. So your friends, Natalie, Susan, Jose and Alex, might look to you as if they were separate individuals. But that is only an impression due on Brahman's side to his (its) skilful 'magic', and on your side to your ignorance. In actual fact they are all of them Brahman, one undivided entity.

Non-dualists, however, maintain that this belief in the ultimate unreality of individuals does not in any way devalue human personality. Brahman is said to rejoice in the endless variety of particular things that his (or, its) 'magical' art produces.[21] But the intrinsic value of the particular individual personality is seriously undermined when the goal of meditation and of life itself is described thus:

> Non-dualists maintain that this belief in the ultimate unreality of individuals does not in any way devalue human personality.

> The most important consequence of these beliefs: that a human being can, within consciousness, reverse the process of creation which proceeded from singularity to diversity: not just retrace it, for example, in science or philosophy, but reverse it, so that one withdraws from the world of change and follows what St. Augustine called the 'hidden footprint of unity' that is there, perhaps covered but never eradicated in our consciousness.[22]

Moreover, we are further warned that if we do not realise properly here on earth that our true Self (as distinct from our false self which imagines that we are distinct, separate individual human beings) is one entity with Brahman and with every other human being and animal, then at death an undesirable consequence will follow. Instead of finding release (*moksha*) from the cycle of birth, death and rebirth (*samsara*), we shall have to suffer a further reincarnation in another human body. And that will mean we shall once more have the misleading and undesirable appearance of being a distinct, individual human personality, or indeed some lesser thing.

---

[21] Shvetashvatara Upanishad, 4.1–5, Easawaran (tr.), *Upanishads*, 126–7.
[22] Nagler, 'Reading the Upanishads', 317.

Katha Upanishad says:

> Come, I'll tell you this secret and eternal
>   formulation of truth (*brahman*);
> And what happens to the Self (*ātman*), Gautama,
>   when it encounters death.
>
> Some enter a womb by which
>   an embodied self obtains a body.
> Others pass into a stationary thing—
>   according to what they have done,
>   according to what they have learned.[23]

Some suggest that the phrase 'a stationary thing' refers to a plant or a tree. Consider also these lines from Katha Upanishad: 'Who sees multiplicity, | But not the one indivisible Self, | Must wander on and on from death to death';[24] and 'If one fails to realise Brahman in this life, | Before the physical sheath is shed, | He must again put on a body | In the world of embodied creatures.'[25]

An appeal to science

Now modern followers of Shankara's system claim that it agrees with contemporary physics. Speaking of the ancient Hindu sages Easwaran says:

> Penetrating below the senses, they found not a world of solid, separate objects but a ceaseless process of change—matter coming together, dissolving, and coming together again in a different form. Below this flux of things with 'name and form', however, they found something changeless: an infinite, indivisible reality in which the transient data of the world cohere. They called this reality Brahman: the Godhead, the divine ground of existence.
>
> This analysis of the phenomenal world tallies well enough with contemporary physics. A physicist would remind us that the things we see 'out there' are not ultimately separate from each other and from us; we perceive them as separate because

---

[23] 5.6–7, Olivelle, *Early Upanishads*, 397; alternative enumeration, Part 2.2.6–7.

[24] 4.10 (Easwaran, *Upanishads*, 85); alternative enumeration, Part 2.1.10.

[25] 6.4 (Easwaran, *Upanishads*, 90); alternative enumeration, Part 2.3.4.

of the limitations of our senses. If our eyes were sensitive to a much finer spectrum, we might see the world as a continuous field of matter and energy. Nothing in this picture resembles a solid object in our usual sense of the word. 'The external world of physics', wrote Sir Arthur Eddington, 'has thus become a world of shadows. In removing our illusions we remove the substance, for indeed we have seen that substance is one of the greatest of our illusions.' Like the physicists, these ancient sages were seeking an invariant. They found it in Brahman.[26]

The danger of the fallacy of reductionism

One of the fascinating goals of science is to find out the basic element of which all the myriad individual objects in the universe are made. At the moment the main candidate proposed is energy. But we must not let this lead us into the trap of thinking that if we can explain what a thing is made of, we then know what a thing is. For that is not so.

Take water, as an example. Knowing what water is made of, namely two gases, hydrogen and oxygen, is far from telling us what water is. Water has properties and functions and significance that neither hydrogen nor oxygen has.

What a thing is, therefore, and what its function is, is much more important than what it is made of. Take a silver teaspoon and a silver flute. To say that the difference between them is illusory, and that the reality is that both are made of silver, or indeed that they are simply part of a continuous field of matter and energy, is to ignore the fact that it is the complexity imposed by the silversmith on the basic silver that gives them their individual significance and value.

> What a thing is, therefore, and what its function is, is much more important than what it is made of.

The continuous field of matter and energy, compared, say, with the human cell, appears to be a comparatively simple thing. The human cell is not simple: it is astonishingly complex. If that is true of the cell, what shall we say of a whole human being, consisting as it

---

[26] Easwaran, *Bhagavad Gita*, 24–5.

does of ten trillion cells? To suggest that the marvellous complexity of even the physical component of a human personality is adequately described by saying that it is simply part, along with cabbages and slime, of a continuous field of matter and energy, is to lose touch with reality altogether. The random buzzing and crackling of electricity wires on a frosty night is not basically one with a symphony by Tchaikovsky. Between them lies a gulf, impassable by mere energy and matter, namely the input of the creative genius of a complex human personality.

The supposed nature of Ultimate Reality

If the complexity of a human being is part of the glory of being human, the claim that Ultimate Reality is pure, undifferentiated, simplex being, must at first sight seen strange. But it is perhaps easy to see how Hindus of this persuasion come to assurance that their belief about the nature of Ultimate Reality is true. They come to it by 'meditation'. They first withdraw awareness from the mind, thus stripping themselves of all ability to make distinctions. They then withdraw their awareness from all reality around them, or within them, and even from their own identity. It is not, perhaps, to be wondered at, that what they then report being aware of is pure undifferentiated consciousness. What else could they be aware of by that method?

That they should then conclude that what they become aware of by this method is Brahman, the Ultimate Reality, is to anyone who believes in God as the transcendent Creator, strange indeed. But it is not surprising, in view of the Hindu concept of our relation to Brahman.

That they should then conclude that what they become aware of by this method is Brahman, the Ultimate Reality, is to anyone who believes in God as the transcendent Creator, strange indeed. But it is not surprising, in view of the Hindu concept of our relation to Brahman. We are not created by Brahman, in the strict sense of that term. We are emanations from Brahman, like sunbeams emanating from the sun, and therefore of the same stuff as the sun. Our being is not simply analogously like God's being in some respects (as in Judaism, Christianity and Islam): our being *is* God's being, the very same substance. We are made out of God.

In the beginning was only Being,
One without a second.
Out of himself he brought forth the cosmos
And entered into everything in it.
There is nothing that does not come from him.
Of everything he is the inmost Self . . .
You are that, Shvetaketu; you are that.[27]

This, then, is classical Indian pantheistic non-dualism. Pantheism of any kind is fraught with serious difficulties, as we shall see in later chapters; but it is an idea that has been incorporated into many philosophies. The ancient Stoics held a form of pantheism: according to them the Intelligence that lay at the heart of the universe, a spark of which was in every human being, was itself part of the stuff of the universe. Similarly nowadays a number of leading scientists (as we shall see in Ch. 3) begin to be attracted to this element in Hindu thought. Compelled by advances in modern science to recognise that there must be an intelligence behind the universe, they do not relish the idea that this intelligence might be the transcendent Lord God Almighty who created the world out of nothing. In that case, the only alternative is something like the impersonal, all pervasive, Brahman of Indian pantheistic non-dualism.

ADDITIONAL NOTE: KEY PROMOTERS OF VEDANTA

Other notable exponents of the Vedanta philosophy have been:

(a) in medieval times:
    1. Ramanuja (trad. AD 1017–1137)
    2. Madhva (thirteenth century AD)

---

[27] Chandogya Upanishad, 6.2.2, 2.3, Easwaran trans.
   The Upanishads often speak of other gods like Shiva, and Vishnu as creating the world, along with Brahmā who is explicitly said to be the Creator. But these, themselves, are emanations of Brahman and therefore can be spoken of as The Self, just as humans can claim to be Brahman. There is felt to be a hierarchy in which some entities, like rocks, have less Brahman in them than humans, and they in turn have less than the gods, and the gods less than the Ultimate Reality.

(*b*) in more modern times:
1. Vivekananda Swami (1863–1902). He popularised Shankara's non-dualist philosophy in the West, in the USA and in England (1893–96), as a result of which the first Vedanta Society was founded in New York (1895).
2. A. C. Bhaktivedanta Swami (1896–1977), who in 1966 founded the International Society for Krishna Consciousness (ISKCON). Hare Krishna devotees are committed to spread awareness and love of the god Krishna in the West as well as in India.
3. Sir Sarvepali Radhakrishnan (1888–1975). He was professor of philosophy at Mysore (1918–21) and Calcutta (1921–31; 1937–41), and the first Spalding Professor of Eastern Religions and Ethics at Oxford University (1936–52); a friend of Mahatma Gandhi; Indian ambassador to the Soviet Union; and President of India (1962–67).

While they all embrace the Vedantic system of philosophy, they do not all adhere to Shankara's rigid non-dualism. Some embrace dualism; some adopt worship, rather than pure intellectualism, or mysticism, as their preferred approach to God. Some regard God as personal. All are pantheists.

CHAPTER 2

GREEK PHILOSOPHY AND MYSTICISM

AN INTELLECTUAL SEARCH FOR ULTIMATE REALITY

Thus mythology overreached itself and discredited the very existence of a spiritual world. Science drew the conclusion, not that the spiritual world had been misconceived, but that there was no such thing: nothing was real except tangible body composed of atoms. . . . The Socratic philosophy is a reaction against this materialistic drift of physical science.

—F. M. Cornford, *Before and After Socrates*

ANCIENT RELEVANCE

Still seeking answers to our questions about the nature of Ultimate Reality, and how we are related to it, we now leave the East and journey to the West, from Indian pantheistic monism to Greek philosophy and mysticism.[1]

Greek philosophy has proved to be one of the most important and influential movements of thought in the history of Western civilisation. The movement is traditionally held to have begun with Thales of Miletus in Ionia (*c*.600 BC). In the course of the following centuries it eventually developed into a formal system of education with its colleges and professors in various cities of the ancient world. As a pagan system of organised education it came to an end in AD 529, for in that year the emperor Justinian shut down the philosophical schools in Athens—an early example of the tendency that religion has to use political power to stifle freedom of thought. However, the influence of Greek philosophy continues with us still in this twenty-first century; for many of the questions that it raised are still debated not only by professional philosophers but by educated people generally.

THE CHIEF SIGNIFICANCE OF GREEK PHILOSOPHY

Perhaps the most significant thing about it is, not so much the results it achieved, but the new approach it brought to the question of man's relation to Ultimate Reality. Abandoning mythological and

---

[1] The ancient Greek word *mystēs* (from which 'mysticism' derives) was originally a religious term. It denoted someone who had been initiated into one of the so-called 'mystery' religions. Such initiates, after preparatory ceremonies, were said to witness manifestations of a god or goddess or to learn secret, and supposedly powerful, names, spells and charms. Nowadays the term is often applied to what is more accurately called 'spiritism' or 'occultism', in which people claim that they can be put in touch with the spirits of the dead (see the biblical prohibition of this practice in Isa 8:9–20). In this section, however, we shall be concerned not with mysticism in either of these senses, but with the particular form of philosophical mysticism advocated by the Neoplatonist Plotinus.

polytheistic interpretations of the origin, composition and workings of the universe and of humankind, it determined to investigate these things by observation and reason.

Faced with the multiplicity of life forms on the earth, the Greek philosophers were no longer content to attribute life to the Sky-god impregnating the Earth-goddess as the myths taught. They were not prepared any more to regard thunder as the loud angry voice of Zeus, the high god of the Greek pantheon. They set themselves to think what stuff the universe was made of, by what natural processes it had reached its present state, what natural forces initiated and maintained the perpetual motion of the heavenly bodies, and the cycles of growth and decay, of birth, life and death; and what human beings were made of, and how they came about.

Abandoning mythological and polytheistic interpretations of the origin, composition and workings of the universe and of humankind, Greek philosophy determined to investigate these things by observation and reason.

Then there came a second stage, when people like Socrates were no longer content to ask what the sun and moon were made *of*: they wanted to know what the human race was made *for*; what is the purpose of humanity's existence; what supreme good should people aim at in life; what principles and laws should guide their behaviour. But here again it was no longer a question of blindly accepting the traditional cultural norms of contemporary society as though they automatically possessed divine authority. Rather such questions as justice and truth and courage and piety had to be thought through rationally.

It is, then, to Greek philosophy that we shall, in this chapter, address our question: What is the nature of Ultimate Reality and how are we related to it? But first we must make some precautionary observations.

PRECAUTIONARY OBSERVATIONS

We have said that the early Greek philosophers abandoned the traditional mythological interpretations of the universe, and relied simply upon observation and reason. But that does not mean that they all forthwith abandoned faith in, or worship of, the gods. It simply means that when it came to their 'scientific' investigations, some of them—particularly the Ionian philosophers—felt the gods to be irrelevant.

For example, Xenophanes (b. 570 BC) lampooned the anthropo-morphic gods of mythology:

> The Ethiopians say that their gods are snub-nosed and black, the Thracians that theirs have light blue eyes and red hair.[2]

> But if cattle and horses or lions had hands, or were able to draw with their hands and do the works that men can do, horses would draw the forms of the gods like horses, and cattle like cattle, and they would make their bodies such as they each had themselves.[3]

This lampoon is well known, and is often quoted nowadays to support the contention that the very idea of God is a human invention. But that is unfair to Xenophanes who appears to have been almost a monotheist when he spoke of:

> One god, greatest among gods and men, in no way similar to mortals either in body or in thought.[4]

> Always he remains in the same place, moving not at all; nor is it fitting for him to go to different places at different times, but without toil he shakes [or, 'controls'] all things by the thought of his mind.[5]

Nor did the majority of his fellow philosophers forthwith abandon all talk of God. Thales, the first of the Ionian philosophers, is reported to have remarked: 'everything is full of gods'. But here we must be careful to understand precisely what he means, since the word 'god' did not necessarily mean to the Greeks what it means to us today. For instance, someone brought up in the Judaeo-Christian tradition may well say 'God is love'. He expects you to know what he means by 'God', namely, the One True God, Creator of the universe; and then he mentions one of God's attributes, namely, love. But an

---

[2] Fr. 16, Clement *Strom.* 7.22.1 (Kirk and Raven, 168).

[3] Fr. 15, Clement *Strom.* 5.109.3 (Kirk and Raven, 169).

[4] Fr. 23, Clement *Strom.* 5.109.1 (Kirk and Raven, 169).

[5] Fr. 26 & 25, Simplicius, *Phys.* 23.11 & 23.20 (Kirk and Raven, 169).

ancient Greek, using his Greek word *theos* (god) is more likely to say 'Love is *theos*'. What he means by that is that love is a wonderful, mysterious, 'divine', power—but only one such power among many. Nor did all these philosophers abandon every preconception that stemmed from the earlier mythologies. Far from it. There are three basic concepts from Greek mythology that recur time and time again in many of even the more advanced philosophers. They are: (1) that matter existed *before* the gods; (2) that some one or other of the gods imposed order and form on the basic stuff of the universe, and in that sense, but only in that sense, can be talked of as a creator; and (3) that even this god, like all the others, arose out of original matter, and is part of the stuff, or one of the forces, of the universe.

The mythologist Hesiod (*c*.700 BC), for example, in his poem *Theogony* ('genealogy of the gods') speaks of:

> The august race of first-born gods, whom Earth
> Bore to broad Heaven.[6]

And again:

> Olympian Muses, tell
> From the beginning which first came to be?[7]

And the answer is given:

> Chaos was first of all, but next appeared
> Broad-bosomed Earth.[8]

> And misty Tartarus, in a recess
> Of broad-pathed earth, and Love [*Eros*], most beautiful
> Of all the deathless gods.[9]

Commenting on Hesiod's poem Professor Werner Jaeger wrote:

> If we compare this Greek hypostasis of the world-creative Eros with that of the *Logos* in the Hebrew account of creation, we may observe a deep-lying difference in the outlook of the two peoples. The *Logos* is a substantialization of an intellectual prop-

---

[6] Theogony, ll. 44-46, Wender (tr.), 24.
[7] Theogony, ll. 114-115, Wender (tr.), 26.
[8] Theogony, ll. 116-117, Wender (tr.), 27.
[9] Theogony, ll. 119-120, Wender (tr.), 27.

erty or power of God the creator, who is stationed *outside* the world and brings that world into existence by his own personal fiat. The Greek gods are stationed *inside* the world; they are descended from Heaven and Earth . . . they are generated by the mighty power of Eros, who likewise belongs within the world as an all-engendering primitive force. Thus they are already subject to what we should call natural law. . . . When Hesiod's thought at last gives way to truly philosophical thinking, the Divine is sought inside the world—not outside it, as in the Jewish–Christian theology that develops out of the book of Genesis.[10]

It has been worth quoting Professor Jaeger at length because he has put his finger on a basic issue that we shall meet again and again in our study, an issue, in fact, that still divides the world's philosophical and religious systems even today, and that is what is meant by *creation*.

The Greek system taught that:

1. Matter has always existed and always will. It is eternal. In its basic state it was formless, unorganised and boundless— what the Greeks call *chaos*. But then some god or other arose and imposed order on this pre-existent material, and turned it into a well-ordered universe—what the Greeks call *cosmos*; and this process is what the Greeks meant by creation.
2. The creator is part of an eternal system in which everything in the universe emanates out of God, like sunbeams out of the sun; and so, in some sense, everything *is* God.
3. God is somehow in the matter of the universe, actively engaged in moving and developing matter to the best effect.

In contrast to ideas of this kind stands the ancient Hebrew tradition, which has been inherited by Christianity and Islam. It was already centuries old in the time of the Ionian philosophers. It taught that

1. Matter is not eternal: the universe had a beginning; and there is only one God, creator of all.
2. God existed before the universe, and is independent of it. The universe is not an emanation out of God. God created

---

[10] *The Theology of the Early Greek Philosophers*, 16–17.

it out of nothing, not out of himself, though he maintains it
and is guiding it to its destined goal.

With those preliminary remarks, then, we turn to study the ancient
Greek philosophers. Not all of them, of course, but representatives of
three main kinds. And we shall be looking to see what conclusions
they reached on the basis of their presuppositions and methods, in
regard to the questions we have asked: What is the nature of Ultimate
Reality, and how are we related to it?

THE SEARCH FOR WHAT THE WORLD IS MADE OF

The interesting thing is that right from the very start the Greek philosophers appear to have assumed that the seemingly endless multiplicity of things must have stemmed from one primal substance,
unknowingly anticipating an aspect of modern scientific methodology. They set themselves to discover this primal stuff—the *archē* as
they called it.

Naturally enough, the early thinkers did not all agree on what
the primal stuff was.

Thales (*c*. mid sixth century BC). For him the primal stuff was
water. Some scholars have suggested that this idea was prompted by
his observation that water could exist in three different forms: gas
(steam), liquid (water) and solid (ice). Others, with perhaps more
plausibility, suggest that he noticed that throughout nature moisture
is always connected with the processes by which seed germinates and
brings forth life. Thales held that the earth floated on water. He is famous for having been able to predict the eclipse which took place in
585 BC. (It would be worthwhile looking up this story in Herodotus,
The Histories, I.74.)

Anaximander (611–547/6 BC). For him the primal stuff was what
he called in Greek *apeiron*, that is, 'indeterminate', 'without boundaries'. Some scholars think he meant that this primal stuff had no external boundaries, and was therefore infinite in extent. Others hold
that he meant that the primal stuff contained in itself all those things
and states which now seem to be different, or even opposites—hot
and cold, moist and dry, etc.—but with no internal boundaries be-

tween them in a single indeterminate mixture. He believed that this *apeiron* was the cause and maintainer of perpetual motion, and he called it divine. In the course of this motion the *apeiron* split up into pieces that then formed the universe, and beings of all kinds. He is famous for his brilliant, new idea that the earth is not supported by something concrete; it stays still because it is equidistant from everything around it, and therefore is in equilibrium. 'The earth is on high, held up by nothing, but remaining on account of its similar distance from all things.'[11] This idea was radically new.

Anaximenes (active about the middle of the sixth century BC). For him the primal stuff was air, the element necessary for breathing, and therefore for life. He held that the earth was broad, flat and shallow in depth, and was supported by air.

THE SEARCH FOR HOW THE UNIVERSE WORKS

Somewhat different was **Heraclitus** (about 40 years old *c*.500 BC), who has become famous for his saying that 'everything is in flux'. He deserves to be known rather for another, more important insight. The unity he looked for behind the multiplicity of things was not so much that of the primal stuff of the universe, as that of the one basic principle—the *logos* as he called it in Greek—which held it all together and made it work. He decided that the world in its working is held together by the interactive tension between opposites; and that these opposites constantly turning into one another, like day and night, cannot exist separately.

> Heraclitus has become famous for his saying that 'everything is in flux'. He deserves to be known rather for another, more important insight.

To illustrate his theory he used the analogy of a bow and its bowstring. The wood of the bow, drawn into an arc by the bowstring, is all the while pulling against the string in an attempt to return to its own original straightness. The bowstring, stretched and held taut by the bow, is all the while pulling in the opposite direction against the wood of the bow. It is this interactive tension between the bow and the string, however,

---

[11] Hippolytus *Ref.* I.6.3 in Kirk and Raven, *Presocratic Philosophers*, 134.

that keeps the two opposite forces working together and thus enables the instrument to function. It is also the stretching of the bow by the archer, and then its sudden relaxation that sends the arrow on its way.

Heraclitus suggested that there were many such opposites-in-tension at work in the universe, with one alternately giving way to the other, and then the other to the one, so restoring the balance and coherence of the forces of nature, and thus maintaining the general harmony of the universe. He cited hot and cold, moist and dry, day and night, up and down, etc. It was much like the principle of yin and yang, the two opposing forces that by their complementary interaction form and maintain the workings of the universe, according to Eastern thought. Still today scientists talk of matter and anti-matter, centripetal and centrifugal forces, gravity and anti-gravity.

Empedocles (*c.* middle of the fifth century BC) made the innovative suggestion that there never was an original unity. There were four basic substances in the universe—Fire, Air, Earth and Water. Between them they filled the whole of space. But they were perpetually shifting, now coming together in different proportions, now separating. Empedocles, however, realised that he had to explain what caused this motion. Motion is something that has to be accounted for: it cannot be taken for granted. He came to the conclusion that the power of love which draws human beings together, and the power of hate that drives them apart, are in fact two forces that operate throughout the universe, and affect matter as well as animate beings.

Anaxagoras (*c.*500/499–428/7 BC) went further. He proposed that the source of movement was the single intellectual force of Mind.

When we read this we could easily forget that we are reading the thoughts of a philosopher who lived two and a half millennia ago. We could rather imagine that we are reading the recent suggestions of some of the world's leading modern scientists. The fantastic fine-tuning of the universe and the irreducible complexity of the cell make it virtually impossible for them to go on believing that the whole universe, including human intellect and reason, have arisen by mindless processes from mindless matter.

Of course, we have to ask how Anaxagoras conceived of this 'Mind'. Was it part of the matter of the universe? Or was it a truly incorporeal entity? G. S. Kirk and J. E. Raven comment:

Anaxagoras in fact is striving, as had several of his predecessors, to imagine and describe a truly incorporeal entity. But as with them, so still with him, the only criterion of reality is extension in space. Mind, like everything else, is corporeal, and owes its power partly to its fineness, partly to the fact that it alone, though present in the mixture, yet remains unmixed.[12]

Christians might be tempted to comment that Anaxagoras was, to use a phrase of Paul's, 'feeling after God' (Acts 17:27).

Different again from Heraclitus, Empedocles and Anaxagoras was **Parmenides** (born c.515–510 BC). He took the search for the One behind the Many to an extreme. He claimed that the universe is one solid block in which no change or motion ever takes place. Any impression of change or movement that we receive through our senses is sheer illusion. In our understanding of the world and of the universe we must be guided solely by reason and not by our senses.

Such a theory seemed in its own day, as it still does today, to fly in the face of common sense and reality. Consideration of the simple fact that people are born, live, grow old and then die might serve to convince anyone that change does in fact take place. And if our sense-impressions are illusions, do not even our illusions change from time to time? Nevertheless Parmenides' theory brought to prominence a question that has occupied philosophers ever since: the conflicting claims of empiricism on the one hand and rationalism on the other.[13]

Parmenides was also the first to force upon the attention of his contemporaries, and on philosophers ever since, the area in philosophy which is labelled ontology. That is the study of what is meant by saying that something exists.

To understand his thinking we should first be aware that the Greek verb 'to be' can be used in two senses:

1. To state 'existence'. So when the Greek of John 1:1 says 'In the beginning was the Word', it means 'In the beginning the Word existed'.
2. To act as a copula: 'Socrates is wise' i.e. 'Socrates = wise'.

---

12 *The Presocratic Philosophers*, 374.
13 We discuss the meaning of these terms in Book 3 of this series: *Questioning Our Knowledge*.

Parmenides, Greek speaker though he was, seems not to have realised that the verb 'to be' had these two meanings. He thought it always implied existence. For him, then, what exists has 'Being'; what does not exist must be regarded as 'Non-Being'. Therefore to define an absolute vacuum by saying that an absolute vacuum is a state in which there is nothing at all, would have been for Parmenides both linguistic and logical nonsense. To say such a vacuum *is* is to say that it exists, 'has Being'. But according to Parmenides such a vacuum cannot exist, cannot have Being: it is Non-Being. A vacuum cannot be anything.

The next stage in his argument was to appeal to an axiom fundamental to Greek thought: 'out of nothing, nothing comes'. From this he then deduced the following points:

1. 'Being' (whatever exists) is eternal, neither coming into being, nor ceasing to be. For had it not always existed, there would have been a time when it was non-existent, 'non-being', and from that 'non-being' nothing could ever have come into existence, and the universe would not now exist. Moreover, if Being could cease to exist, everything would eventually become non-being and thereafter nothing could ever come into being.

2. 'Being' is the same all the way through. Since every part of reality has 'Being', the only way in which one part could differ from another would be in not being something that the rest is. But not being does not exist. If you differ in 'nothing', you do not differ at all.

3. 'Being' (what exists) cannot change or move. For the only way Being could change or move would be by not being what it was before, or by not being where it was before. But there is no such thing as 'not-being'. Not-being does not exist.

Now after many centuries of analysis of language and logic we can see the mistakes in Parmenides' reasoning. To start with, the verb 'to be' does not always imply existence. If we say 'a unicorn is a horse with a single horn protruding from its forehead', we do not imply by the verb 'is' that such an animal actually exists; we are merely defining what the term 'unicorn' in fairy tales means.

Secondly Parmenides assumed that the term 'being' must always be used univocally, that is, it always implies only one kind of being. But that is not necessarily so. A chair does not have the same kind of being (existence) as the carpenter who made it. The chair's being was manufactured by the carpenter; the carpenter's being was not manufactured by the chair. Similarly Christians would argue that God's Being and the universe's being are not exactly the same kind of being. The universe is dependent on God for its being. There was a time when it did not exist; it was created out of nothing and one day will cease to exist. It is, as philosophers would say, contingent being. God's being is not dependent on anything or anyone. It is not contingent.

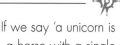

If we say 'a unicorn is a horse with a single horn protruding from its forehead', we do not imply by the verb 'is' that such an animal actually exists; we are merely defining what the term 'unicorn' in fairy tales means.

But it has not been a waste of time studying Parmenides' attempts at arguing philosophically; for it can teach us how critical we have to be of the meanings of the words and terms we use when we try to argue. Nor should we underestimate the importance of the issues that Parmenides raised by his pioneer thinking. They are still relevant to advanced physics and cosmology, as Karl Popper has shown in his book *The World of Parmenides*.

In contrast to Parmenides, **Leucippus** (*fl. c.*440–435 BC) and **Democritus** (born *c.*460–457 BC), the inventors of the atomic theory of matter, could rightly be said to have been, not monists, but dualists in the sense that they taught that two things exist eternally: void (empty space) and atoms. They held, moreover, that the void did actually exist and that its existence was necessary for the movements of the atoms (Parmenides held that there was no such thing as movement). In addition they claimed that the void was infinite in extent, and the atoms infinite in number. Both existed eternally. The atoms were indestructible.

They do not appear to suggest how this infinite number of atoms was originally set in motion. Taking it for granted that they were all moving randomly in all directions, they then argued that by the laws of dynamics the atoms would necessarily and irresistibly be drawn into a vortex. In that process atoms would collide with other atoms, rebound and collide again with still other atoms. Since, according to them, the atoms were of different shapes, there would result multitudinous conglomerations that for a while would stick together. Thus evolved worlds and beings of all kinds, both human and animal. These conglomerations would hold together by their interlocking shapes, helped by the continual external bombardment by the other atoms that surrounded them.

But eventually the atoms in the conglomerations would come unstuck and would disperse. Then whatever these conglomerates had been, whether universes, or individual human beings, or anything else, they would cease to exist; and their component atoms, being themselves indestructible, would go off and become part of other conglomerates.

To have conceived of even their version of the atomic theory in those early centuries was, it must be said, brilliant, all the more so because it was arrived at, not empirically through the senses—in their day even their kind of atoms could not be seen or individually touched— but by reason.

They were dualists, then, to this extent at least that they believed in both space and atoms. Modern atomic theory, as we all know, is very different from theirs. But to have conceived of even their version of the atomic theory in those early centuries was, it must be said, brilliant, all the more so because it was arrived at, not empirically through the senses—in their day even their kind of atoms could not be seen or individually touched—but by reason.

Yet in another sense they were monists, for their theory was unrelievedly materialistic: matter was everything. For them there was no Mind behind the world's, or man's, existence, not even with the limited function that Anaxagoras gave to Mind of getting the original cosmic motion going. There was, therefore, no purpose behind the human race's existence. All happened by a mixture of necessity and chance. The mindless laws of physics (necessity) would remorselessly draw the atoms into a vortex. Which atoms then collided with which might well be due to chance. But the shape and size of the atoms would necessarily dictate the formation of the conglomerations. (Similar arguments are still used in connection with evolutionary theory.)

The human soul, moreover, was made of atoms, finer than other atoms, but still nothing but matter, like all other atoms. At death the atoms dispersed: nothing of the man or his personality survived.

Nowadays this bleak theory would be labelled physical monism.

Democritus' younger contemporary, Plato, rigorously criticised Democritus' theory on the ground that it denied any purpose behind the human race's existence; and so have many since. The Cambridge classicist F. M. Cornford summed it up well:

> The essential feature of this Atomism is that it is a materialist doctrine . . . in the sense that it declares that material substance, tangible body, is not only real but the whole of reality. Everything that exists or happens is to be explained in terms of these bodily factors. The world is resolved into an invisible game of billiards. The table is empty space. The balls are atoms; they collide and pass on their motion from one to another. That is all: nothing else is real. There are no players in this game. If three balls happen to make a cannon, that is a mere stroke of luck— necessary, not designed. The game consists entirely of flukes; and there is no controlling intelligence behind.[14]

Then Cornford proceeds to offer his account of how Greek philosophy came to ignore or deny the spiritual aspect of humans and of the universe in this way (as indeed do many people still):

> If the world has a spiritual aspect, man can only give an account of it in terms of his own spirit and mind. At first he projected elements of his own personality into external things. Then the Greek imagination developed these elements into the complete human personalities of anthropomorphic gods. Sooner or later the Greek intelligence was bound to discover that such gods do not exist. Thus mythology overreached itself and discredited the very existence of a spiritual world. Science drew the conclusion, not that the spiritual world had been misconceived, but that there was no such thing: nothing was real except tangible body composed of atoms. The result was a doctrine that philosophers call materialism, and religious people call atheism.

> The Socratic philosophy is a reaction against this materialistic drift of physical science.[15]

---

[14] *Before and After Socrates*, 24–5.
[15] *Before and After Socrates*, 27.

THE SEARCH FOR HUMANITY'S PURPOSE AND GOAL

Socrates (470–399 BC)

It would be a mistake to suppose that all the Greek philosophers be-fore Socrates were interested solely in the physical universe, and had no concern for moral philosophy and theology; and equally and more obviously wrong to suppose that from Socrates onward Greek philos-ophers abandoned interest in the physical universe and concentrated solely on moral philosophy and theology. But with Socrates a notice-ably new emphasis entered Greek philosophy.

Socrates was at first interested in the new physical theories that were being propounded, and was excited when he learned of Anax-agoras' suggestion that Mind was the first cause of the universe's de-velopment. Socrates thought this would mean that Mind must have had some rational purpose in creating the universe, and that it would have designed the universe in the best possible way to achieve that purpose. Merely to explain, as Anaxagoras did, what the universe was made of, and what caused its motion, still left unexplained what, for Socrates, were the most important things requiring explanation:

1. What purpose was the universe created to fulfil?
2. Can it be shown that Mind has designed the universe in the best possible way so as to fulfil that purpose?
3. What is the point and purpose of human existence?

We can easily understand Socrates' dissatisfaction with Anax-agoras. If you were called on to explain a telescope to someone who had never seen one before, would you start by first explaining what it was made of? Would it not be more sensible to point out first what it was made for? And then to point out how skilfully it was engineered in order to achieve the purpose for which it was made; and then what theory of optics controlled the production of the lenses; and only fi-nally, what the lenses and the casing were made of?

According to Plato, Socrates was sitting in prison when he made his criticism of Anaxagoras.[16] Socrates had been condemned to death by the Athenian court and was awaiting execution. Some of

---

[16] *Phaedo* 97c–99d.

his friends would gladly have supplied the money to bribe his way out of prison. But he refused their offer, and that for two reasons. First, he had taught others that as citizens of a state, if they could not get the laws changed by democratic means, they ought to submit to the laws of the state, and not act as anarchists. He would not now disobey those laws himself, simply for his own advantage. Secondly, he believed that god had appointed him to act as his fellow-citizens' moral mentor, and he would not desert his god-given charge just to save his life. Truth and justice, he held, were more important than physical life.

If, then, someone asked 'Why is Socrates sitting in prison, and not trying to escape execution?' it would be silly, Socrates maintained, to answer in terms of what Socrates was made of: arms, legs, spine, joints and muscles, and to point out that all those things were at this moment bent in the right position for sitting. It was his mind—his profoundly intellectual and moral mind—that controlled his body and directed him to stay in prison. And it was Socrates' belief that mind in man, which is meant to control his body, must be akin to the Mind that controls the universe.

Humanity's proper work and virtue

Two words stand out in Socrates' vocabulary, as being keys to his thought: 'work' and 'virtue'. Both need explanation.

Socrates argued that the proper work of a shoemaker, qua shoemaker, his *ergon* as the Greeks called it, was to make shoes; that of a doctor was to heal sick people; that of a naval captain to navigate the seas. 'What, then,' he asked, 'was the proper work of man qua man?' In other words, what was the chief purpose that men and women were meant to aim at and achieve in life? His answer was 'To perfect that part of him that is eternal, and therefore most important, that is, his soul'.

Some modern philosophers would dispute his analogy. 'Shoemaker' is, they say, a 'functional' word; and so is 'doctor', or 'engineer' or 'farmer'. It is legitimate, therefore, to enquire what is the nature of the functions that these words imply. But 'human being', they point out, is not a 'functional' word. It does not itself imply any function. And that is true, if one argues simply on the basis of semantics. But given Socrates' presupposition that there is a Mind behind the universe, then man's function would be to fulfil the purpose for which the Mind created him.

The Old Testament would here agree with Socrates. It says for instance, that man was made in the image of God to act as God's steward and manager of earth's ecosystem (Gen 1). This is a function and responsibility that people of the twentieth and twenty-first centuries have woken up to, more perhaps than previous generations; and they have become aware that the proper discharge of this function raises profound moral questions. Is it morally right, for the sake of maximising profits, to destroy the fish stocks in the sea by overfishing? Is it just to pollute the rivers and oceans with poisonous industrial discharges? Is it morally justifiable to hunt rhinoceros almost to extinction in order to get their horns for superstitious customers in wealthy countries? Is it fair for one industrial nation to pollute the atmosphere, increase global warming, and destroy the forest in neighbouring countries by acid rain, or radiation fallout?

> The Old Testament would here agree with Socrates. It says for instance, that man was made in the image of God to act as God's steward and manager of earth's ecosystem.

The second key word in Socrates' thought was 'virtue' (Gk. *aretē*). As Socrates used it, it did not denote moral virtue so much as the quality of being good at something. So the *aretē* of a farmer was to produce good crops. The *aretē* of a shoemaker was to be good at making shoes. And to be good at that a shoemaker would have to have precise knowledge about feet, their shape and action, and about the component parts of a shoe, and how to fit a shoe comfortably to a foot, so that the foot could function properly.

The human race's *aretē*, then, was to be good at the proper development of that part of him that distinguishes man from animal, that is, his soul; and for that purpose he would need to have precise and accurate knowledge about such things as justice, and courage, and self-control, and piety, etc.

Socrates' search for definitions

Socrates, therefore, set himself to find answers to such questions as: What is justice? What is courage? What is temperance? He was not looking simply for particular instances of those qualities, such as, this or that act was courageous, or this law was more just than that one. He was looking for definitions. (See, as a good example of this, his questioning of Euthyphro in Plato's dialogue of that name.)

This, in itself was a great contribution to clear thinking, to get people to distinguish between properties of a thing, and definitions of that thing. If, for instance, someone is asked to say what ice cream is, and replies that ice cream is something which little boys like, what he says is certainly true in itself; but it is not a definition of ice cream. It is simply one of the properties that ice cream happens to have, an 'accidental' property, as we say. There are many other things that little boys like, and the property of being liked by little boys, doesn't tell us what ice cream *is* in itself, nor distinguish it from other things liked by small boys.

But in insisting on the search for definitions, Socrates was not teaching logic for the sake of abstract reasoning. In his society, what was held by some people to be just, was regarded by others as totally unjust; and the conventional exercise of justice was often distorted. It was Socrates' contention that one cannot rightly decide whether a particular law, or a particular business deal, is just or not, if one does not know what justice is.

Socrates himself seems not to have discovered the definitions he was seeking for, though in the process of searching for them in his conversations with his fellow citizens he exposed the fact that many of his city's conventional ideas on such things as justice were not rationally thought through, but seriously defective. Calling attention to that was what in the end caused his death at the hands of the State.

> Socrates exposed the fact that many of his city's conventional ideas on such things as justice, were not rationally thought through, but seriously defective.

Socrates' concept of Ultimate Reality

Suppose, then, we put to Socrates our double question as to the nature of Ultimate Reality and how we are related to it. His answer is much debated by the experts. Socrates certainly believed that Mind, not matter, was the Ultimate Reality behind the universe. If Plato's *Apology* and the early dialogues (as distinct from the later dialogues in which Plato puts his own ideas in the mouth of Socrates) coupled with Xenophon's *Memorabilia* can be trusted, the historical Socrates spoke of god or the gods indiscriminately as though he accepted the traditional mythologies. On the other hand, there are places where he seems to imply one supreme Creator God. For instance, he refers in the singular to the Supreme Being as 'he who created man from the beginning';[17] and in another place he mentions, as distinct from other gods, 'he who coordinates and holds together the universe.'[18]

Was he a pantheist? It seems not. He certainly believed that mind in humans that controls their bodies was akin to the Mind that controls the universe; but he seems to have meant it analogously, and not to assert strict identity between the two. Moreover, in the passage already quoted (iv.3.13), not only are the gods (however Socrates envisaged them) kind to men, but in particular 'he who coordinates and holds together the universe' ceaselessly supplies the good and beautiful contents of the universe for our use. That is language which, as we have seen, the pantheist Shankara could never have used of Brahman, and which Plotinus could never use of the One.[19]

As to man's relationship with God or the gods, Socrates certainly held that it is a relationship of moral responsibility; and, without dogmatising, he seems to have considered that, after death, man will be judged according to his works.[20]

Whatever, then, Socrates' exact answer to our double question would have been, if we could have put it to him, we cannot doubt the noble sincerity of a man who for conscience's sake was prepared to submit to execution by the State, and paid with his life for his insistence on the search for the truth.

Plato (c.428–347 BC)

Plato was not only a philosopher and a fervent moralist but a literary artist with a poet's imaginative powers. His influence on subsequent thought has been massive. We cannot here even begin to comment on the vast range of his philosophical system. Our particular interest lies in his answer to our double question: What is the nature of Ultimate Reality and how are we related to it? To understand Plato's answer we

---

[17] Xenophon, *Memorabilia*, i.4.5.
[18] *Memorabilia*, iv.3.13.
[19] We shall think more about Plotinus' thinking about the One in the following pages.
[20] Plato, *Apology* 40e–41a.

must recall the teachings of earlier philosophers and mark how Plato developed and modified them.

Heraclitus had taught that everything in the universe is continually changing and in a constant state of flux. If, then, one regards reality as that which really exists, and then one has to admit that that which really exists is constantly changing, it would follow that one could not have complete and permanent knowledge of reality, but only tentative impressions and opinions of it.

Parmenides had taught the opposite. Change, becoming, i.e. coming into existence, perishing, i.e. passing out of existence, and movement of any kind, were illusions, not real, mere appearances that deceive our senses. Only intellect and reason could tell us the truth. Reality, that is what really exists, is one solid undifferentiated whole, eternally existing, unchanging, in which there is no motion, no 'becoming', but only 'Being'.

Plato's reaction to these two sets of doctrines was to develop Socrates' insistence on the difference between particular instances of a quality, like beauty or justice, and the definition of that quality. Particular instances of, say, beauty can vary in duration and extent; by contrast the definition of beauty will be always the same.

> Particular instances of, say, beauty can vary in duration and extent; by contrast the definition of beauty will be always the same.

In our changing world, such as Heraclitus saw it, a particular example of, say, beauty can be mixed in with other qualities. Beauty can be seen in a woman who is tall, blonde, young, with long hair, or in a woman who is short, brunette, middle-aged, and close-cropped. By contrast, the definition of beauty must describe beauty itself apart from any other qualities.

In our changing and imperfect world various objects show varying degrees of beauty. But beauty itself, as truly defined, must admit of no degrees.

Again in our changing world beauty can gradually increase and then subsequently decay and perish. A plain child may develop into a beautiful adult, and then in old age become ugly. Beauty itself, as truly defined, must be unchanging and eternal.

Now there is no evidence to suggest that Socrates ever gave thought to the question what kind of entities beauty itself, justice itself, courage itself, piety itself might be. He seemed to have looked on them simply as definitions. But Plato came to think that they were substantial entities—he called them 'Forms' or 'Ideas'[21] and he made the following distinctions:

1. The Forms, Beauty itself, Justice itself, etc., exist, not in our changing world but in an eternal, unchanging world such as Parmenides imagined our world to be; and they are themselves eternal and unchanging. They are 'really real'.[22] Particular things or acts are beautiful or just, as long as, and to the extent that, they 'share in' the Form of Beauty or the Form of Justice. Being part of this changing world, they have some kind of reality but they are not 'really real', like the Forms are.

2. Since the Forms and the world they exist in are eternal and unchanging, we can arrive at true knowledge of them by means of reason, after suitable education to awaken memory of the Forms that Plato believed the soul had seen before birth. But of particular things in this changing world, we cannot have true knowledge, but only more or less tentative opinion.

The question of motion

Parmenides had denied that there was any such thing as motion. Plato disagreed with him about that; and not only with him, but with the professional itinerant lecturers of the time, called sophists. To understand the point at issue between Plato and the sophists we should first understand that what the Greeks called *kinēsis*, that is, 'motion', included not merely movement, like that of the sun and the stars, but growth and development, such as those of an acorn into an oak tree.

The sophists held that the universe itself and all its most important contents are the product of nature, nature being understood as an inanimate mindless force. The world, the cycles of the sun, moon, stars and seasons are all the results of chance movements of matter.

---

[21] Hence the philosophical term 'idealism' as distinct from 'realism'. Plato's 'Forms' raise similar questions to those raised by the problem of 'universals' in modern philosophy. Wittgenstein denied their existence; D. H. Armstrong argues for universals that play a role in scientific laws.
[22] Some mathematicians, like Penrose of Oxford, still think that the great truths of mathematics exist independently of us. We discover them but do not invent them.

The human race's activities in art, design, engineering and law are secondary phenomena, not necessarily inherent in nature, and often contrary to it. The gods are merely products of the human mind.

Plato countered those assertions by calling attention to movement in the world and in the universe. Like Empedocles and Anaxagoras, he felt that motion has to be accounted for; it cannot just be taken for granted. Some things communicate to other things the motion that they first receive from some other source. They, therefore, cannot be the original source of motion. That original source must be something that can move other things but did not itself receive its motion from any other source. It has the source of motion in itself.

The sophists held that the universe itself and all its most important contents are the product of nature, nature being understood as an inanimate mindless force.

The only thing, Plato argued, that has the source of motion in itself is what the Greeks called soul, or life-principle, *psychē*. Therefore, he went on to argue, the human soul must come before the body, and its powers of mind, morality and intelligent design before the body's merely material powers of strength and size. From this he concluded that while there are evil powers at work in the world, the Prime Mover and Subsequent Controller of the universe must likewise be an Intelligent, Moral World Soul infinitely superior to the human soul. For how could the Prime Mover and Controller of the universe be less intelligent than man?

The question naturally arises: how did Plato conceive of this World Soul? To answer that, we must return to his theory of the Forms.

The Form of 'the Good'

Having posited the existence of the Forms, Plato realised something that they each had in common. Each of the different Forms—Justice itself, Courage itself and so forth—could be said to be good. From this he deduced that there must also exist a Form of the Good. If so, this Form of the Good, could not be just one more Form along with the other Forms. They were instances of goodness; the Form of the Good was the source of their goodness; it therefore must be above them just as the other Forms were above the instances of beauty, justice, courage and so forth, which we encounter in this world.

What, then, was this Universal Good common to them all? We notice, to start with, that the term the Good (Gk. *to agathon*) does not denote moral goodness. It means rather what we should mean if we were to ask: what is the good of physical exercise, or the good of playing chess? What is the good of justice, of trying to be courageous? The good of a thing is what makes us value it and long after it.

> The good of a thing is what makes us value it and long after it.

To Plato, then, the knowledge of the Good was the highest form of knowledge. 'It's no use', he writes, 'possessing anything if you can't get any good out of it. Or do you think that there's any point in possessing anything if it's no good? Is there any point in having all other forms of knowledge without that of the good, and so lacking knowledge about what is good and valuable?'[23]

The Good, therefore, is the end, the supreme object of all desire and aspiration, the thing a human being lives for, would do anything, or give anything, to get:

> The Good, then, is the end of all endeavour, the object on which every heart is set, whose existence it divines, though it finds it difficult to grasp just what it is.[24]

In addition the Good is 'the condition of knowledge, or that which makes the world intelligible and the human mind intelligent'.[25] The sun, Plato points out, is not itself sight; but without the light it sheds, the human eye would not be able to see anything. So it is in the light of the Good that the human intellect is able to make sense of the intelligible world.[26] And just as the sun is also visible, so the Good is intelligible.[27]

Thirdly, according to Plato, the Good is the creating and sustaining cause of the world.

> The Good therefore may be said to be the source not only of the intelligibility of the objects of knowledge, but also of their being

---

[23] *Republic* 505b–c; Book 6, Lee (tr.), 304.
[24] *Republic* 505e; Book 6, Lee (tr.), 304.
[25] Nettleship, *Republic of Plato*, 218.
[26] *Republic* 507c–509a (Book 6).
[27] *Republic* 508b (Book 6).

and reality; yet it is not itself that reality, but is beyond it, and superior to it in dignity and power.[28]

Finally, though the Good is the cause of knowledge and truth and is itself known, yet it is something other than, and even more splendid than, knowledge and truth.[29]

What, then, does Plato say that the Form of the Good is? He says it is beyond Being; so obviously he is not thinking, like the early Ionian philosophers, that it is some primal stuff of which the universe is made. But by 'beyond Being', he may also mean that while one may rightly ask what is the good of, say, justice or beauty, one cannot, with any sense, ask what is the good of the Good. While the Good is the reason why all else exists, the Good itself does not need any reason for its existence. Uncaused itself, it is, as Aristotle will say, the Final Cause of everything else. It is the Ultimate Reality.

Now the thought process by which Plato reached these conclusions may seem to us moderns somewhat tortuous. But the question he raises is still for us of the highest practical importance. If there is some supreme good that we are meant to serve in life, that supreme good must have been the cause of our existence in the first place. What then is the Good? All the major philosophical schools in Greece—Platonists, Aristotelians, Stoics, Epicureans—all asked this question, and gave their various answers. We should be wise to ask the same questions ourselves.

What, then, was Plato's answer?

Plato's identification of 'the Good'

Plato, then, has described in detail what he thought Ultimate Reality was like. We notice that in calling it 'the Good' he has combined the moral aspect of absolute good with the metaphysical concept of the origin of all reality. But when it comes to identifying 'the Good', Plato, it must be said, disappoints us. Let Professor W. K. C. Guthrie explain:

Some have thought that the Good in the *Republic* is itself Plato's god, but so far as his words go there is no suggestion that it is

---

[28] *Republic* 509b; Book 6, Lee (tr.).

[29] *Republic* 508e–509a (Book 6).

personal, or anything but the final *object* of thought. Is it anachronistic to suggest that, as in the philosophy of Plato's greatest pupil [i.e. Aristotle], 'Mind and its object are the same'? I do not know, nor, I believe, does anyone else. But that it is godlike or divine is certain. So are all the Forms of which it is the chief, for by turning his mind to them the philosopher 'through his familiarity with the divine and orderly becomes himself orderly and divine so far as a man may be'.[30]

Yet when in the *Timaeus* Plato comes to talk about the creator, he does so in terms of the older mythologies. The creator is a kind of master-craftsman who is not the omnipotent originator of the material universe, but simply imposes order on a pre-existent chaos and produces from it the best he can according to a pre-existent model.[31]

Aristotle (384–322 BC)

Aristotle was undoubtedly Plato's most able student, and as a young man he seemed to have accepted all Plato's teachings. But his disposition was very different from Plato's. He was much more of a scientist than Plato ever was, and eventually he abandoned many of Plato's theories.

The starting point in his philosophy was not contemplation of ideal Forms in some other realm; but the study of actual things in this world that we know by our senses. His pioneer work in biology was based on the systematic collection and study of specimens with a view to understanding the function and interrelationship of their constituent parts. His findings in biology remain, perhaps, the most significant part of his work.

If he were going to study, say, dogs in order to arrive at a definition of what a dog is, he would start by collecting a number of actual dogs, examining them all to see what essential features they all had in common—as distinct from accidental features such as that one or two of the dogs might have only three legs, because the fourth had been bitten off in a dogfight. He would then proceed to establish a definition of the species, dog, which could be used to decide whether

---

[30] *History of Greek Philosophy*, 4:512.
[31] *Timaeus* 29e–34.

a particular animal that you subsequently encountered was a dog, or a leopard.

But in Aristotle's thinking this did not mean that there existed in some separate, intelligible world the Form of Dog, Dog itself, as Plato might have said. The form of dog existed in each actual dog here on earth. The form could logically be distinguished from the matter of which the dog was composed, but practically it was inseparable from the matter; just as the form of a shuttle is inseparable from the wood of which it is made.

Aristotle's four causes

Aristotle analysed man-made things under four headings: their Material Cause, their Efficient Cause, their Formal Cause, and their Final Cause. Take a weaver's shuttle as an example.

1. Its Material Cause was the material it was made of.
2. Its Efficient Cause was the carpenter who made it.
3. Its Formal Cause was the shape and function he had in mind when he set about making it.
4. Its Final Cause was the purpose it was meant to serve, namely, to produce cloth.

To explain, therefore, what a shuttle was, it was utterly insufficient to analyse what it was made *of*; you must discover and describe the purpose which it was made *for*. Its final purpose, though not achieved until the end of the process, was responsible for the form it was given, and indeed for its being made at all. The end purpose determined the beginning. We call this the *telic* view of things.

Aristotle also applied this analysis to living things, human beings included, though in these cases the terms had to be modified. Aristotle did not believe in a creator, at least not in the Judaeo-Christian sense of the term. To Aristotle both the forms of all living things and the matter they were composed of were eternal. Therefore, instead of the 'efficient cause', it would be better to talk of the 'moving cause', for reasons we shall see in a moment.

Then in addition to the four causes, he made great use of the concepts 'potential' and 'actual'.

Take an acorn. Its final cause is the fully-grown oak tree into which it will develop. The acorn is not yet an actual oak tree, but it is a potential oak tree. What is more, it already has within it the 'form' of an oak tree that will control its development so that it eventually develops into an oak tree, and not into, say, a silver birch or a palm tree. And the moving cause is the life that is in it, moving it along towards the fully-grown oak tree that it unconsciously aspires to be.

Aristotle noticed that in living things the form is contributed to the seed by a fully-grown and mature specimen of the species. It requires an oak tree to produce an acorn and to contribute to the acorn the 'form' that will eventually develop the acorn into an oak tree. The chicken has to supply the egg with its inherent chicken form within it; adult human beings have to produce the human embryo with its inherent human form. The human embryo is therefore already a potential human being, since it already contains the 'form' of a human being; and this 'form' will develop the embryo eventually into an actual, mature human being. What is more the 'form' will be passed on and persist through many subsequent generations. One cannot help observing how close Aristotle came to the modern theory according to which the information necessary for developing a human being from embryo, through birth, to adulthood and beyond, is carried by the chemicals of the genes; and while the original chemicals perish, the information remains constant and is passed on to subsequent generations.

> One cannot help observing how close Aristotle came to the modern theory according to which the information necessary for developing a human being from embryo, through birth, to adulthood and beyond, is carried by the chemicals of the genes; and while the original chemicals perish, the information remains constant and is passed on to subsequent generations.

Aristotle's idea of God

Like many other pagan philosophers Aristotle rejected the idea of a creator who created the universe out of nothing. He held that matter and the natural forms of everything are eternal. There never was a beginning; there never will be an end. Birth–life–death–and the succession of the generations is an endless cycle. Given the eternality of matter and the eternal activity of natural forms, one might have thought that Aristotle would have felt no need in his system for a god of any sort. But he did; and it will be interesting to see why, and what kind of a Being he imagined God to be.

Aristotle's theory of motion

Like Plato and Anaxagoras before him Aristotle believed that the phenomenon of motion in the universe had to be accounted for; it could not be taken for granted. Since he thought that the universe was eternal, without beginning and without end, he supposed that motion within the universe was similarly without beginning and without end. Circular motion was, in his view, the optimum form of motion, since it could be said to have no beginning or end, and could maintain itself eternally.

Yet a question remained. What was the powerhouse within the system that produced and maintained the motion?

In addition, he regarded the cycle of birth, growth and death in this terrestrial world to be a form of movement. The form of the oak tree within the acorn would give the acorn an unconscious 'aspiration' to develop into an oak tree, and the human form in an embryo would give it its aspiration to develop into a mature adult. But what was it that made it work, and kept the process going?

Aristotle, therefore, had to decide and describe the source of movement within the universe. He argued that the source of movement must by definition (of the idea of source) be something that owes its own movement to nothing else, but at the same time moves everything else: hence the term he used, 'the Unmoved Mover'. The next question was: How, and by what kind of mechanism did this Unmoved Mover exert its power over all other things?

At this point in his theory Aristotle introduced the idea of Mind (Gk. *nous*). In human beings, he thought, mind was a part of the human soul. Yet mind, he felt, was so much the superior part of the soul, that it was (in the Greek sense) divine, akin to the nature of god, and could possibly survive the death of the body and of the rest of the soul.

He concluded that if the Unmoved Mover was, as it must be, utter perfection, the highest thing in the universe, it must be perfect Mind. Yet, to be perfect, it must not be in a potential state, it must be pure actuality, not potential Being but actual Being.

Then again, for this divine Mind to be perfect it must be engaged in the highest kind of mental activity; and Aristotle had no doubt what kind of thinking that was. The thinking of, say, a builder is not an end in itself: its goal is the building of houses. The thinking of a politician is not an end in itself. It does not manufacture anything; but it has as its goal the ordering and governing of society. But genuine theoretical thinking is an end in itself. It is not aimed at producing, or managing, anything. It is engaged in thinking for its own sake. It is the highest kind of happiness (see the final chapters of his *Nicomachean Ethics*). It was the kind of thinking that Aristotle himself enjoyed most.

Aristotle concluded therefore that the divine Mind, the Unmoved Mover, is eternally engaged in the highest kind of thinking. But thinking about what?

He (or it) could not be engaged in creating things, for that involved a lower kind of thinking, and meant beginning with mere potential and proceeding to actuality. Nor could he be concerned with, or care about, things in this world, not even about human beings, because they were all in the process of moving from potential to actuality, through birth, maturity, and then to old age and death. The Unmoved Mover, Aristotle concluded, was pure thought, thinking about itself, thinking about thinking; 'for', said Aristotle, 'the activity of mind is life'.

If then, the divine Unmoved Mover is not interested in the universe of men and things, how does he move anything? Aristotle answers that the sheer activity of his pure thought exerts a powerful attractive power that instigates and maintains motion in the rest of the universe. It is, as some have said, like a beautiful woman whose beauty attracts many admirers to aspire after her, while she herself is not interested in any of them.

Reflections on Aristotle's concept of God

F. M. Cornford

It has always seemed to me unfortunate that the word 'God' (which is, after all, a religious word) should have been retained by philosophers as the name for a factor in their systems that no one could possibly regard as an object of worship, far less of love. In the Middle Ages, the subtlety of scholastic rationalism was strained to the utmost in the attempt to reconcile Aristotle's God with the God proclaimed in the Gospels. . . . The plain truth is that the Being described as the object of the world's desire, the goal of aspiration, has ceased to be an object that could excite anything recognisable as desire. When the God of feeling is rationalised into a logical abstraction, the feeling itself dwindles and fades.[32]

Marjorie Grene

Aristotle's God is finite through and through, wholly determinate Being, pure thought and the purest object of thought, delimited sharply from all other beings, the point of reference for our knowledge of them as beings but not, most emphatically not, the source of their existence as Father or creator. Aristotle's God cannot love the world; he can be no more than the self-sufficient object of its love, the self-contained being which other beings imitate. How can such a being be said to live? I do not know.[33]

W. K. C. Guthrie

The conclusion is that the only possible object of the eternal thought of God is himself.... There is no way by which he could include in his thought the creatures of the physical world.... Thus all possibility of divine providence is excluded. God cannot care for the world: he is not even aware of it.... God does not go out to the world, but the world cannot help going out to him.... 'He moves as the object of desire.' ... Since the world was never created but is coeval with time itself, no initial act of creation in time is called for, and the last consideration is removed which could cause God to display even a momentary interest in the world.[34]

After this there is no need to point out the difference between the God of Aristotle and the God made known by Jesus Christ, who notices the fall of a sparrow (Matt 10:29), who numbers the hairs of our head (Matt 10:30), and who 'so loved the world that he gave his only Son, that whoever believes in him should not perish but have eternal life' (John 3:16).

---

[32] *Before and After Socrates*, 102–5.

[33] *A Portrait of Aristotle*, 246–7.

[34] *The Greek Philosophers from Thales to Aristotle*, 129–31.

NEOPLATONIC MYSTICISM

We now leave Socrates, Plato and Aristotle, and travel through the centuries to Plotinus (AD 204/5–270), the founder of so-called Neo-platonism. On the way we can afford, for our present purposes, to bypass the Stoics and the Epicureans. Both of these systems of philosophy were forms of monistic materialism. True, the Stoics believed that there was Reason behind the universe; but that Reason was part of the stuff of the universe (though a very refined form of stuff like fire), and it was immanent in everything. Stoics were *panentheists*. Epicureans, for their part, adopted the atomism of Leucippus and Democritus (see above); they were virtual atheists.

We pass on, then, to Plotinus. He was the last of the great Greek philosophers, and in him we meet something that we, in this study of Greek philosophy, have not so far encountered, namely a vigorous intellectualism, equal or even excelling that of the previous Greek philosophers, yet coupled with a kind of religious mysticism.[35] His writings are known as *The Enneads*.[36]

Plotinus on reality

If we put our double question to Plotinus as to the nature of Ultimate Reality, and how we are related to it, he will reply that there are four levels of reality:

1. **The Ultimate, Supreme Reality**, which he calls 'the One' and also 'the Good'. Below the One there is:

2. **Mind**, at the first remove from the One; and therefore in some sense less real than the One, but nonetheless part of Reality. Below Mind there is:

3. **The World Soul**, again less real than Mind but still part of Reality.

Then below these three comes:

4. **Matter**. But this is so far from the One, which is the perfection of being, that it is almost non-being, verging on formless chaos; and it is evil.

---

[35] There were of course elements of mysticism in some earlier philosophical writings.

[36] There has recently been a rising tide of interest in the professional study of Plotinus with the effect that older interpretations are being challenged. See e.g. O'Meara, *Plotinus*; Gerson, *Plotinus*.

Plotinus' argument for the existence of the four levels of reality

Let's start by remembering Aristotle. He pointed out that the 'form' of a chair is more important than the material it is made of. It is the form, chair, which is the cause of the shape that is given to the material.

Plotinus argues that it is Soul that forms, organises, directs and controls the matter of our bodies, and of all bodies of every kind. Soul is not in the matter: the matter is taken up by Soul. Matter, therefore, is dependent on the kind of being above it in the hierarchy, namely Soul.

But from where did Soul get the necessary wisdom to know how to organise and govern matter aright? The answer is from the next stage above it, that is Mind; for Mind contained all the Platonic Forms, on the pattern of which Soul created and governed matter.

But then again, since Mind contains all the Forms and they are the topic of its thinking, Mind is not truly One: it is composite. It is made up of a subject (the thinker) and an object (the Forms).

Now it was axiomatic in Greek thought that anything that is composite must depend on something that itself is simple, that is, non-composite. Therefore, Plotinus argued, above even the World-Mind there must exist a Being which is an absolute, non-composite, through and through undifferentiable, simple entity, 'The One', which cannot be said to think even about itself; for if it did it would form a duality of thinker and object.

The answer, then, to the question of how Plotinus came to believe in these hierarchical orders of Reality is, simply by the use of his reason. His concept of God, however, was different from Aristotle's, for whom Mind, (Gk. *nous*), the Ultimate Reality, was pure thought, thinking about itself.

What then was the One like, according to Plotinus?

The nature of the One

According to Plotinus, the only way that we can know anything about the nature of the One is through the effects it has on the rest of the universe. What it is like in itself, about that we can say nothing. It is completely ineffable. If, for instance, for convenience of expression, we say the One is good, all we are, or should be, saying is that in our experience 'The One' is good *for us*; we are not thereby saying anything about 'The One' itself.

But in spite of that Plotinus identifies 'the One' with the Platonic Form of the Good (see above on Plato), which provokes from Professor Anthony Kenny the comment: 'In a way which remains mysterious, The One is identical with the Platonic Idea of the Good. As The One, it is the basis of all reality; as the Good, it is the standard of all value; but it is itself beyond being and beyond goodness.'[37]

Here is a sample of Plotinus' own exposition of the nature of 'The One':

> How then do we ourselves speak about it? We do indeed say something about it, but we certainly do not speak it, and we have neither knowledge nor thought of it. . . . But we have it in such a way that we speak about it, but we do not speak it. For we say what it is not, but we do not say what it is; so that we speak about it from what comes after it.[38]

Christians will feel a certain sympathy for Plotinus in his difficulty. He is coming to the question of Ultimate Reality, that is, God, by means of pure, unaided reason. He can therefore deduce certain things about the One 'from what comes after it', that is, from observing the effects of God's power seen in creation. The New Testament says the same thing: 'For his invisible attributes, namely, his eternal power and divine nature, have been clearly perceived, ever since the creation of the world, in the things that have been made' (Rom 1:20). But when it comes to saying what God himself is like, all Plotinus can do, on the basis of his unaided reason without the light of revelation, is to resort to what has come to be called 'negative theology', that is, to say not what God is, but what he is not: he is not this, he is not that.

In this Plotinus is in the same position as exponents of Shankara's non-dualist Hindu philosophy who when asked to give a precise definition of Brahman reply '*Neti, neti*', i.e. (He is) not this, not that.

It is not, then, in any disdainful spirit, but simply as stating the sheer fact of the matter, that the Christian Apostle Paul remarks: 'the world did not know God through wisdom [i.e. philosophy]' (1 Cor 1:21). The living God is not the end product of a chain of syl-

---

[37] *A Brief History of Western Philosophy*, 97.
[38] *Enneads*, v.3.14.1–8.

logistic reasoning, nor the solution of a mathematical equation. God is a person. If we are to know what he is like as a person, we can know it only through his self-revelation. 'No one knows the Father,' says Christ, 'except the Son and anyone to whom the Son chooses to reveal him' (Matt 11:27). 'No one has ever seen God,' comments John, 'but the one and only Son, who is himself God and is in the closest relationship with the Father, has made him known' (John 1:18 NIV).

But Plotinus had decided that the One must be an absolute non-dualistic unity. Therefore nothing could be predicated of him. Not only could one not say of him that he thinks about the world, or about human beings, because that would imply a duality (subject and object) in his thinking; one could not even say he thinks about himself, because that too would imply a duality, the thinker and what he is thinking about. All therefore that Plotinus can do is to say what the One is not.

> He is coming to the question of Ultimate Reality, that is, God, by means of pure, unaided reason. He can therefore deduce certain things about the One 'from what comes after it', that is, from observing the effects of God's power seen in creation.

Plotinus was, in fact, trying to make reason do what reason was never meant to do. C. S. Lewis put it this way:

> When it becomes clear that you cannot find out by reasoning that the cat is in the linen cupboard, it is Reason herself who whispers 'Go and look. This is not my job: it is a matter for the senses.' So here. The materials for correcting our abstract conception of God cannot be supplied by Reason: she will be the first to tell you to go and try experience—'Oh, taste and see!' [*scil.* 'that the Lord is good', Ps 34:5].[39]

The relationship of the One to the universe

The One, according to Plotinus, is the source of everything; but how it manages to be so, and what kind of relationship that sets up between itself and all the rest requires some explanation.

Put briefly, Plotinus' scheme is that the One, as the source of the existence of everything else, is the direct source of Mind, the second

---

[39] *Miracles*, 144–5.

stage of the hierarchy of existence. Mind, being one stage of existence below the One, is not, like the One, an absolute unity, but a duality. It contains, and constantly thinks about, the Forms that will become the patterns according to which all other things are formed. Even so, Mind does not produce all the other things directly. As a result of the power of Mind's contemplation of the One and of the Forms, the World Soul comes into existence; and then it in turn creates and orders everything else.

What Plotinus is seeking to preserve by this sophisticated, but hyper-artificial, theory is the absolute non-duality of the One. His theory must not allow the One even to think about things below itself in the hierarchy; for even thinking would imply, as we have seen, a duality in the One.

How, then, and by what process, does the One cause Mind—and through Mind everything else—to come into existence? Plotinus confesses he has a problem here,[40] and uses the best metaphor he can think of to describe the process:

> It must be a circumradiation—produced from the Supreme but from the Supreme unaltering—and may be compared to the brilliant light encircling the sun and ceaselessly generated from that unchanging substance.[41]

In other words, the process is not creation as, say, in the Bible's sense of that term, but—to use another of Plotinus' own metaphors— an overflowing, or emanation, of energy from the One that leaves the One undiminished.[42]

It would be unfair to push Plotinus' metaphor too far. He maintains that the One does not begrudge this outflowing of creative energy from itself. On the other hand, the process seems to be just as automatic as is the emanation of sunshine from the sun. What is more, Plotinus explicitly says that the One has no interest in its 'products':

> Not that God has any need of His derivatives: He ignores all that produced realm, never necessary to Him, and remains identi-

---

[40] *Enneads*, v.1.6.

[41] *Enneads*, v.1.6 (MacKenna).

[42] Plotinus imagined that the sun is not in any way diminished by its vast output of energy. Nowadays we know this to be untrue.

cally what He was before He brought it into being. So too, had the secondary never existed, He would have been unconcerned.[43]

Or again:

It is not that the Supreme reaches out to us seeking our communion: we reach towards the Supreme.[44]

Once more this contrasts vividly with the God revealed in Christ, who became man that he might 'seek and save the lost' (Luke 19:10), and of whom it is said 'This is love: not that we loved God, but that he loved us and sent his Son as an atoning sacrifice for our sins' (1 John 4:10). R. T. Wallis's comment on Plotinus' exposition of the motives of the One is apposite: 'not even here is the One said to love anything other than itself'.[45]

Plotinus' mysticism

It would be wrong to suggest that Plotinus' mysticism formed a large part of his philosophical system; nor does he anywhere offer it as a logical proof of the truth of his system. On the other hand he does seem to regard it as the full-flowering and the reward of all his intellectual striving to discover what the One is really like. In this mystical experience he claims to achieve direct vision of the One.

Our curiosity is naturally aroused, for hitherto he has consistently asserted that the One is unknowable, and that nothing can properly be said about what the One is like in itself. How, then, will he get to know any more about the One by seeing it, since by his own definition the One remains eternally unknowable?

Here is his account of the vision:

We no longer see the Supreme as an external.[46]

We pause here because Plotinus is making a notable point. Because, according to him, man's soul is an emanation, via various agents (Mind and the World Soul), from the One itself, man's soul is

---

[43] *Enneads,* v.3.12.40–49 (MacKenna, 404).
[44] *Enneads,* vi.6.9.8 (MacKenna, 545).
[45] *Neoplatonism,* 64.
[46] *Enneads,* vi.7.36 (MacKenna, 505).

akin in substance to the One, and since his intellect comes via Mind from the One itself, his intellect, too, is akin to the One. Therefore, as Plotinus points out elsewhere, to turn to the One is actually to turn inwards and upwards *to yourself*. This is what we found Hindu philosophy saying: a man's own true Self *is* Brahman.

To look to God, then, according to this theory, is to look, not outside of oneself but to something within oneself. This stands in vivid contrast to the Bible, which exhorts its followers: 'Seek the things that are above, where Christ is, seated at the right hand of God. Set your minds on things that are above, not on things that are on earth' (Col 3:1–2), or again 'Looking to Jesus' (Heb 12:2).

Anyone, not already convinced of Plotinus' philosophy, might very well wonder how one could be sure that what one eventually saw, by this method, would be anything more than, say, an electrical discharge in the depths of one's brain.

But to continue with the quotation from Plotinus:

> we are near now, the next is That and it is close at hand, radiant above the Intellectual.

> Here, we put aside all learning . . . the quester holds knowledge still of the ground he rests on, but, suddenly, swept beyond it all by the very crest of the wave of Intellect surging beneath, he is lifted and sees, never knowing how; the vision floods the eyes with light, but it is not a light showing some other object, the light is itself the vision. No longer is there something seen and light to show it, no longer Intellect and object of Intellection; this is the very radiance that brought both Intellect and Intellectual object into being. . . . With This he [the viewer] himself becomes identical.[47]

We notice three elements in this experience:

1. To achieve it Plotinus had to put aside, or leave behind, all his learning.

2. He saw nothing but light. There was no voice, no message from the One, no communication of itself, no hint that the One was even aware of Plotinus.

---

[47] *Enneads*, VI.7.36 (MacKenna, 505).

3. In observing this light he became—but only temporarily—identical with it.

Again, it is interesting to notice that all three of these items bear striking similarity to the mystical experiences claimed by devotees of Shankara's philosophy (see Ch. 1).[48]

To grasp the distinctive nature of Plotinus' mystical vision, we could begin by comparing it with the visions of God reported by various people in the Bible. In biblical visions the person involved invariably hears a voice proclaiming the name and character of God, thus communicating in understandable language some feature or other of what God is like, or of what he is going to do. The person experiencing the vision, therefore, has not to leave his intellect behind, or empty his mind of rational, cognitive thought.

The experience of Saul of Tarsus is a case in point. He saw a light above the brightness of the sun, but in addition he heard a voice speaking to him, identifying the author of the light as 'Jesus whom you are persecuting', and then commissioning Saul to spread the gospel of Christ (Acts 26:13–18).[49]

Another feature of biblical visions, as distinct from those of Plotinus and Hindu mysticism, is this: never in any biblical vision is the human participant said to find himself becoming merged with God or Christ.

It would be unreasonable to doubt that Plotinus saw what he describes himself as seeing, or to doubt his motives in reporting it. It is also understandable that both Plotinus and Shankara should seek some more satisfying experience of Ultimate Reality than what bare reason could provide. Their 'God', however, was an abstract idea constructed by their intellects. Again an outsider might wonder why they would welcome being merged with the 'God' they had defined by their reason. The One, Plotinus has already told us, was not interested in any of its products—and that would include Plotinus himself—and would

---

[48] Plotinus at one stage in life went with the Roman emperor to visit the East. But the visit was aborted. There is no positive evidence that he got his mystical ideas from Hinduism.

[49] See also Gen 15; Exod 3,34; Isa 6; Ezek 1–2; Luke 9:28–36; Acts 10; 2 Cor 12:1–4; Rev 1.

not have cared if Plotinus had never existed; could not think of any object, not even of itself; and would never have taken any notice of Plotinus even were he merged with the One.

Plotinus' 'God' had never hitherto spoken to Plotinus and never would to all eternity. An abstract idea, of course, cannot speak. Only the living God, creator of the human heart as well as of their intellect, could do that. Perhaps, the Spanish philosopher, Don Miguel de Unamuno, was not too severe when, having spoken of the God of the Old Testament, he remarked:

> Subsequently reason—that is, philosophy—took possession of this God . . . and tended to define him and convert him into an idea. For to define a thing is to idealize it, a process which necessitates the abstraction from it of its incommensurable or irrational element, its vital essence. Thus the God of feeling, the divinity felt as a unique person and consciousness external to us, although at the same time enveloping and sustaining us, was converted into the idea of God.
>
> The logical, rational God . . . the Supreme Being of theological philosophy . . . is nothing but an idea of God, a dead thing.[50]

Plotinus and the problem of evil

The problem of evil is a problem that any philosophy or religion that believes in an almighty, all-loving, and all-wise creator has to face and try to answer.[51] But Plotinus has a very severe difficulty in trying to deal with this problem in terms of his system, and that for the following reasons:

Matter is evil, says Plotinus, in the sense that it actually exists as an evil entity.[52] It is evil because, in Plotinus' scheme, it is formless, without boundary, without intelligent order. Compared with Mind and World Soul it is at the farthest remove from the One; and if the One is the sum total of Goodness, matter is at the other extreme, and is Absolute Evil.

At this stage, Plotinus is talking of what we may call metaphys-

---

[50] *The Tragic Sense of Life*, 183.

[51] We examine this question later in this series in Book 6 – *Suffering Life's Pain*.

[52] See *Enneads*, 1.8 throughout.

ical evil like the material chaos that in Greek thought existed eternally before God imposed order on it.

But even at this level Plotinus had a problem, because according to his scheme matter emanated from the One; not directly, but through the agency of Mind and then of Soul, Matter was created by the One. How then could the Absolute Good create the Absolute Evil?

Matter is also the cause of moral evil. This comes about because when the human soul gets too involved with matter it gets enslaved and corrupted by the evil of matter, and forgets the One.

The New Testament likewise warns us that if we allow the attractive things of life to make our hearts forget God, then this is sinful. But that is not because these things are material and matter itself is evil. According to the New Testament matter is not evil in itself. But in Plotinus matter is evil in itself, and yet, as we have seen, emanates from the One.

Moreover, the Bible teaches that both matter and humans, like the rest of the universe, were created out of nothing, not out of God himself. They are not emanations out of God, like sunbeams are emanations from the sun and therefore of the same substance as the sun. But in Plotinus, the soul of man is part of the World Soul (as in Hinduism) and an emanation out of God himself. How could such a soul emanating from God be overcome by evil matter which likewise has ultimately emanated from God?

Plotinus never really comes to grips with this problem. It is a problem that haunts all versions of pantheism.

Salvation according to Plotinus

Salvation is achieved simply by turning away from excessive absorption with material things, by moral living, and pre-eminently by developing one's intellectual powers, and thus ascending to a contemplation of the World Soul, and Mind, and ultimately to become merged with the One.

Salvation, then, is by moral, and above all intellectual, discipline. Forgiveness from a personal God has, by definition, no place in the process. The One, we remember, is not concerned with human beings. But if salvation depends on the development of such a massive intellect as Plotinus had, how realistic would it be as a way of salvation for the average man and woman?

But, then, Plotinus belonged to an intellectual elite. Here in his own words is how he looked upon the 'lower classes':

> The life which is merely human is two-fold, the one being mindful of virtue and partaking of a certain good; but the other pertaining to the general populace, and to artificers who minister to the necessities of more worthy men.[53]

Plotinus' theory of reincarnation

What happens, then, to sinners? They will, according to Plotinus, be punished. How? To answer this question Plotinus, like Pythagoras and Plato, teaches the reincarnation and the transmigration of souls.

That means, for example, that a man who rapes a woman in this life, will not simply be reincarnated as a man. His soul will migrate into the body of a woman, and will then suffer being raped himself.

> It is not an accident that makes a man a slave; no one is a prisoner by chance; every bodily outrage has its due cause. The man once did what he now suffers. A man that murders his mother will become a woman and be murdered by a son; a man that wrongs a woman will become a woman, to be wronged.[54]

Once more this is very similar to what many forms of modern (as well as ancient) Hindu philosophy teach (see Ch. 1). If it were true, it would mean that a girl who is raped, does not suffer it by chance: she deserved to be raped because as a man in a previous incarnation she raped some other woman. A child who is murdered, deserved to be killed because in a previous incarnation it murdered someone else. Slave labour is justified because the people who are now enslaved, enslaved others in a previous life. It is a baseless, hideously cruel and unjust doctrine.

Nowadays a growing number of people seem to find the idea of reincarnation attractive for one reason or another. It is important, therefore, to understand what the moral implications of this ancient myth are.

---

[53] *Enneads*, II.9.9.
[54] *Enneads*, III.2.13 (MacKenna).

ADDITIONAL NOTE: NEOPLATONISM'S LONG REACH

Neoplatonism subsequently exercised considerable influence on Islamic, Jewish and Christian thinkers particularly in the early centuries up until the Middle Ages, and in some cases beyond.

Islamic philosophers

The early Islamic philosophers were indebted to Plato and above all to Aristotle. But they also knew and studied a work entitled *Theology of Aristotle*. It was not in fact by Aristotle: it was Porphyry's paraphrase of Plotinus' *Enneads*. From this work some of the early Islamic philosophers took over markedly Neoplatonic ideas: (1) Plotinus' typical approach to the knowledge of God by so-called 'negative theology' (as distinct from faith in divine revelation); and (2) his theory of *emanation* rather than *creation out of nothing* (which latter was, and still is, the orthodox Islamic doctrine. We may cite just two examples.

Al-Kindī (died *c*.866–73) is generally regarded as the first Islamic philosopher; he commissioned a translation of the Greek philosophers into Arabic. Of him Felix Klein Franke says:

> According to al-Kindī, the philosopher is unable to make any positive statement concerning God. All he is able to state is in the negative: that 'He is no element, no genus, no species, no individual person, no part (of something), no attribute, no contingent accident.' Thus al-Kindī's philosophy leads to a negative theology, i.e. where God is described only in negative terms. In this he followed Plotinus.[55]

Similarly, **Al-Fārābī** (*c*.870–950), embraced the emanational cosmology of Neoplatonism, even though, in his case, he was aware that the so-called *Theology of Aristotle*, was not Aristotle's work but stemmed originally from Plotinus. Following Th.-A. Druart,[56] Deborah L. Black writes:

> al-Fārābī personally upheld the emanational cosmology central to Neoplatonism, even while he recognised that it was not

---

[55] Klein-Franke, 'Al-Kindī', 168.
[56] 'Al-Fārābī and Emanationism.'

Aristotelian. Emanation was, in short, adopted to fill in the lacuna that al-Fārābī felt had been left by Aristotle's failure to complete his account of the part of metaphysics that comprises theology or divine science. . . .

Viewed from this perspective, al-Fārābī's emanational theories form an integral part of his contribution to the discussion within Islamic philosophy of the nature and scope of metaphysics in relation to natural philosophy. . . .

The major doctrine of Neoplatonic metaphysics known to al-Fārābī, the theory of emanation, has as its focal point divine beings and their causal links to the sublunar world. . . .

It is God's intellectual activity which, in al-Fārābī's scheme, underlies God's role as the creator of the universe. As a result of his self-contemplation, there is an overflow or emanation (*fayḍ*) from God of a second intellect. This second intellect, like God, is characterized by the activity of self-contemplation; but it must, in addition to this, contemplate God himself. By virtue of its thinking of God, it generates yet a third intellect; and by virtue of its self-contemplation, it generates the celestial sphere that corresponds to it, the first heaven.[57]

The similarities between this and Plotinus' philosophical system are obvious. Equally important would be the differences between them.[58]

A Jewish Neoplatonic thinker

Solomon ibn Gabirol (*c.*1022–*c.*1058), otherwise known as Avicebron, is most famous for his poetry. His poem '*Keter Malkhut*', 'The Crown of the Kingdom', or 'Royal Crown' (the title is taken from the book of Esther 2:17), is to this day included in the Sephardic liturgy on the Day of Atonement. But he is generally regarded as the father of

---

[57] Black, 'Al-Fārābī', 187, 188, 189.
[58] For a discussion of these similarities and differences, and of the place and significance of emanational theories in the thought of later Islamic philosophers and for an assessment of the relation between Islamic philosophy and Islamic faith in the medieval period, see Charles Genequand, 'Metaphysics'.

Jewish Neoplatonic thought in Spain (he was born in Malaga, lived in Saragossa and died in Valencia); and his attempt to explain the relationship between the unity of God and the multiplicity of the universe is certainly derived from the Neoplatonic idea of emanation, though with some modification. In Plotinus all originally emanated from the One automatically, or even fatalistically; but ibn Gabirol maintained that this emanation was activated by God himself. He posited two aspects of God's will: one he identified with God himself, but the other he seems to have regarded as a functional entity separate from God. God then allowed the Will (in this second sense) to emanate from himself through his wisdom, and hence ultimately to produce the universe.

The influence of Plotinus' mysticism on Christian thought

Christianity was already two hundred years old by the time of Plotinus. His successors, Porphyry and Proclus, were energetically hostile to Christianity. Of the Neoplatonist schools, the Athenian school was the most avowedly pagan. In the late fifth, or early sixth, century a member of that school (apparently) wrote a work entitled *Mystical Theology* in which he tried to combine his pagan doctrines and negative theology with the positive declaration of God by Christ. He published this work pseudonymously, making out that it came from the pen of the Apostle Paul's Athenian convert, Dionysius the Areopagite (see Acts 17). Strangely enough, it was later received into some sections of the Christian church as though it were truly Christian. Subsequently it was translated into Latin by the Irish scholar, John Scotus Eriugena (*c*.810–*c*.877). In the late fourteenth century it was translated into a modified English version by the anonymous author of *The Cloud of Unknowing*; and this work in turn[59] continues to foster in various countries the practice of Plotinus' pagan mysticism as though it were Christian.[60]

> *The Cloud of Unknowing* continues to foster in various countries the practice of Plotinus' pagan mysticism as though it were Christian.

---

[59] Translated into modern English by Clifton Wolters.
[60] See R. T. Wallis, *Neoplatonism*, 160–1.

CHAPTER 3

NATURALISM AND ATHEISM
A SEARCH FOR ULTIMATE REALITY IN NATURE ALONE

Our obligation to survive is owed, not just to ourselves, but also to the Cosmos, ancient and vast, from which we spring.

—Carl Sagan, *Cosmos*

DEFINING OUR TERMS

Naturalism, as interpreted by the majority of those who hold it, asserts that Nature is all there is: there is nothing supernatural, nothing outside Nature. The late Carl Sagan expressed this worldview concisely: 'The COSMOS is all that is, or ever was, or ever will be.'[1] John H. Randall states it more robustly:

> naturalism finds itself in thoroughgoing opposition to all forms of thought which assert the existence of a supernatural or transcendent Realm of Being, and which make knowledge of that realm of fundamental importance to human living.[2]

Atheism, by its very name, positively asserts what this form of naturalism implies: there is no God.

It might seem obvious, therefore, what answers these twin philosophies of naturalism and atheism will give to our double question as to the nature of Ultimate Reality and how we are related to it. But in actual fact the answers that we get nowadays are not all of them so clear-cut as they would have been a few decades ago.

Atheism, of course, true to its name, will unvaryingly assert that there is no God of any kind. So will most forms of naturalism. But in recent times other versions of naturalism have sprung up which are prepared to envisage a 'God' of some kind. Only, this 'God' is not outside, or above, Nature, but inside it. It may be superhuman, but it is not supernatural. It is part of Nature's processes. It is not personal.[3] We must, therefore, proceed to discuss the various nuances that are to be found in modern naturalism.

---

[1] *Cosmos*, 20.

[2] 'The Nature of Naturalism', 358.

[3] In saying this we are not referring to the New Age Movement with its Earth goddess and its supposed planetary influences, and occult practices; for these are but a recrudescence of ancient pagan superstitions, and in some cases, demonism. We are talking about scientific and philosophical worldviews.

MATERIALISTIC NATURALISM: ULTIMATE REALITY IS INANIMATE MINDLESS MATTER

Those who hold this view do so for two main reasons among others. First, they feel that there is no valid evidence for the existence of a supernatural or transcendent realm, and that in the absence of such evidence they are entitled to hold, as a fallback position, the view that Nature is all there is.[4]

The second major reason that atheists give for not believing in the existence of God is the prevalence of evil and suffering in the world. If there is an all-loving, all-powerful, all-wise creator, they say, why do so many people suffer such bad things? Why did God allow evil in the first place? And why does he not put an end to it?

This, we admit, is a genuine problem, which weighs heavily with many people, and not just with atheists. It is too large to be dealt with here; but we shall devote the last book in this series to it.[5]

The difficulties inherent in materialistic naturalism

Materialistic naturalism, however, itself involves severe difficulties. Because it holds that the Ultimate Reality is matter, it is obliged also to hold that matter has always existed eternally; for if matter had a beginning, it could no longer be considered Ultimate Reality. Instead, we should have to ask where it came from, and who or what created it; in other words, to what Ultimate Reality did matter owe its existence.

The first difficulty, then, with this view is raised by the majority modern theory that the matter of the universe did have a beginning, at the so-called Big Bang.[6]

The second difficulty with this version of naturalism is even more severe: it subverts the status and validity of human reason, and, therefore, the validity of its own arguments by which it tries to support its theory. Let's see how that is.

---

[4] See, by contrast, the cumulative evidence that there is a Creator God behind the universe, as discussed in the books *God's Undertaker* and *Gunning for God*, both by John Lennox.

[5] Book 6: *Suffering Life's Pain*.

[6] For a critique of the view that quantum cosmology has proved that in theory at least, science will one day be able to explain how the universe came to exist out of nothing without any supernatural Creator, see John Lennox's *Gunning for God*, Ch. 4 – 'Designer Universe?'.

Since naturalism holds that there is no creator, it must accept the only alternative explanation of how things began, that is, some form of materialistic evolution. It teaches that matter, from which everything evolved, was itself mindless; and that mind did not, and could not, exist until mindless matter mindlessly evolved it.

Worse still, naturalism holds that mind, having evolved from mindless matter, remains essentially material in that it is composed of, and involves nothing but, impersonal, mindless matter and electrochemical, physical processes. If that is so, what validity could possibly be ascribed to thoughts produced by such substances and processes, or even to the supposedly rational arguments that the proponents of naturalism use to support their position?

In this context, then, we may set out the case against materialistic naturalism in the following propositions:

1. It is absurd to claim that human rationality owes its existence to non-rational matter.
2. It is absurd to claim that human rationality was mindlessly produced by non-rational matter by non-rational processes.
3. It is absurd to claim that human rationality is a function of mindless matter.
4. It is absurd to claim that the creative source of mind is less rational than mind itself is.
5. It is absurd to claim that rationality and logic were produced by small, purposeless, evolutionary permutations, each one of which was unintentional and accidental.

But not all versions of naturalism are so crassly materialistic. So let's consider another slightly more nuanced version.

The Ultimate Reality is energy

According to Nobel Laureate physicist Richard Feynman, 'It is important to realise that in physics today, we have no knowledge of what energy *is*.'[7] On the other hand, according to our school textbooks, Einstein's equation, $E = mc^2$, allows us to think that mass and energy are related. Could we not then appeal to the First Law of

---

[7] *Six Easy Pieces*, 71.

Thermodynamics—'energy can be neither created nor destroyed'—and argue, as many atheists do, that energy, if not matter, is eternal: no god was needed to create it, no god can destroy it; it is self-existent and eternal, and therefore Ultimate Reality?

Well, we could, but the argument would not be logically watertight. The First Law is formulated on the basis of scientific observations of how the universe, as presently constituted, works.[8]

Heat is measured in calories of energy, and these calories can migrate from one object to another, can be converted into mechanical work, or be stored. But no calorie of energy goes out of existence. It simply changes form.

If this, then, is what the First Law is stating, it could equally well be expressed in a less misleading way: 'the amount of *actual* energy in the universe remains constant'. Put this way it is talking of the *conservation* of energy, and not about where the energy came from in the first place.

When the First Law, as presently phrased, asserts that energy can be neither created nor destroyed, it is merely denying that we human beings or any other systems, activities, or events within the universe can create or destroy energy.

When, therefore, the First Law, as presently phrased, asserts that energy can be neither created nor destroyed, it is merely denying that we human beings or any other systems, activities, or events within the universe can create or destroy energy. It would be logically gratuitous, however, to deduce from this that energy was not, and did not need to be, created by God in the first place, and maintained by him thereafter for as long as he pleased. It would be on a par with the mistaken idea of the earliest Greek philosophers, that motion within the universe can just be assumed to be eternal, and does not require an initiating source, such as Anaxagoras's Mind or Aristotle's Unmoved Mover (see Ch. 2).

---

[8] See Russell and Adebiyi, *Classical Thermodynamics*, 5: 'As stated earlier, the only basis of thermodynamics is the observation of the physical world and the experimental measurements related to the observation. No other theoretical proof exists for thermodynamics. Thus, if a case were observed in nature that was contrary to what is implied by an existing law of thermodynamics, the law would be declared invalid.'

Another difficulty for materialistic naturalism

Some modern scientists have come to see that there is something more fundamental in the universe than matter or energy, and that is the laws of physics. The well-known physicist Paul Davies puts it this way:

> An atheist will argue that the world is thoroughly rational and logical at every step: there is a causal or explanatory chain for everything, which we can trace either backwards in time to the Big Bang or down to the ultimate laws of physics. But if you ask, 'Why the Big Bang?' or 'Why those laws?' you'll be told, 'Well, there is no reason'. In other words, the laws of physics exist reasonlessly. Having argued that the world is thoroughly rational at all points, the atheist says it is ultimately founded in absurdity.
>
> My point of view is that the world is rational all the way down to the lowest level—which is beyond the domain of science. There is a reason why things are as they are: the universe is not just arbitrary and absurd. Physics can tell us about the phenomena of the world, but asking 'Why those laws?' is the domain of metaphysics, and at that point I would part company with the atheist.[9]

Yet another difficulty for materialistic naturalism

This time the difficulty is information; and once more we shall let Professor Davies tell us about it:

> there is not the slightest shred of scientific evidence that life is anything other than a stupendously improbable accident. It's often said that life is written into the laws of physics; well, it's not—any more than houses or television sets are. It is consistent with those laws, but they alone will not explain how it came to exist.
>
> For a hundred years the debate has been dominated by chemists, who think it's like baking a cake: if you know the recipe, you can just mix the ingredients, simmer for a million years,

---

[9] From an interview by David Wilkinson published in *Third Way*, 'Found in space?', 18–19.

add a pinch of salt, and life emerges. I don't think that is ever going to be the explanation, because life is not about stuff, about magic matter; it's about a very special type of information processing system. And the whole subjects of information theory and complexity theory are very much in their infancy.[10]

Now this is refreshingly different from fashionable materialistic naturalism. The rationality behind the basic laws of physics, the genes as carriers of the coded information necessary for the production of life, and the astonishing complexity of the biochemical machinery within each cell which is self-evidently designed to achieve a foreseen end—all this constitutes severe difficulties for supporters of that form of naturalism which declares mindless matter to be the Ultimate Reality.

But it also constitutes grave difficulty for those who wish on the one hand to recognise the evident intelligence behind the universe and yet on the other hand to retain naturalism's basic contention that neither the universe nor life within the universe was created by the direct action of a personal creator.

Presently we shall investigate examples of this particular difficulty, one from the ancient world and two others from the modern. But for the moment let us pause and ask ourselves some questions.

REACTIONS TO MATERIALISTIC NATURALISM

The Stoic concept of God

Stoicism was founded by Zeno of Citium (334–262 BC). Its influence, particularly on Roman thinkers like Cicero and Seneca, and through them on the Enlightenment, and thus on the modern world, has been large and persistent.

Stoicism stood at the opposite extreme from the materialistic philosophy of the atomists, Leucippus and Democritus (see Ch. 2). These latter had taught that the universe was composed of an infinite number of tiny, unsplittable pieces of matter, moving eternally through infinite space. There was nothing else. No mind created the

---

[10] Wilkinson, 'Found in space?', 20.

atoms for they were eternal. No mind initiated their movement; no mind controlled it. Each human being, body and soul, was but a temporary conglomeration of material atoms. In a word, atomists were thoroughgoing believers in materialistic naturalism.

Stoics rejected this mindless, materialistic system altogether as being totally unreasonable. They insisted that the universe is everywhere permeated by reason, which they called by the Greek word *logos*. *Logos* is related to the verb *legein*, 'to speak', but it covers a wide range of meaning. It means, of course, 'speech' or 'expression'; but it can also mean 'the explanation of a thing', or 'the formula of its constitution', or 'the statement of its purpose'. It can

> Stoics rejected this mindless, materialistic system altogether as being totally unreasonable. They insisted that the universe is everywhere permeated by reason, which they called by the Greek word 'logos'.

be used of 'an architect's plan of a house' indicating the point and purpose of its design. It can also refer to an army general's 'plan of campaign', showing what ultimate goal the general had in mind right from the outset, and the method he chose to achieve that goal.

Logos, then, so the Stoics held, permeated the whole of Nature.[11]

Interestingly enough, the Stoics said that this *Logos* was God. Now, the New Testament uses this same word *Logos* as a title of the Son of God in relation to the creation of the universe:

> In the beginning was the Word [*Logos*], and the Word was with God, and the Word was God. . . . All things were made through him, and without him was not any thing made that was made. (John 1:1–3)

But having noticed the similarity, we should at once notice the crucial difference between the Stoic concept of God, and the New Testament's teaching. God, in the Bible, is personal, and though he made the universe, and constantly upholds it, and is omnipresent throughout it, he is not part of the universe, and certainly not embodied in its matter.

But according to Stoicism, there were two ultimate principles in the universe: God and matter. God is active; matter is passive. But

---

[11] See Sandbach, *The Stoics*, 72–3.

God and matter are always conjoined. God, who is *Logos*, is in everything in the world, both in matter and in man. God is spoken of as breath (Gk. *pneuma*), but this breath likewise is always embodied in matter. In that sense the whole universe can be called God, or Cosmic Nature, since in Stoic thought, Nature and God refer to the same thing. Hence Professor A. A. Long can write:

> They were convinced that the universe is amenable to rational explanation, and is itself a rationally organised structure. The faculty in man which enables him to think, to plan and to speak—which the Stoics called *logos*—is literally embodied in the universe at large. The individual human being at the essence of his nature shares a property which belongs to Nature in the cosmic sense. And because cosmic Nature embraces all that there is, the human individual is a part of the world in a precise and integral sense. Cosmic events and human actions are therefore not happenings of two quite different orders: in the last analysis they are both alike consequences of one thing—*logos*. To put it another way, cosmic Nature or God (the terms refer to the same thing in Stoicism) and man are related to each other at the heart of their being as rational agents.[12]

In the end, then, Stoicism reduced everything to Nature. Nature, or *Logos*, or God—it did not matter which term you used—was in everything, in matter and in man. Man's ideal, therefore, was to live according to Nature (Gk. *physis*), that is, according to the Cosmic Reason. But whether an individual cooperated with this Cosmic Reason or not, Cosmic Reason was ultimately in control. Therefore the evil behaviour of wicked men had to be regarded as part of the all-controlling rational *Logos*. It meant also, for instance, that if you saw a man abusing a child, or a dictator gassing six million Jews, it was a reasonable thing to do to attempt to stop the outrage. But if you failed to stop it, it would be unreasonable to grieve over it. You had to accept that this outrage, too, was ultimately the work of Cosmic *Logos*, that is, God.

The Stoics, then, as we have said, reduced everything to Nature—rational Nature, not materialistic Nature, but in the end simply all-

---

12 *Hellenistic Philosophy*, 108.

embracing Nature. Whether, therefore, their philosophy should be called naturalism, or not, is a debatable point. Normally it is said to be a form of panentheism (i.e. the view, not that everything is God, but that God is in everything). But it certainly suffered from this glaring moral problem: it made God, not only the source of, but the active agent in, moral evil.

New naturalism's concepts of God

The Cosmos takes the place of God

Carl Sagan (1934–96) was a thoroughgoing adherent of naturalism. He admitted that 'the neurochemistry of the brain is astonishingly busy, the circuitry of a machine more won-derful than any devised by humans'.[13] Nev-ertheless he insisted that humans emerged by a powerful but random process.[14] No God, then, as we deduce from his assertion, which we quoted earlier: 'The Cosmos is all that is or ever was or ever will be'.[15] Yet, interestingly enough, the way he talks of the Cosmos and of our relationship to it suggests that in his system of thought, the cosmos acts as a sub-stitute for God.

> The ocean calls. Some part of our being knows this is from where we came. We long to return. These aspirations are not, I think, irreverent, although they may trouble whatever gods may be.
> —Carl Sagan, *Cosmos*

Christians, for instance, will say of God 'Thou hast made us for thyself, nor can our hearts find rest until they rest in thee.'[16] Carl Sagan apparently rec-ognises the existence of this instinct in the human heart; but accord-ing to him the creator from which we came and to which we long to return is the ocean!

> The ocean calls. Some part of our being knows this is from where we came. We long to return. These aspirations are not, I think, irreverent, although they may trouble whatever gods may be.[17]

---

[13] *Cosmos*, 305.

[14] *Cosmos*, 309.

[15] *Cosmos*, 20.

[16] Augustine of Hippo, *Confessions*, I.1.

[17] *Cosmos*, 20.

Christians maintain that as creatures of a personal Creator, we have an undeniable duty of gratitude and thankfulness to him, and likewise a moral responsibility towards him (Rom 1:21; 14:11–12). Carl Sagan similarly owns that humans have a moral responsibility to their creator, but for him the creator is the cosmos:

> Our obligation to survive is owed, not just to ourselves, but also to the Cosmos, ancient and vast, from which we spring.[18]

But how can humanity have any moral obligation to an impersonal system, when, in addition, humanity itself is supposed to be merely the product of a long series of impersonal biological accidents?[19]

We can only conclude that it is very difficult to eradicate from the human heart its instinctive awareness that we owe a duty of gratitude and of moral obligation to the living personal God, our Creator; and so, naturalists like Sagan, unwilling to recognise him, transfer these aspirations to a surrogate god, the Cosmos. As the New Testament puts it, 'they worship and serve the created thing, rather than the Creator' (Rom 1:25).

Ultimate Reality, or God, is a set of very clever mathematical laws

For our second example of new naturalism's concept of God we revert to Paul Davies and the interview that he gave, and from which we quoted earlier.[20] We cite him because he is known worldwide as a scientist and has written a stream of books informing the educated public of the ongoing scientific debate.

In 1983 he published a book that he entitled *God and the New Physics*; and in the interview to which we refer he explains his reasons for giving it this title:

> I make no bones about the fact that I was being deliberately mischievous. I wrote it at a time when most people felt that science was totally hostile to religion. By saying that science actually can lead us to God, I think I made a lot of people sit up and take notice.

---

[18] *Cosmos*, 374, in 'Cosmos' the capital letter is his.

[19] Sagan, *Cosmic Connection*, 52.

[20] Wilkinson, 'Found in space?', 17–21.

In the interview he confesses that he is uneasy with the term 'God';[21] nonetheless throughout the interview he frequently refers to his views about God. Moreover, another of his many books is entitled *The Mind of God*; and the last sentence of this book, referring to our existence as human beings on this planet, declares: 'We are truly meant to be here.' From this, one might easily conclude that Ultimate Reality, according to Davies, must be at least personal. For how could an impersonal anything *mean* us to be here?

Davies's own basic position, to which his research has led him, is that 'the world is rational all the way down to the lowest level—which is beyond the domain of science', down to, in fact, 'the domain of metaphysics'.[22] If, then, at this 'lowest' level there is something rational that is responsible for, or the source of, the rationality of the world all the way 'up' to the level of human intelligence, most people would find it easy to suppose that that something rational was God. What else could it be?

But Davies has a difficulty. His science has convinced him that the world is rational from its lowest level all the way up to intelligent human beings. But he is a Darwinian evolutionist,[23] and for naturalistic Darwinists it is normally a non-negotiable article of faith that no mind, and certainly no divine mind, was involved in the process of evolution either from inorganic to organic matter or from the emergence of the lowliest form of life to the body and mind of *Homo sapiens*.

Davies's own view

What, then, according to Davies is the Ultimate Reality that brought the universe into existence? Here are some of his statements:

On the origin of life

It's often said that life is written into the laws of physics; well, it's not.[24]

there is not the slightest shred of scientific evidence that life is anything other than a stupendously improbable accident.[25]

---

[21] Wilkinson, 'Found in space?', 18.

[22] Wilkinson, 'Found in space?', 19.

[23] See his book *The Fifth Miracle*, 89.

[24] Wilkinson, 'Found in space?', 20.

[25] Wilkinson, 'Found in space?', 20.

I'm assuming that God did not intervene to make life. I don't want that.[26]

To that extent, life and mind are written into the underlying laws of physics: the tendency for them to emerge is there at the beginning.[27]

On the origin of the universe

I want to be very clear. I've long disliked the idea of God as a cosmic magician, a sort of super being who existed before the universe and then waved a magic wand and brought it into being—and from time to time intervenes by moving atoms around.[28]

On the possibility of divine revelation

It's very hard to see how God could be any sort of a being who could bring about a revelation without coming back to moving atoms around. I mean if someone's going to implant a thought in your mind that would not be there otherwise, they have got to move atoms around.[29]

There is something very odd about this. We grant, of course, that if we implant a thought in a friend's mind—as we very frequently do—it has the effect that in so doing we 'move atoms around in our friend's head'. But if we are allowed to do this, and can do it without breaking the laws of physics, why can't God be allowed to do it? Even Davies's 'God' was responsible for creating atoms in the first place and for their ceaseless movements throughout the universe. Why must God be forbidden to implant thoughts in people's mind because it would involve moving a few atoms around?

---

[26] Wilkinson, 'Found in space?', 20.

[27] Wilkinson, 'Found in space?', 21.

[28] Wilkinson, 'Found in space?', 18. This is, of course, a grotesque caricature of the Bible's account of creation. The Bible says that God created the world by his Word, thus supplying the information necessary for the formation of life, which information, we now know, is carried by the genes.

[29] Wilkinson, 'Found in space?', 20.

On a God who answers prayer

> at no point would I want a miracle-working Deity who inter-
> venes to fix things.[30]

> I just don't like the idea that there are electromagnetic forces
> and nuclear forces and gravitation and oh, then there's God
> from time to time.[31]

On the incarnation and resurrection of Christ

> The Incarnation means God intervenes in history by taking on
> human flesh, not as an inevitable process but as a free act.[32]

> the Resurrection . . . to my mind is a miracle.[33]

A problem with intervention

What Davies means is that if the incarnation had happened as the
inevitable result of the laws of physics and biochemistry, he could
believe it. But he cannot allow God to bypass the laws of physics and
biochemistry and do a miracle such as the incarnation and the resurrection. God, apparently, must not intervene in our world unless he
submits to the laws of physics and chemistry which he himself made,
and those especially which humans have so far discovered.

From all this it would appear that, for all his talk about 'God',
and about a rationality that goes beyond science, Paul Davies is a
thoroughgoing believer in naturalism. Nature is everything. He just
doesn't like, to use his own phrase, 'a Super-Natural God', particularly one who could intervene in our world.

Then what exactly is his concept of 'God', or of Ultimate Reality?
Here are a few more quotations:

> And so my God is a rather abstract God . . . a timeless being, a
> being outside of time, a being that will explain space and time,
> and therefore cannot be part of them . . . a rather remote being,
> who is unlikely to appeal to those who are seeking for some

---

30 Wilkinson, 'Found in space?', 19.
31 Wilkinson, 'Found in space?', 20.
32 Wilkinson, 'Found in space?', 19.
33 Wilkinson, 'Found in space?', 19.

personal salvation. . . . The phrase 'intellectual input' comes to mind . . . 'something clever'.[34]

There's no need to invoke anything supernatural in the origins of the universe or of life. I have never liked the idea of divine tinkering: for me it is much more inspiring to believe that a set of mathematical laws can be so clever as to bring all these things into being.[35]

So Ultimate Reality, according to Davies, is a set of clever mathematical laws! This is astonishing. In the world I live in, the simple law of arithmetic, 1 + 1 = 2, by itself never brought anything into being, and certainly never put any money into my bank account. If I first put £1000 into the bank, and later another £1000 into the bank, the laws of arithmetic will then rationally explain how it is that I now have £2000 in my account. But if I never put any money in to the bank myself, and simply leave it to the laws of arithmetic to bring money into being in my bank account, I shall remain permanently bankrupt. The world of non-supernatural naturalism in which clever mathematical laws all by themselves bring a whole universe into being and life itself into the bargain, is more like science fiction than science. The intelligence that formed the real world must have belonged to a supernatural personal agent, namely God.

THE ROLE OF PREJUDICE IN THE DECISION WHETHER TO BELIEVE IN GOD OR NOT

It is perfectly true that many people want there to be a God, because, they believe, he satisfies their needs. To that extent their belief may be said to be prejudiced. But unbelief in God can be prejudiced too; and it is healthy to recognise that fact.

It is noticeable, for instance, in the interview with Professor Davies cited above, that much of what he says about what God cannot be and cannot do is governed by what Davies himself doesn't like.

---

[34] Wilkinson, 'Found in space?', 19.

[35] From another interview reported by Clive Cookson, 'Scientist Who Glimpsed God', 20.

Thomas Nagel, Professor Emeritus of Philosophy at New York University, expresses his prejudice even more strongly and more explicitly:

> In speaking of the fear of religion, I don't mean to refer to the entirely reasonable hostility toward certain established religions . . . in virtue of their objectionable moral doctrines, social policies, and political influence. Nor am I referring to the association of many religious beliefs with superstition and the acceptance of evident empirical falsehoods. I am talking about something much deeper—namely, the fear of religion itself. . . . I want atheism to be true and am made uneasy by the fact that some of the most intelligent and well-informed people I know are religious believers. It isn't just that I don't believe in God and, naturally, hope that I'm right in my belief. It's that I hope there is no God! I don't want there to be a God; I don't want the universe to be like that.[36]

On the other hand, the most vigorous intellectualism cannot always entirely suppress the heart's deeper longings for God. For all his anti-Christian agnosticism Bertrand Russell once wrote:

> Even when one feels nearest to other people, something in one seems obstinately to belong to God and to refuse to enter into any earthly communion—at least that is how I should express it if I thought there was a God. It is odd, isn't it? I care passionately for this world, and many things and people in it, and yet . . . what is it all? There *must* be something more important, one feels, though I don't *believe* there is.[37]

---

[36] *The Last Word*, 130.
[37] *Autobiography*, 320 (ellipsis in original).

CHAPTER 4

CHRISTIAN THEISM
THE SEARCH FOR ULTIMATE REALITY IN GOD'S SELF-REVELATION

Long ago, at many times and in many ways,
God spoke to our fathers by the prophets, but
in these last days he has spoken to us by his
Son, whom he appointed the heir of all things,
through whom also he created the world.

—Hebrews 1:1–2

GOD IS THE ULTIMATE REALITY AND HE CAN BE KNOWN

Central to Christian theism is its proclamation that God is the Ultimate Reality and he can be known. God has not left it to our unaided human reason to work out what Ultimate Reality might be like. God has himself taken the initiative to make himself known to us. He has done so in many ways:

- (*a*) through creation;
- (*b*) through the voice of conscience;
- (*c*) through history, especially through the Old Testament prophets;
- (*d*) but supremely by himself becoming man in the person of Jesus Christ.

By this divine act of self-communication God has transcended two obstacles in the way of our getting to know him:

Obstacle 1: The essential limitation of abstract human reasoning

At its best, abstract human reasoning can only produce an idea of God. Now, in any subject an idea of a thing is always substantially less than the thing itself. An idea of a thing is only a mental concept; the thing itself is the reality. So an idea of God, arrived at by abstract philosophical reasoning, is a very different thing from the living God himself in active self-revelation through the word and person of the incarnate Son of God and through the illumination of the Spirit of God.

Obstacle 2: The incarnation has bridged a gulf that human reason by itself could never cross

Critics of Christianity have often called attention to this gulf. If God is the transcendent Lord, they argue, the Altogether Other, how could human concepts and language ever cross the gulf between our world, which we know by experience, and God and his world, which is altogether different? The language Christianity uses to talk of God, they say, is all metaphorical and analogical. But those metaphors and analogies are not valid. They are based on experience of this world; and we have no rational ground for supposing that they can tell us anything about the realities of God and that other world—even if such exist. The gulf between the two worlds is conceptually and linguistically uncrossable. So runs the criticism.

Christian theism admits the gulf but asserts that, by the incarnation, God has himself crossed the gulf, and entered our time and space. Not only has he spoken to us in human language, but he has himself become man without ceasing to be God. In his self-communication he of course uses metaphors and analogies drawn from our world in order to facilitate our understanding. But those metaphors and analogies are valid, since he came from the other side of the gulf and knows that world, and knows what metaphors can reliably be used to describe it (John 3:12–13; 6:62; 8:14, 23, 26; 16:28).

> Unless God had first revealed himself to us, we would have nothing to use our intellects on. It is with the knowledge of God as it is in science: God had first to create the universe before the human intellect could study it.

Now when we point to the inadequacy of unaided human reason to decide what God is like, we are not implying that reason has no place in our knowing and understanding of God. The Bible itself commands us to love the Lord our God with all our mind as well as with our heart (see Mark 12:30). 'In your thinking be mature', says 1 Corinthians 14:20. But unless God had first revealed himself to us, we would have nothing to use our intellects on. It is with the knowledge of God as it is in science: God had first to create the universe before the human intellect could study it.

Here to start with, then, is a key passage in the New Testament that declares not only that God does communicate himself to humanity, but that it is part of his very nature to do so. Let's first read it through and then study its main features:

> In the beginning was the Word, and the Word was with God, and the Word was God. He was in the beginning with God. All

things were made through him, and without him was not any thing made that was made. In him was life, and the life was the light of men. The light shines in the darkness, and the darkness has not overcome it.

There was a man sent from God, whose name was John. He came as a witness, to bear witness about the light, that all might believe through him. He was not the light, but came to bear witness about the light.

The true light, which enlightens everyone, was coming into the world. He was in the world, and the world was made through him, yet the world did not know him. He came to his own, and his own people did not receive him. But to all who did receive him, who believed in his name, he gave the right to become children of God, who were born, not of blood nor of the will of the flesh nor of the will of man, but of God.

And the Word became flesh and dwelt among us, and we have seen his glory, glory as of the only Son from the Father, full of grace and truth. (John bore witness about him, and cried out, 'This was he of whom I said, "He who comes after me ranks before me, because he was before me."') And from his fullness we have all received, grace upon grace. For the law was given through Moses; grace and truth came through Jesus Christ. No one has ever seen God; the only God, who is at the Father's side, he has made him known. . . . The next day he saw Jesus coming towards him, and said, 'Behold, the Lamb of God, who takes away the sin of the world!' (John 1:1–18; 29)

This passage makes a number of assertions. Let's first list them and then comment on the detail of the passage.

1. God exists. He is eternal, uncreated and distinct from the contingent, created universe.
2. God speaks. It is part of his essential nature to speak and to communicate himself.
3. The creation of the universe was by the Word of God, and is an expression of his mind.
4. Humanity's original rejection of God's word resulted in a universal darkness. Yet God continued to speak, and his light to shine.

5. God's supreme self-revelation has been through the incarnation of the Word, and through Christ's sacrificial death.
6. The incarnation of the Word of God gives insight into the inner relationships of the triunity that is the one God.

The difference between 'being' and 'becoming' (John 1:1–3)

Here we meet the New Testament's comment on a subject that had long exercised the Greek philosophers, that is, the important difference between 'being' and 'becoming', or 'coming to be' (see the sections on Heraclitus, Parmenides, Leucippus, Democritus, and Plato, in Ch. 2). In a world of constant change and becoming, some argued, there can be no fixed, complete, unchanging knowledge of anything. Are there, then, asked Plato, no eternal, unchanging truths and values on which we can build our lives and guide them through this changing world? As if in answer to this question, the passage from John's Gospel points to the eternal being that lies behind our individual 'coming-to-be'.

Three times in verse 1 and once in verse 2 the verb 'to be' (Gk. *einai*) is used of the Word. Deliberately so, for it denotes his eternal, timeless, Being that had no beginning.

In verse 3, by contrast, the other verb, 'to become', 'to begin to be', 'to come into existence' (Gk. *gignesthai*), is used of the creation of all things. It tells us that matter did not exist eternally as the Greeks thought. It had a beginning.

> The universe, then, is not part of the very being of God, eternally emanating from him, as Plotinus thought, and, like God, eternal itself. Matter is not eternal. It had a beginning. Unlike God, there was a time when it did not exist.

Now return to verse 1 and notice how precise the language is. 'In the beginning'—that is, the beginning of the universe—'the Word *was*', not 'began to be' or 'came into existence', for the Word had no beginning. He already was, with a being that was eternal; and it was through him, the eternally pre-existent Word, that the time-bound universe, by contrast, eventually came into existence.

The universe, then, is not part of the very being of God, eternally emanating from him, as Plotinus thought, and, like God, eternal itself.

Matter is not eternal. It had a beginning. Unlike God, there was a time when it did not exist.

'The Word was with God and the Word was God' (John 1:1–2)

Here we meet again the Greek word *Logos*, which we encountered when we studied Stoic philosophy (see Ch. 3). Its basic meaning (though it has many connotations) is 'word', not in the sense of an individual word—the Greek for that would be *rhēma*—but speech, expression, communication.

Two things are here said about this Word:

1. 'The Word was with God'

This is said twice, once in verse 1 and then again in verse 2, and on both occasions in connection with the Beginning. Verse 1 says 'In the beginning the Word [already] was and the Word was with God', thus enjoying eternal existence equally with God. Verse 2 says 'He was in the beginning with God.' It thus indicates that not only eternally, but at creation, the Word was with God, participating so completely with God in the creation of the universe that nothing in all the vast universe was created without him, as verse 3 goes on to explain. In other words, it was not the case that God made some things by the Word, and other things by some other agent. All came into existence through the Word.

The preposition in Greek is *pros* (and not the more usual *syn* or *meta*). Normally in the New Testament this preposition is used in the sense 'with' only when it applies to persons, when one person is in some kind of relationship with another person.[1]

Here in these two verses it indicates that the Word was a person in eternal fellowship and intimate relationship with God. Now normally if we say that one person is with another person, it implies that each of the two persons is distinct from the other. To say, then, that the Word was with God, implies that the Word was, and is, in some

---

[1] Cf. 'Are not his sisters here with us?' (Mark 6:3); 'Day after day I was with you' (Mark 14:49); 'at home with the Lord' (2 Cor 5:8); 'I would have been glad to keep him with me' (Phlm 13); 'the eternal life, which was with the Father' (1 John 1:2).

sense, distinct from God. That is certainly true; but it is immediately followed in the biblical text by another statement about the Word:

2. 'And the Word was God'

What this phrase tells us is that the Word was not only with God, but was nothing less than God himself. What can this mean? How can the Word be said to be 'with God', and so distinct from God, and yet at the same time be said to be nothing less than God? Is the Apostle John saying that there were originally two Gods? Certainly not! John was not a pagan Greek polytheist. John was a strict, Jewish, monotheist for whom polytheism was a denial of Judaism's basic tenet: 'The LORD our God is one LORD' (Deut 6:4 ESV mg).

Some have argued that the word for 'God' (Gk. *theos*), though a noun, is being used in this sentence as an adjective: The Word was 'God-like', or 'divine'. But if John had intended to say that, he had

> We must concentrate on the significance that the statement, 'the Word was God', carries for God's revelation of himself to humankind. It means that the very nature of God is to speak, to communicate, to make himself known.

a word at his disposal that meant exactly that (Gk. *theios*), and he could have used it to make his meaning clear. He didn't use it, because he did not want to say that Christ was God-like. He intended to say that the Word was nothing less than God. We know that, because—to take one example—John tells us that he was present when Thomas addressed Christ as 'My Lord and my God', and Christ neither rebuked nor restrained him (John 20:28).

Here, then, we have an early insight into the fact that God, though One, is not simplex as Plotinus thought, but a triunity of distinct persons; and of that we shall talk presently. But for the moment we must concentrate on the significance that the statement, 'The Word was God', carries for God's revelation of himself to humankind. It means that the very nature of God is to speak, to communicate, to make himself known. It is not that God is silent, and occasionally gets some lesser being to make some announcement about him. The true God is the God who speaks. When the Word speaks, it is God who is speaking, for the Word is God.

It is this feature in God which according to the Bible distinguishes him from man-made idols, whether those idols are material statues, or merely human concepts of God: Their idols have mouths, but they don't speak (see e.g. Ps 115:5). It also stands in vivid contrast to those philosophies that depict Ultimate Reality as not being concerned to speak to humankind. The fact is that the Word has spoken, and the Word is God.

God spoke at creation, and still speaks through the created order (John 1:3–4)

All things came into existence through the Word, says verse 3. Genesis 1, with its repeated 'and God said' at each stage in the process of creation, emphasises the same point. Says Psalm 33:6, 9:

> By the word of the LORD the heavens were made,
> and by the breath of his mouth all their host

> ... for he spoke, and it came to be;
> he commanded, and it stood firm.

The New Testament repeats the observation:

> By faith we understand that the universe was created by the word of God, so that what is seen was not made out of things that are visible. (Heb 11:3)

Hebrews 1:2–3 adds that God, who created the universe through the Word, now maintains it through that same Word. He upholds all things by the word of his power.

This consistent emphasis throughout the Bible on the fact that the universe was created by the Word of God, has special resonance for us who in the past several decades have become aware that the physical substances in the human cell act as a code that carries the 'information' necessary for the production and reproduction of life (see Appendix).[2]

But the very existence of created life in our world carries another message. It acts as light, says our passage (John 1:4), inviting us, indeed compelling us, to ask where it came from. If we are walking along a dark country road at night and suddenly a beam of light crosses our path, we instinctively ask where it comes from. If someone suggested it didn't come from any source, it just came from nowhere, we should

---

[2] See Appendix: The Scientific Endeavour, p. 169.

dismiss the suggestion as nonsense. Light has to have a source, and so does life.

What then was life's source? Our passage answers: 'In him [i.e. in the Word] was life, and the life was the light of men' (1:4). He, the Word, was the source of all created life. So if we, as human beings, would make sense of our life, and discover what is the point and purpose of it, and what is its goal, we must trace it back to its source, God the Word, and learn to live in his light and according to his purpose in creating us.

God spoke all through earth's 'dark ages' (John 1:5–9)

Through general revelation

'The light shines in darkness', says John 1:5. What darkness? According to Genesis 3 (see also Rom 5:12–21) the fall of humankind came about not through any lack of evidence for God's existence, nor through some crude sin like murder or unnatural vice, but through rejection of God's word and an attempt to achieve moral and intellectual independence of God. It resulted in centuries of darkness (Acts 17:11–23; Rom 1:21–22; Eph 4:17–18).

In saying so, the Bible is not denying or despising the progress that the early human race made in music and metalwork (Gen 4:21–22), or the brilliance of subsequent civilisations like those of Egypt, Babylon, Persia, Greece and Rome. But as regards knowledge of God the nations at large fell into the darkness of polytheism and idolatry with their resultant superstitions, fear and religious slavery. Nevertheless God continued to speak: (1) through the constancy of seedtime and harvest, and the repeated 'miracle' of the provision of daily bread (humans still cannot manufacture a kernel of wheat); see Acts 14:16–17); (2) through the majesty of the heavens with their stars and galaxies (Ps 19:1); (3) through the voice of conscience reacting to the law of God written on the human heart (Rom 2:1–15). And, of course, he still speaks to our modern world through these same means.

Through special revelation

But God had in mind to reveal himself more directly than through general revelation, namely, by the incarnation of the Word, the Son of God, the God-man. Necessarily that involved centuries of preparation so that when this revelation was eventually made, its significance would be unmistakable. The world's idea of God was everywhere perverted by polytheism. How then could the claim of Christ to be the Son of God have been rightly understood, if even the nation in which he was born, like all the others, believed in numerous gods and goddesses, with endless supposed sons and daughters? Or if it had believed in a succession of avatars of one among thousands of gods, as Hinduism still does?

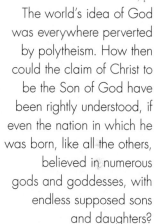

> The world's idea of God was everywhere perverted by polytheism. How then could the claim of Christ to be the Son of God have been rightly understood, if even the nation in which he was born, like all the others, believed in numerous gods and goddesses, with endless supposed sons and daughters?

God's preparation for the incarnation, therefore, took the form first of the raising up, the training, and, where necessary the severe discipline, of one nation, Israel, so that this nation would eventually stand clear of all the polytheism of the other nations in its uncompromising witness to the One True God. Such monotheism, so history shows us, was virtually unique in the ancient world. It took centuries to establish it without compromise, for Israel often lapsed into the polytheism of the surrounding nations (witness the Old Testament prophets). But the necessary objective was finally achieved. When the Word became flesh, the nation into which he was born was strictly and uniquely monotheistic.

The preparatory function of the Law and the Prophets

In addition the law, given by God to Israel at Sinai through Moses, proclaimed God's character, his holiness and righteousness, and set the standards of behaviour he demanded from men. Then came the long line of Hebrew prophets. They were unique: there is nothing in the ancient world to match their denunciation of merely external, formal religion unaccompanied by true morality, and their powerful call for social, religious and political reformation. If people had not developed awareness of God's holiness, and of the seriousness of personal, social, religious and political sin, it would have made no sense for the Son of God to come and to offer himself as a sacrifice for the sins of the world.

The climax of the preparatory period

Eventually the preparatory period was over, and there came the last and the greatest of the Old Testament prophets (Matt 11:11), John the Baptist, as Christ's precursor, to prepare the way of the Lord and to introduce Christ to the people (see Isa 40:3–5; John 1:6–8, 19–28).

God has spoken finally through the incarnation of the Word (John 1:14–18)

Our passage puts it thus:

> And the Word became flesh and dwelt among us, and we have seen his glory, glory as of the only Son from the Father, full of grace and truth. . . . No one has ever seen God; the only God, who is at the Father's side, he has made him known. (John 1:14, 17–18)

Commenting on this climax of God's self-revelation the New Testament elsewhere says:

> Long ago, at many times and in many ways, God spoke to our fathers by the prophets, but in these last days he has spoken to us by his Son, whom he appointed the heir of all things, through whom also he created the world. He is the radiance of the glory of God and the exact imprint of his nature, and he upholds the universe by the word of his power. After making purification for sins, he sat down at the right hand of the Majesty on high. (Heb 1:1–3)

Ultimate Reality is personal

Even in Old Testament times God's self-revelation made it clear that he is personal. He is not only spoken of as God: he has a name, expressive of his character. To Moses at the burning bush (Exod 3:13–14) he declared that name to be 'I AM THAT I AM', indicating his self-existent, eternal, unchanging being. Later God proclaimed the name of the LORD thus:

> Yahweh, Yahweh, a God full of compassion and gracious, slow to anger and plenteous in mercy and truth; keeping mercy for thousands, forgiving iniquity and transgression and sin; and that will by no means clear the guilty. (Exod 34:5–7 own trans.)

and these are all personal qualities and activities.

But the supreme evidence that God is personal is, of course, the fact that the Word, who was eternally with God and was God, has not only talked to us about God, but has himself become man, and thus fully expressed God in human form and human terms, without ceasing to be God. 'Whoever has seen me', he declared, 'has seen the Father' (John 14:9).

Moreover, since the one who became man was eternally with God and was God, yet spoke also of the Father, and the Spirit of God, his incarnation has given us genuine insight into the nature of God. Christian theism does not believe in three Gods. It proclaims as vigorously as Judaism and Islam do, that there is only one God (1 Tim 2:5). But that one God is not simplex.

Relying simply on their human concept of ultimate perfection, Greek philosophers could not conceive of Ultimate Reality being anything other than an absolute, simplex, Oneness; so much so that both Aristotle and Plotinus argued that the One could not think of anyone or anything outside of Itself—for that would imply a duality: the Thinker and the thing thought. Mere reason pushed Plotinus even further: he argued that the One could not even think about Itself—for that same reason: it would imply the same duality: the Thinker and the Thing thought (see Ch. 2). Reason thus concluded that Ultimate Reality was something that had less powers than human beings have!

The Godhead revealed to us through the incarnation of the Word, then, is a triunity of Father, Son and Holy Spirit. Not three Gods, but three centres of relationship within the One God. It has been customary, in Christian theology, to speak of these three relationships as three persons. But in this context 'three persons' does not mean 'three separate people'. Yet each centre of relationship is distinct, and thus the Godhead is a divine fellowship.

God is love, says the Bible. He not only loves his creatures, but long before any creatures existed, the Godhead was a fellowship of love. Moreover, when it comes to God's attitude and activities towards us his creatures, the Bible makes it clear that each person in the Godhead is involved in what is nonetheless the distinctive work of the other two.[3]

---

[3] Christian theologians refer to this phenomenon as the 'Coinherence of the Trinity', the technical term for which is the Greek word *perichōrēsis*. Examples are: The miracles that the Son did were done by him (John 5:35); yet he could also say that it was the Father abiding in him that did the miracles (John 14:10). What the Son speaks to his churches (Rev 2:1) is what the Spirit speaks to the churches (Rev 2:11).

Some people think that all talk about the Trinity is idealistic nonsense. But it is interesting to notice that in a completely different sphere scientists who investigate the quantum behaviour of particles report that at this level particles can no longer be understood as isolated, unrelated, individual things. They appear to sustain ongoing relationships with one another in an interconnected continuous field, witness quantum entanglement. We are not saying, of course, that the persons of the Trinity are like particles in a quantum field. The Holy Trinity is unique, and cannot be compared with anything else, except in the vaguest of senses. But what we are saying is that if matter at the quantum level behaves in this mysterious and counter-intuitive way, it is not to be wondered at if the facts that God has revealed to us about the interrelationships of the persons of the Trinity very soon exceed our ability to visualise them or to understand them fully.

> We cannot, and shall never, know everything about God. In his infinity, he will always go beyond our full understanding. But we can know a great deal about him.

We cannot, and shall never, know everything about God. In his infinity, he will always go beyond our full understanding. But we can know a great deal about him. Moreover, what he has made known to us about the persons of the Trinity, is of fundamental practical importance for us in the process of getting to know God personally. We may map out that process in three parts:

1. *God the Father.* He is the one who is to be known, and it is the Son of God who has made him known (John 1:18; 17:26).

2. *God the Son.* As the Word he is the message, the full declaration of God, told out not only in words, but by his virgin birth, life, works, death, burial and resurrection.

3. *God the Holy Spirit.* He is not the message. He has never been incarnated in human form, nor was he ever crucified for us. He is not the subject matter of the gospel. On the other hand we are not left to our own unaided powers to perceive the truth of the message, to understand it, to receive it and to be transformed by it. According to the New Testament it is the ministry of God, the Holy Spirit to convict the world of sin (John 16:8–9); to convince them of Christ's resurrection (Acts 2); to glorify Christ so that people's hearts and faith are

drawn out to him (John 16:14–15); to effect within them that spiritual renewal that Christ spoke of as being born from above (John 3); to pour out God's love in the hearts of those who receive Christ (Rom 5:5); to empower them to develop, bit by bit, a truly Christian style of living (Rom 8:1–17); to make it possible for them to explore even more fully the deep things of God (1 Cor 2:1–12); to be with them and in them (John 14:17); to guide their prayers and deepest longings and aspirations (Rom 8:26–27); and thus to be for them their foretaste and guarantee of their eventual eternal inheritance (Eph 1:13–14).

Knowledge of God, then, according to Christian theism, certainly involves the reception and understanding of much information. But it is not just a matter of assimilating facts. The ever-present danger with theology is that it can tend to objectivise the knowledge of God so that it becomes nothing more than a system of abstract truths. It is the work of the living, personal, Holy Spirit of God to maintain the process of getting to know God as an ever-deepening personal relationship between the creature and the Creator.

HOW WE ARE RELATED TO ULTIMATE REALITY

Hitherto we have concentrated on the first half of our double question: What is the nature of Ultimate Reality? Now we must answer the second half: How are we related to it?

We are related to Ultimate Reality as creatures to a Creator

In that connection we should notice a number of points:

God himself is our Creator

In Plato's thought the creator, or the Demiurge, as he is called, is not the Ultimate Reality; and when he makes the universe by imposing order on pre-existent chaotic matter, he does so according to the pre-existent eternal Forms (see Ch. 2).

In Shankara's system of philosophy the Ultimate Reality, Brahman, is not the Creator; creation is the work of a lesser deity, Brahmā (see Ch. 1).

Similarly in Neoplatonism the Ultimate Reality, the One, is not the creator. The creator is the third entity in the hierarchy, the World Soul (see Ch. 2).

In all three systems the matter that the world, and our bodies, are made of is regarded as either an illusion, or of no real value, if not positively evil. In all three philosophies humanity's ideal goal is to escape from his material body and from the world of matter.

In vivid contrast the Bible teaches that God himself, the Ultimate Reality, created the universe and humankind. Far from our bodies being undesirable or evil, God himself made our bodies, male and female, and pronounced them very good (Gen 1:31). Far from being something that we should aim to escape from, the Christian gospel declares, as we have seen, that the second person of the Trinity, the Word of God, eventually took a real human body; and in resurrection he was not a disembodied spirit, but had a body of flesh and bones (Luke 24:34–43). Finally, when redemption is complete, the redeemed will have bodies like Christ's glorified body (Phil 3:21). God's material creation, then, is not an unfortunate, regrettable thing, and certainly not evil. It is God's own handiwork, and therefore good.

The human race is made in the image and likeness of its Creator

This refers, first, to the status and function of man and woman in the world. They were to be God's representatives and stewards over the earth's ecosystem.

Secondly, it refers to the moral and spiritual nature of men and women, conscious of God and of his moral standards. And though that image has been in part defaced by human sinfulness and turning away from God, it remains the basis of the dignity and essential value of each individual human being (Gen 1:26–27; 9:6; Jas 3:9).

We are created by God; we are not emanations from God. God made the whole universe out of nothing

Stoic panentheism taught that God is in everything. Indian philosophy and Greek Neoplatonism teach that everything, humankind included, emanates from God like sunbeams from out of the sun. If that were so, we should each be able to regard ourselves as being, in some sense, God. Indian philosophy's famous dictum 'Tat tvam asi', 'THOU

ART THAT', asserts this very thing, that a human's inner self is God, part of God's very substance (see Ch. 1).

If that were true, it would have some strange implications. It would mean that part of us, at least, existed eternally even before we were born, and never had a beginning. It would also mean that our ignorance and evil behaviour would be attributable to God.

Sri Ramakrishna, a pantheist, spelled out the implications of emanational pantheism when he remarked:

> God alone is, and it is He who has become this universe. . . . 'As the snake, I bite, as the healer I cure.' God is the ignorant man and God is the enlightened man. God as the ignorant man remains deluded. Again, He as the guru gives enlightenment to God in the ignorant.[4]

On this basis one could presumably say that God in Adolf Hitler was a diabolical fiend, and God in the Jews whom Hitler gassed was gassed by God.

The Bible denies this outright. God had occasion to remark at one point in history: 'The Egyptians are man, and not God' (Isa 31:3); and that is true of all of us. God alone has immortality, says the Bible (1 Tim 6:16). The idea that matter is an emanation from God's own substance and is indestructible, coupled with the twin idea that 'soul' has existed eternally without beginning, is the reason why in emanational thought history just goes round in endless circles—birth, life, death, reincarnation, life, death, rebirth—and never reaches any goal. By contrast the Bible teaches that the progress of history is linear; one day it will reach its destined goal.

According to the Bible, then, the universe is not an emanation from God, and neither are we. God created the universe out of nothing. As C. S. Lewis put it: 'He is so brim-full of existence that He can give existence away, can cause things to be, and to be really other than Himself, can make it untrue to say that He is everything.'[5]

The relation of the universe to the Son of God

The Christian Apostle Paul explained it this way:

---

[4] See Isherwood, *Vedanta for Modern Man*, 246.

[5] *Miracles*, 141.

> For by him all things were created, in heaven and on earth, visible and invisible . . . all things were created through him and for him. And he is before all things, and in him all things hold together. (Col 1:16–17)

The universe had its beginning, then, in the Son of God, as, say, a hospital can be said to have had its beginning in the mind of the person, or persons, who first thought it up and in the mind of the architect. But the hospital was not built out of the 'stuff' of the architect, nor the universe out of the substance of God.

The Son of God was also the agent in the creation of the universe. What is more, he is the goal for which it was created; and he holds the universe together until it reaches its designed goal.

We are related to God as subjects to a king

God not only set the physical laws by which we exist: he has also set the moral and spiritual laws according to which we are commanded to behave. And he will call us to account and be our judge. Christ summed up those laws under two heads:

1. 'You shall love the Lord your God with all your heart and with all your soul and with all your mind';

2. 'You shall love your neighbour as yourself' (Matt 22:35–40).

On the other hand God did not make us as robots.

God has placed us in a world that combines fixed physical laws with a great deal of openness and freedom. It matters what we do. We can have real effects on our world and our fellow humans. We can explore nature and develop its potentials wisely and well; or we can abuse the ecosystem. This reminds us that life is worth living—but that it is a serious and responsible business.

We are fallen creatures

The tragic state our world is in, for which humankind is largely responsible, is undeniable evidence that we human beings are sinful and blameworthy. God does not excuse our sin; but he foresaw our failure, and estrangement from him, and offers himself in Christ as our personal Redeemer. Moreover, the redemption God has initiated will eventually involve the restoration of the whole of creation (Rom 8:18–25).

ARGUMENTS AGAINST CHRISTIAN THEISM

Several metaphysical arguments are raised against Christian theism. Prominent among them is the fact that it involves miracles: the virgin birth, the resurrection and the ascension of Christ, and the whole idea that Jesus somehow 'came down from heaven', and is simultaneously God and man. No scientifically educated person, it is claimed, could bring himself to accept miracles like this.

Secondly stands the moral charge that all religion in general, and Christianity in particular, have been the cause of social discrimination, wars and massacres all down the centuries.

Perhaps the most powerful argument against Christianity, however, is the problem of evil and pain. How can there be an all-loving, all-powerful, all-knowing God, when gross evil is allowed to persist unchecked, and natural disasters, plagues and illnesses torment and destroy so many innocent people? If God exists, and he does not care about these things, then he must be some kind of a monster.

These are genuine problems. Certainly they are too big to be answered in a few sentences at this point. We shall endeavour to answer them at length in Book 5 of this series—*Claiming to Answer: How One Person Became the Response to our Deepest Questions.*

EPILOGUE

Now that we have reached the end of this discussion of physical and metaphysical concerns, a question naturally arises: Which, if any, of these systems of thought that we have covered seems likely to be anywhere near the truth?

That in turn raises a second question: How could we know which, if any, was true?

And that raises a third question: How can we know the truth about anything?

The branch of philosophy that deals with this problem is called epistemology. But we will not try to cover that subject now; it deserves its own book. And that is precisely what we have given it in the third book in this series—*Questioning Our Knowledge,* which asks whether we can know what we need to know.

APPENDIX:
THE SCIENTIFIC ENDEAVOUR

The doing of successful science follows
no set of cosy rules. It is as complex as
the human personalities that are involved
in doing it.

THE CLEAR VOICE OF SCIENCE

Science rightly has the power to fire the imagination. Who could read the story of how Francis Crick and James D. Watson unravelled the double helix structure of DNA without entering at least a little into the almost unbearable joy that they experienced at this discovery? Who could watch an operation to repair someone's eye with a delicately controlled laser beam without a sense of wonder at human creativity and invention? Who could see pictures from space showing astronauts floating weightless in the cabin of the International Space Station or watch them repair the Hubble telescope against the background of the almost tangible blackness of space without a feeling akin to awe? Science has a right to our respect and to our active encouragement. Getting young people into science and giving them the training and facilities to develop their intellectual potential is a clear priority for any nation. It would be an incalculable loss if the scientific instinct were in any way stifled by philosophical, economic or political considerations.

But since one of the most powerful and influential voices to which we want to listen is the voice of science, it will be very important for us, whether we are scientists or not, to have some idea of what science is and what the scientific method is before we try to evaluate what science says to us on any particular issue. Our aim, therefore, first of all is to remind ourselves of some of the basic principles of scientific thinking, some of which we may already know. Following this, we shall think about the nature of scientific explanation and we shall examine some of the assumptions that underlie scientific activity—basic beliefs without which science cannot be done.

Then what is science? It tends to be one of those things that we all know what it means until we come to try to define it. And then we find that precise definition eludes us. The difficulty arises because we use the word in different ways. First of all, *science* is used as shorthand for:

1. sciences—areas of knowledge like physics, chemistry, biology, etc.;
2. scientists—the people who work in these areas;
3. scientific method—the way in which scientists do their work.

Often, however, the word *science* is used in expressions like 'Science says . . .', or 'Science has demonstrated . . .', as if science were a conscious being of great authority and knowledge. This usage, though understandable, can be misleading. The fact is that, strictly speaking, there is no such thing as 'science' in this sense. Science does not say, demonstrate, know or discover anything—scientists do. Of course, scientists often agree, but it is increasingly recognised that science, being a very human endeavour, is very much more complex than is often thought and there is considerable debate about what constitutes scientific method.

SCIENTIFIC METHOD

It is now generally agreed among philosophers of science that there is no one 'scientific method', so it is easier to speak of the kind of thing that doing science involves than to give a precise definition of science.

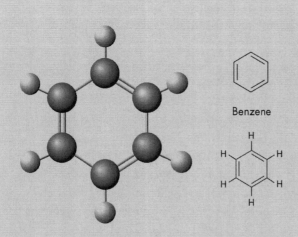

Benzene

FIGURE Ap.1. Benzene Molecule.

In 1929 crystallographer Kathleen Lonsdale confirmed Kekulé's earlier theory about the flat, cyclic nature of benzene, an important milestone in organic chemistry.

Reproduced with permission of ©iStock/hromatos.

Certainly observation and experimentation have primary roles to play, as well as do the reasoning processes that lead scientists to their conclusions. However, a glance at the history of science will show that there is much more to it than this. We find, for example, that inexplicable hunches have played a considerable role. Even dreams have had their place! The chemist Friedrich August Kekulé was studying the structure of benzene and dreamed about a snake that grabbed its own tail, thus forming itself into a ring. As a result he was led to the idea that benzene might be like the snake. He had a look and found that benzene indeed contained a closed ring of six carbon atoms! The doing of successful science follows no set of cosy rules. It is as complex as the human personalities that are involved in doing it.

Observation and experimentation

It is generally agreed that a revolution in scientific thinking took place in the sixteenth and seventeenth centuries. Up to then one main method of thinking about the nature of the universe was to appeal to authority. For example, in the fourth century BC Aristotle had argued from philosophical principles that the only perfect motion was circular. Thus, if you wanted to know how the planets moved, then, since according to Aristotle they inhabited the realm of perfection beyond the orbit of the moon, they must move in circles. In a radical departure from this approach, scientists like Galileo insisted that the best way to find out how the planets moved was to take his telescope and go and have a look! And through that telescope he saw things like the moons of Jupiter which, according to the Aristotelian system, did not exist. Galileo comes to embody for many people the true spirit of scientific enquiry: the freedom to do full justice to observation and experimentation, even if it meant seriously modifying or even abandoning the theories that he had previously held. That freedom should be retained and jealously guarded by us all.

Data, patterns, relationships and hypotheses

In summary form, the most widespread view, often attributed to Francis Bacon and John Stuart Mill, is that the scientific method consists of:

1. the collection of data (facts, about which there can be no dispute) by means of observation and experiment, neither of them influenced by presuppositions or prejudices;
2. the derivation of hypotheses from the data by looking for patterns or relationships between the data and then making an inductive generalisation;
3. the testing of the hypotheses by deducing predictions from them and then constructing and doing experiments designed to check if those predictions are true;
4. the discarding of hypotheses that are not supported by the experimental data and the building up of the theory by adding confirmed hypotheses.

Scientists collect data, experimental observations and measurements that they record. As examples of data, think of a set of blood pressure measurements of your class just before and just after a school examination, or of the rock samples collected by astronauts from the surface of the moon.

There are, however, many other things that are equally real to us, but which scarcely can count as data in the scientific sense: our subjective experience of a sunset, or of friendship and love, or of dreams. With dreams, of course, heart rate, brain activity and eye movement can be observed by scientists as they monitor people who are asleep and dreaming, but their subjective experience of the dream itself cannot be measured. Thus we see that the scientific method has certain built-in limits. It cannot capture the whole of reality.

Scientists are in the business of looking for relationships and patterns in their data and they try to infer some kind of hypothesis or theory to account for those patterns. Initially the hypothesis may be an intelligent or inspired guess that strikes the scientists from their experience as being a possible way of accounting for what they have observed. For example, a scientist might suggest the (very reasonable) hypothesis that the blood pressure measurements in your class can be accounted for by the fact that examinations cause stress in most people! To test the hypothesis a scientist will then work out what he or she would expect to find if the hypothesis were true and then will proceed to devise an experiment or a series of experiments to check if such is indeed the case. If the experiments fail to confirm expectation, the hypothesis may be modified or discarded in favour of another and the process repeated. Once a hypothesis has been successfully tested by repeated experimentation then it is dignified by being called a theory.[1]

It is now generally agreed by scientists themselves and philosophers of science that our account so far of what the scientific method is, is not only highly idealised but also flawed. In particular, contrary to what is asserted about observation and experimentation above, it is now widely accepted that no scientist, however honest and careful, can come to his or her work in a completely impartial way, without presuppositions and assumptions. This fact will be of importance for our understanding of science's contribution to our worldview. It is easier, however, to consider that topic after we have first had a look at some of the logical concepts and procedures that underlie scientific argumentation and proof.

Induction

Induction is probably the most important logical process that scientists use in the formulation of laws and theories.[2] It is also a process that is familiar to all of us from a very early age whether we are scientists or not, though we may well not have been aware of it. When we as young children first see a crow we notice it is black. For all we know, the next crow we see may well be white or yellow. But after observing crows day after day, there comes a point at which our feeling that any other crow we see is going to be black is so strong that we would be prepared to say that all crows are black. We have taken what is called an inductive step based on our own data—we have seen, say, 435 crows—to make a universal statement about all crows. Induction, then, is the process of

---

[1] The terms *hypothesis* and *theory* are in fact almost indistinguishable, the only difference in normal usage being that a hypothesis is sometimes regarded as more tentative than a theory.

[2] Note for mathematicians: the process of induction described above is not the same as the principle of mathematical induction by which (typically) the truth of a statement $P(n)$ is established for all positive integers n from two propositions:

(1) $P(1)$ is true;

(2) for any positive integer k, we can prove that the truth of $P(k+1)$ follows from the truth of $P(k)$.

The key difference is that (2) describes an infinite set of hypotheses, one for each positive integer, whereas in philosophical induction we are generalising from a finite set of hypotheses.

generalising from a finite set of data to a universal or general statement.

A famous example of the use of induction in science is the derivation of Mendel's laws of heredity. Gregor Mendel and his assistants made a number of observations of the frequency of occurrence of particular characteristics in each of several generations of peas, like whether seeds were wrinkled or smooth, or plants were tall or short, and then made an inductive generalisation from those observations to formulate the laws that now bear his name.

> Induction, then, is the process of generalising from a finite set of data to a universal or general statement.

But, as may well have occurred to you, there is a problem with induction. To illustrate this, let's turn our minds to swans rather than the crows we thought about just now. Suppose that from childhood every swan you have seen was white. You might well conclude (by induction) that all swans are white. But then one day you are shown a picture of an Australian black swan and discover that your conclusion was false. This illustrates what the problem with induction is. How can you ever really know that you have made enough observations to draw a universal conclusion from a limited set of observations?

But please notice what the discovery of the black swan has done. It has proved wrong the statement that all swans are white, but it has not proved wrong the modified statement that if you see a swan in Europe, the high probability is that the swan will be white.

Let's look at another example of induction, this time from chemistry.

Particular observations:

Time	Date	Substance	Litmus test result
0905	2015-08-14	sulphuric acid	turned red
1435	2015-09-17	citric acid	turned red
1045	2015-09-18	hydrochloric acid	turned red
1900	2015-10-20	sulphuric acid	turned red

Universal or general statement (law): litmus paper turns red when dipped in acid.

This law, based on induction from the finite set of particular observations that are made of particular acids at particular times in particular places, is claimed to hold for all acids at all times in all places. The problem with induction is, how can we be sure that such a general statement is valid, when, in the very nature of things, we can only make a finite number of observations of litmus paper turning red on the application of acid? The story of the black swan makes us aware of the difficulty.

Well, we cannot be absolutely sure, it is true. But every time we do the experiment and find it works, our confidence in the litmus test is increased to the extent that if we dipped some paper in a liquid and found it did not go red we would be likely to conclude, not that the litmus test did not work, but that either the paper we had was not litmus paper or the liquid was not acid! Of course it is true that underlying our confidence is the assumption that nature behaves in a uniform way, that if I repeat an experiment tomorrow under the same conditions as I did it today, I will get the same results.

Let's take another example that Bertrand Russell used to illustrate the problem of induction in a more complex situation: Bertrand Russell's inductivist turkey. A turkey observes that on its first day at the turkey farm it was fed at 9 a.m. For two months it collects observations and notes that even if it chooses days at random, it is fed at 9 a.m. It finally concludes by induction that it always will be fed at 9 a.m. It therefore gets an awful shock on Christmas Eve when, instead of being fed, it is taken out and killed for Christmas dinner!

So how can we know for certain that we have made enough observations in an experiment? How many times do we have to check that particular metals expand on heating to conclude that all metals expand on heating? How do we avoid the inductivist turkey shock? Of course we can see that the problem with the turkey is that it did not have (indeed could not have) the wider experience of the turkey farmer who could replace the turkey's incorrect inductivist conclusion with a more complicated correct one: namely the law that each turkey will experience a sequence of days of feeding followed by execution!

The point of what we are saying here is not to undermine science by suggesting that induction is useless, nor that science in itself cannot lead us to any firm conclusions. It simply teaches us to recognise the limits of any one method and to found our conclusions, wherever possible, on a combination of them.

The role of deduction

Once a law has been formulated by induction, we can test the validity of the law by using it to make predictions. For example, assuming Mendel's laws to be true, we can deduce from them a prediction as to what the relative frequency of occurrence, say, of blue eyes in different generations of a family, should be. When we find by direct observation that the occurrence of blue eyes is what we predicted it to be, our observations are said to confirm the theory, although this sort of confirmation can never amount to total certainty. Thus deduction plays an important role in the confirmation of induction.

Deduction plays an important role in the confirmation of induction.

It may be that what we have said about induction has given the impression that scientific work always starts by looking at data and reasoning to some inductive hypothesis that accounts for those data. However, in reality, scientific method tends to be somewhat more complicated than this. Frequently, scientists start by deciding what kind of data they are looking for. That is, they already have in their mind some hypothesis or theory they want to test, and they look for data that will confirm that theory. In this situation deduction will play a dominant role.

For example, as we mentioned above regarding observation and experimentation, in the ancient world, Greek philosophers supposed as a hypothesis that the planets must move in circular orbits around the earth, since, for them, the circle was the perfect shape. They then deduced what their hypothesis should lead them to observe in the heavens. When their observations did not appear to confirm their original hypothesis completely, they modified it. They did this by replacing the original hypothesis by one in which other circular motions are imposed on top of the original one (epicycles, they were called). They then used this more complicated hypothesis from which to deduce their predictions. This theory of epicycles dominated astronomy for a long time, and was overturned and replaced by the revolutionary suggestions of Copernicus and Kepler.

Kepler's work in turn again illustrates the deductive method. Using the observations the astronomer Tycho Brahe had made available, Kepler tried to work out the shape that the orbit of Mars traced against the background of 'fixed' stars. He did not get anywhere until he hit on an idea that was prompted by geometrical work he had done on the ellipse. That idea was to suppose as a hypothesis that the orbit of Mars was an ellipse, then to use mathematical calculations to deduce what should be observed on the basis of that hypothesis, and finally to compare those predictions with the actual observations. The validity of the elliptical orbit hypothesis would then be judged by how closely the predictions fit the observations.

This method of inference is called the deductive or hypothetico-deductive method of reasoning: deducing predictions from a hypothesis, and then comparing them with actual observations.

Since deduction is such an important procedure it is worth considering it briefly. Deduction is a logical process by which an assertion we want to prove (the conclusion) is logically deduced from things we already accept (the premises). Here is an example of logical deduction, usually called a syllogism:

P1: All dogs have four legs.
P2: Fido is a dog.
___

C: Fido has four legs.

Here statements P1 and P2 are the premises and C is the conclusion. If P1 and P2 are true then C is true. Or to put it another way, to have P1 and P2 true and C false, would involve a logical contradiction. This is the essence of a logically valid deduction.

Let's now look at an example of a logically invalid deduction:

P1: Many dogs have a long tail.
P2: Albert is a dog.
___

C: Albert has a long tail.

Here statement C does not necessarily follow from P1 and P2. It is clearly possible for P1 and P2 to be true and yet for C to be false.

It all appears to be so simple that there is danger of your switching off. But don't do that quite yet or you might miss something very important. And that is that deductive logic cannot establish the truth of any of the statements involved in the procedure. All that the logic can tell us (but this much is very important!) is that if the premises are true and the argument is logically valid, then the conclusion is true. In order to get this clear let us look at a final example:

P1: All planets have a buried ocean.

P2: Mercury is a planet.

C: Mercury has a buried ocean.

This is a logically valid argument even though statement P1 and statement C are (so far as we know) false. The argument says only that if P1 and P2 were true, then C should be true, which is perfectly valid.

This sort of thing may seem strange to us at first, but it can help us grasp that logic can only criticise the argument and check whether it is valid or not. It cannot tell us whether any or all of the premises or conclusion are true. Logic has to do with the way in which some statements are derived from others, not with the truth of those statements.

> Logic has to do with the way in which some statements are derived from others, not with the truth of those statements.

We should also note that deductive inference plays a central role in pure mathematics where theories are constructed by means of making deductions from explicitly given axioms, as in Euclidean geometry. The results (or theorems, as they are usually called) are said to be true if there is a logically valid chain of deductions deriving them from the axioms. Such deductive proofs give a certainty (granted the consistency of the axioms) that is not attainable in the inductive sciences.

In practice induction and deduction are usually both involved in establishing scientific theories. We referred above to Kepler's use of deduction in deriving his theory that Mars moved in an ellipse round the sun. However, he first thought of the ellipse (rather than, say, the parabola or the hyperbola) because the observations of Brahe led Kepler to believe the orbit of Mars was roughly egg-shaped. The egg shape was initially conjectured as a result of induction from astronomical observations.

Competing hypotheses can cover the same data

But here we should notice that when it comes to interpreting the data we have collected, different hypotheses can be constructed to cover that data. We have two illustrations of this.

Illustration from astronomy. Under the role of deduction above we discussed two hypotheses from ancient astronomy that were put forward to explain the motion of the planets. Successive refinements of the epicyclic model appeared to cover the data at the expense of greater and greater complication in that more and more circles were necessary. Kepler's proposal, by contrast, covered the data by the simple device of replacing the complex array of circles by one single ellipse, which simplified the whole business enormously. Now, if we knew nothing of gravity and the deduction of elliptical orbits that can be made from it by means of Newton's laws, how would we choose between the two explanations?

At this point, scientists might well invoke the principle sometimes called 'Occam's razor', after William of Occam. This is the belief that simpler explanations of natural phenomena are more likely to be correct than more complex ones. More precisely, the idea is that if we have two or more competing hypotheses covering the same data, we should choose the one that involves the least number of assumptions or complications. The metaphorical use of the word 'razor' comes from this cutting or shaving down to the smallest possible number of assumptions. Occam's razor has proved very useful but we should observe that it is a philosophical preference, and it is not something that you can prove to be true in every case, so it needs to be used with care.

Illustration from physics. Another illustration of the way in which different hypotheses can account for the same data is given by a common exercise in school physics. We are given a spring, a series of weights and a ruler and asked to plot a graph of the length of the spring against the weight hanging on the end of it. We end up with a series, say, of 10 points on the paper that look as if they might (with a bit of imagination!) lie on a straight line. We take an inductive step and draw a straight line that goes through most of the points and we claim that there is a linear relationship between the length of spring and the tension it is put under by the weights (Hooke's law). But then we reflect that there is an infinite number of curves that can be drawn through our ten points. Changing the curve would change the relation between spring length and tension. Why not choose one of those other curves in preference to

> The principle sometimes called 'Occam's razor', after William of Occam . . . is the belief that simpler explanations of natural phenomena are more likely to be correct than more complex ones.

the straight line? That is, in the situation just described, there are many different hypotheses that cover the same set of data. How do you choose between them?

Application of Occam's razor would lead to choosing the most elegant or economical solution—a straight line is simpler than a complicated curve. We could also repeat the experiment with 100 points, 200 points, etc. The results would build up our confidence that the straight line was the correct answer. When we build up evidence in this way, we say that we have cumulative evidence for the validity of our hypothesis.

So far we have been looking at various methods employed by scientists and have seen that none of them yields 100% certainty, except in deductive proofs in mathematics where the certainty is that particular conclusions follow from particular axioms. However, we would emphasise once more that this does not mean that the scientific enterprise is about to collapse! Far from it. What we mean by 'not giving 100% certainty' can be interpreted as saying that there is a small probability that a particular result or theory is false. But that does not mean that we cannot have confidence in the theory.

Indeed there are some situations, as in the litmus-paper test for acid where there has been 100% success in the past. Now whereas this does not formally guarantee 100% success in the future, scientists will say that it is a fact that litmus paper turns red on being dipped in acid. By a 'fact', they mean, as palaeontologist Stephen Jay Gould has delightfully put it, 'confirmed to such a degree that it would be perverse to withhold provisional assent to it'.[3]

On other occasions we are prepared to trust our lives to the findings of science and technology even though we know we do not have 100% certainty. For example, before we travel by train, we know that it is theoretically possible for something to go wrong, maybe for the brakes or signalling to fail and cause the train to crash. But we also know from the statistics of rail travel that the probability of such an event is very small indeed (though it is not zero—trains have from time to time crashed). Since the probability of a crash is so small, most of us who travel by train do so without even thinking about the risk.

On the other hand we must not assume that we can accept all

---

[3] Gould, 'Evolution as Fact and Theory', 119.

proposed hypotheses arrived at by scientific method as absolute fact without testing them.

One of the criteria of testing is called falsifiability.

Falsifiability

Karl Popper put the emphasis not on the verifiability of a hypothesis but on its falsifiability. It is unfortunate that Popper's terminology can be a real source of confusion, since the adjective 'falsifiable' does not mean 'will turn out to be false'! The confusion is even worse when one realises, on the other hand, that the verb 'to falsify' means 'to demonstrate that something is false'! The term 'falsifiable' has in fact a technical meaning. A hypothesis is said to be falsifiable if you can think of a logically possible set of observations that would be inconsistent with it.

It is, of course, much easier to falsify a universal statement than to verify it. As an illustration, take one of our earlier examples. The statement 'All swans are white' is, from the very start, falsifiable. One would only have to discover one swan that was black and that would falsify it. And since we know that black swans do exist, the statement has long since been falsified.

However, there can be problems. Most scientific activity is much more complex than dealing with claims like 'All swans are white'!

For example, in the nineteenth century observations of the planet Uranus appeared to indicate that its motion was inconsistent with predictions made on the basis of Newton's laws. Therefore, it appeared to threaten to demonstrate Newton's laws to be false. However, instead of immediately saying that Newton's laws had been falsified, it was suggested by French mathematician Urbain Le Verrier and English astronomer John Couch Adams (unknown to each other) that there might be a hitherto undetected planet in the neighbourhood of Uranus that would account for its apparently anomalous behaviour. As a result another scientist, German astronomer Johann Galle, was prompted to look for a new planet and discovered the planet Neptune.

> The term 'falsifiable' has in fact a technical meaning: a hypothesis is said to be falsifiable if you can think of a logically possible set of observations that would be inconsistent with it.

It would, therefore, have been incorrect to regard the behaviour of Uranus as falsifying Newton's laws. The problem was ignorance of the initial conditions—there was a planet missing in the configuration being studied. In other words, some of the crucial data was missing. This story demonstrates one of the problems inherent in Popper's approach. When observation does not fit theory, it could be that the theory is false, but it could equally well be that the theory is correct but the data is incomplete or even false, or that some of the auxiliary assumptions are incorrect. How can you judge what is the correct picture?

Most scientists in fact feel that Popper's ideas are far too pessimistic and his methodology too counter-intuitive. Their experience and intuition tell them that their scientific methods in fact enable them to get a better and better understanding of the universe, that they are in this sense getting a tighter grip on reality. One benefit of Popper's approach, however, is its insistence that scientific theories be testable.

Repeatability and abduction

The scientific activity we have been thinking of so far is characterised by *repeatability*. That is, we have considered situations where scientists are looking for universally valid laws that cover repeatable phenomena, laws which, like Newton's laws of motion, may be experimentally tested again and again. Sciences of this sort are often called inductive or nomological sciences (Gk. *nomos* = law) and between them they cover most of science.

However there are major areas of scientific enquiry where repeatability is not possible, notably study of the origin of the universe and the origin and development of life.

Now of course we do not mean to imply that science has nothing to say about phenomena that are non-repeatable. On the contrary, if one is to judge by the amount of literature published, particularly, but not only, at the popular level, the origin of the universe and of life, for example, are among the most interesting subjects by far that science addresses.

But precisely because of the importance of such non-repeatable phenomena, it is vital to see that the way in which they are accessible to science is not the same in general as the way in which repeatable phenomena are. For theories about both kinds of phenomena tend to be presented to the public in the powerful name of science as though they had an equal claim to be accepted. Thus there is a real danger that the public ascribes the same authority and validity to conjectures about non-repeatable events that are not capable of experimental verification as it does to those theories that have been confirmed by repeated experiment.

Physical chemist and philosopher Michael Polanyi points out that the study of how something originates is usually very different from the study of how it operates, although, of course, clues to how something originated may well be found in how it operates. It is one thing to investigate something repeatable in the laboratory, such as dissecting a frog to see how its nervous system functions, but it is an altogether different thing to study something non-repeatable, such as how frogs came to exist in the first place. And, on the large scale, how the universe works is one thing, yet how it came to be may be quite another.

How the universe works is one thing, yet how it came to be may be quite another.

The most striking difference between the study of non-repeatable and repeatable phenomena is that the method of induction is no longer applicable, since we no longer have a sequence of observations or experiments to induce from, nor any repetition in the future to predict about! The principal method that applies to non-repeatable phenomena is *abduction*.

Although this term, introduced by logician Charles Peirce in the nineteenth century, may be unfamiliar, the underlying idea is very familiar. For abduction is what every good detective does in order to clear up a murder mystery! With the murder mystery a certain event has happened. No one doubts that it has happened. The question is: who or what was the cause of it happening? And often in the search for causes of an event that has already happened, abduction is the only method available.

As an example of abductive inference, think of the following:

Data: Ivan's car went over the cliff edge and he was killed.

Inference: If the car brakes had failed, then the car would have gone over the cliff.

Abductive conclusion: There is reason to suppose that the brakes failed.

However, an alternative suggests itself (especially to avid readers of detective stories): if someone had pushed Ivan's car over the cliff, the result would have been the same! It would be fallacious and very foolish to assume that just because we had thought of one explanation of the circumstances, that it was the only one.

The basic idea of abduction is given by the following scheme:

Data: A is observed.

Inference: If B were true then A would follow.

Abductive conclusion: There is reason to suppose B may be true.

Of course, there may well be another hypothesis, C, of which we could say: if C were true A would follow. Indeed, there may be many candidates for C.

The detective in our story has a procedure for considering them one by one. He may first consider the chance hypothesis, B, that the brakes failed. He may then consider the hypothesis C that it was no chance event, but deliberately designed by a murderer who pushed the car over the cliff. Or the detective may consider an even more sophisticated hypothesis, D, combining both chance and design, that someone who wanted to kill Ivan had tampered with the brakes of the car so that they would fail somewhere, and they happened to fail on the clifftop!

Inference to the best explanation. Our detective story illustrates how the process of abduction throws up plausible hypotheses and forces upon us the question as to which of the hypotheses best fits the data. In order to decide that question, the hypotheses are compared for their explanatory power: how much of the data do they cover, does the theory make coherent sense, is it consistent with other areas of our knowledge, etc.?

In order to answer these further questions, deduction will often be used. For example, if B in the detective story is true, then we would expect an investigation of the brakes of the wrecked car to reveal worn or broken parts. If C is true we would deduce that the brakes might well be found in perfect order, whereas if D were the case, we might expect to find marks of deliberate damage to the hydraulic braking system. If we found such marks then D would immediately be regarded as the best of the competing explanations given so far, since it has a greater explanatory power than the others.

Thus, abduction together with the subsequent comparison of competing hypotheses may be regarded as an 'inference to the best explanation'. This is the essence not only of detective and legal work but also of the work of the historian. Both detective and historian have to infer the best possible explanation from the available data after the events in which they are interested have occurred.

For more on the application of abduction in the natural sciences, particularly in cosmology and biology, see the books by John Lennox noted at the end of this Appendix. Here we need to consider a few more of the general issues related to the scientific endeavour.

EXPLAINING EXPLANATIONS

Levels of explanation

Science explains. This, for many people encapsulates the power and the fascination of science. Science enables us to understand what we did not understand before and, by giving us understanding, it gives us power over nature. But what do we mean by saying that 'science explains'?

In informal language we take an explanation of something to be adequate when the person to whom the explanation is given understands plainly what he or she did not understand before. However, we must try to be more precise about what we mean by the process of 'explanation', since it has different aspects that are often confused. An illustration can help us. We have considered a similar idea in relation to roses. Let's now take further examples.

Suppose Aunt Olga has baked a beautiful cake. She displays it to a gathering of the world's top scientists and we ask them for an explanation of the cake. The nutrition scientists will tell us about the number of calories in the cake and its nutritional effect; the biochemists will inform us about the structure of the proteins, fats, etc. in the cake and what it is that causes them to hold together; the chemists will enumerate the elements involved and describe their bonding; the physicists will be able to analyse the cake in terms of fundamental particles; and the mathematicians will offer us a set of beautiful equations to describe the behaviour of those particles. Suppose, then, that these experts have given us an exhaustive description of the cake, each in terms of his or her scientific discipline. Can we say that the cake is now completely explained? We have certainly been given a description of how the cake was made and how its various constituent elements relate to each other. But suppose we now ask the assembled group of experts why the cake was made. We notice the grin on Aunt Olga's face. She knows the answer since, after all, she made the cake! But if she does not reveal the answer by telling us, it is clear that no amount of scientific analysis will give us the answer.

Thus, although science can answer 'how' questions in terms of causes and mechanisms, it cannot answer 'why' questions, questions of purpose and intention—teleological questions, as they are sometimes called (Gk. *telos* = end or goal).

However, it would be nonsensical to suggest that Aunt Olga's answer to the teleological question, that she made the cake for Sam's birthday, say, contradicted the scientific analysis of the cake! No. The two kinds of answer are clearly logically compatible.

And yet exactly the same confusion of categories is evidenced when atheists argue that there is no longer need to bring in God and the supernatural to explain the workings of nature, since we now have a scientific explanation for them. As a result, the general public has come to think that belief in a creator belongs to a primitive and unsophisticated stage of human thinking and has been rendered both unnecessary and impossible by science.

> Although science can answer 'how' questions in terms of causes and mechanisms, it cannot answer 'why' questions, questions of purpose and intention.

But there is an obvious fallacy here. Think of a Ford motor car. It is conceivable that a primitive person who was seeing one for the first time and who did not understand the principles of an internal combustion engine, might imagine that there was a god (Mr Ford) inside the engine, making it go. He might further imagine that when the engine ran sweetly that was because Mr Ford inside the engine liked him, and when it refused to go that was because Mr Ford did not like him. Of course, if eventually this primitive person became civilised, learned engineering, and took the engine to pieces, he would discover that there was no Mr Ford inside the engine, and that he did not need to introduce Mr Ford as an explanation for the working of the engine. His grasp of the impersonal principles of internal combustion would be altogether enough to explain how the engine worked. So far, so good. But if he then decided that his understanding of the principles of the internal combustion engine made it impossible to believe in the existence of a Mr Ford who designed the engine, this would be patently false!

FIGURE Ap.2. Model T Ford Motor Car.

Introducing the world's first moving assembly line in 1913, Ford Motor Company built more than 15 million Model Ts from 1908 until 1927.

Reproduced with permission of ©iStock/Peter Mah.

It is likewise a confusion of categories to suppose that our understanding of the impersonal principles according to which the universe works makes it either unnecessary or impossible to believe in the existence of a personal creator who designed, made and upholds the great engine that is the universe. In other words, we should not confuse the mechanisms by which the universe works with its Cause. Every one of us knows how to distinguish between the consciously willed movement of an arm for a purpose and an involuntary spasmodic movement of an arm induced by accidental contact with an electric current.

Michael Poole, Visiting Research Fellow, Science and Religion, at King's College London, in his published debate on science and religion with Richard Dawkins, puts it this way:

> There is no logical conflict between reason-giving explanations which concern mechanisms, and reason-giving explanations which concern the plans and purposes of an agent, human or divine. This is a logical point, not a matter of whether one does or does not happen to believe in God oneself.[4]

---

[4]   Poole, 'Critique of Aspects of the Philosophy and Theology of Richard Dawkins', 49.

One of the authors, in a debate with Richard Dawkins, noted how his opponent was confusing the categories of mechanism and agency:

> When Isaac Newton, for example, discovered his law of gravity and wrote down the equations of motion, he didn't say, 'Marvellous, I now understand it. I've got a mechanism therefore I don't need God.' In fact it was the exact opposite. It was because he understood the complexity of sophistication of the mathematical description of the universe that his praise for God was increased. And I would like to suggest, Richard, that somewhere down in this you're making a category mistake, because you're confusing mechanism with agency. We have a mechanism that does XYZ, therefore there's no need for an agent. I would suggest that the sophistication of the mechanism, and science rejoices in finding such mechanisms, is evidence for the sheer wonder of the creative genius of God.[5]

In spite of the clarity of the logic expressed in these counterpoints, a famous statement made by the French mathematician Laplace is constantly misappropriated to support atheism. On being asked by Napoleon where God fitted in to his mathematical work, Laplace replied: 'Sir, I have no need of that hypothesis.' Of course, God did not appear in Laplace's mathematical description of how things work, just as Mr Ford would not appear in a scientific description of the laws of internal combustion. But what does that prove? Such an argument can no more be used to prove that God does not exist than it can be used to prove that Mr Ford does not exist.

To sum up, then, it is important to be aware of the danger of confusing different levels of explanation and of thinking that one level of explanation tells the whole story.

This leads us at once to consider the related question of reductionism.

---

[5] Lennox's response to Dawkins's first thesis 'Faith is blind; science is evidence-based', 'The God Delusion Debate', hosted by Fixed Point Foundation, University of Alabama at Birmingham, filmed and broadcast live 3 October 2007, http://fixed-point.org/index.php/video/35-full-length/164-the-dawkins-lennox-debate. Transcript provided courtesy of ProTorah, http://www.protorah.com/god-delusion-debate-dawkins-lennox-transcript/.

Reductionism

In order to study something, especially if it is complex, scientists often split it up into separate parts or aspects and thus 'reduce' it to simpler components that are individually easier to investigate. This kind of reductionism, often called methodological or structural reductionism, is part of the normal process of science and has proved very useful. It is, however, very important to bear in mind that there may well be, and usually is, more to a given whole than simply what we obtain by adding up all that we have learned from the parts. Studying all the parts of a watch separately will never enable you to grasp how the complete watch works as an integrated whole.

Besides methodological reductionism there are two further types of reductionism, epistemological and ontological. *Epistemological reductionism* is the view that higher level sciences can be explained without remainder by the sciences at a lower level. That is, chemistry is explained by physics; biochemistry by chemistry; biology by biochemistry; psychology by biology; sociology by brain science; and theology by sociology. As Francis Crick puts it: 'The ultimate aim of the modern development in biology is in fact to explain all biology in terms of physics and chemistry.'[6] The former Charles Simonyi Professor of the Public Understanding of Science at Oxford, Richard Dawkins, holds the same view: 'My task is to explain elephants, and the world of complex things, in terms of the simple things that physicists either understand, or are working on.'[7] The ultimate goal of reductionism is to reduce all human behaviour, our likes and dislikes, the entire mental landscape of our lives, to physics.

> The ultimate goal of reductionism is to reduce all human behaviour, our likes and dislikes, the entire mental landscape of our lives, to physics.

However, both the viability and the plausibility of this programme are open to serious question. The outstanding Russian psychologist Leo Vygotsky (1896–1934) was critical of certain aspects of this reductionist philosophy as applied to psychology. He pointed out that such reductionism often conflicts

---

6 Crick, *Of Molecules and Men*, 10.
7 Dawkins, *Blind Watchmaker*, 15.

with the goal of preserving all the basic features of a phenomenon or event that one wishes to explain. For example, one can reduce water (H_2O) into H and O. However, hydrogen burns and oxygen is necessary for burning, whereas water has neither of these properties, but has many others that are not possessed by either hydrogen or oxygen. Thus, Vygotsky's view was that reductionism can only be done up to certain limits. Karl Popper says: 'There is almost always an unresolved residue left by even the most successful attempts at reduction.'[8]

Furthermore, Michael Polanyi argues the intrinsic implausibility of expecting epistemological reductionism to work in every circumstance.[9] Think of the various levels of process involved in building an office building with bricks. First of all there is the process of extracting the raw materials out of which the bricks have to be made. Then there are the successively higher levels of making the bricks, they do not make themselves; bricklaying, the bricks do not self-assemble; designing the building, it does not design itself; and planning the town in which the building is to be built, it does not organise itself. Each level has its own rules. The laws of physics and chemistry govern the raw material of the bricks; technology prescribes the art of brick making; architecture teaches the builders, and the architects are controlled by the town planners. Each level is controlled by the level above, but the reverse is not true. The laws of a higher level cannot be derived from the laws of a lower level (although, of course what can be done at a higher level will depend on the lower levels: for example, if the bricks are not strong there will be a limit on the height of a building that can be safely built with them).

Consider the page you are reading just now. It consists of paper imprinted with ink or, in the case of an electronic version, text rendered digitally. It is obvious that the physics and chemistry of ink and paper can never, even in principle, tell you anything about the significance of the shapes of the letters on the page. And this is nothing to do with the fact that physics and chemistry are not yet sufficiently advanced to deal with this question. Even if we allow these sciences another 1,000 years of development, we can see that it will make no

---

8 Popper, 'Scientific Reduction.'
9 Polanyi, *Tacit Dimension.*

difference, because the shapes of those letters demand a totally new and higher level of explanation than that of which physics and chemistry are capable. In fact, explanation can only be given in terms of the concepts of language and authorship—the communication of a message by a person. The ink and paper are carriers of the message, but the message certainly does not emerge automatically from them. Furthermore, when it comes to language itself, there is again a sequence of levels—you cannot derive a vocabulary from phonetics, or the grammar of a language from its vocabulary, etc.

As is well known, the genetic material DNA carries information. We shall describe this later on in some detail, but the basic idea is simply this. DNA, a substance found in every living cell, can be looked at as a long tape on which there is a string of letters written in a four-letter chemical language. The sequence of letters contains coded instructions (information) that the cell uses to make proteins. Physical biochemist and theologian Arthur Peacocke writes: 'In no way can the concept of "information", the concept of conveying a message, be articulated in terms of the concepts of physics and chemistry, even though the latter can be shown to explain how the molecular machinery (DNA, RNA and protein) operates to carry information.'[10]

In each of the situations we have described above, we have a series of levels, each one higher than the previous one. What happens on a higher level is not completely derivable from what happens on the level beneath it, but requires another level of explanation.

In this kind of situation it is sometimes said that the higher level phenomena 'emerge' from the lower level. Unfortunately, however, the word 'emerge' is easily misunderstood to mean that the higher level properties emerge automatically from the lower level properties. This is clearly false in general, as we showed by considering brick making and writing on paper. Yet notwithstanding the fact that both writing on paper and DNA have in common the fact that they encode a 'message', those scientists committed to materialistic philosophy insist that the information carrying properties of DNA must have emerged automatically out of mindless matter. For if, as materialism insists, matter and energy are all that there is, then it logically follows

---

[10] Peacocke, *Experiment of Life*, 54.

that they must possess the inherent potential to organise themselves in such a way that eventually all the complex molecules necessary for life, including DNA, will emerge.[11]

There is a third type of reductionism, called *ontological reductionism*, which is frequently encountered in statements like the following: The universe is nothing but a collection of atoms in motion, human beings are 'machines for propagating DNA, and the propagation of DNA is a self-sustaining process. It is every living object's sole reason for living'.[12]

Words such as 'nothing but', 'sole' or 'simply' are the telltale sign of (ontological) reductionist thinking. If we remove these words we are usually left with something unobjectionable. The universe certainly is a collection of atoms and human beings do propagate DNA. The question is, is there nothing more to it than that? Are we going to say with Francis Crick, who won the Nobel Prize jointly with James D. Watson for his discovery of the double helix structure of DNA: '"You", your joys and your sorrows, your memories and your ambitions, your sense of personal identity and free will, are in fact no more than the behaviour of a vast assembly of nerve cells and their associated molecules'?[13]

What shall we say of human love and fear, of concepts like beauty and truth? Are they meaningless?

Ontological reductionism, carried to its logical conclusion, would ask us to believe that a Rembrandt painting is nothing but molecules of paint scattered on canvas. Physicist and theologian John Polkinghorne's reaction is clear:

> There is more to the world than physics can ever express.
>
> One of the fundamental experiences of the scientific life is that of wonder at the beautiful structure of the world. It is the pay-off for all the weary hours of labour involved in the pursuit of research. Yet in the world described by science where would that wonder find its lodging? Or our experiences of beauty? Of moral obligation? Of the presence of God? These seem to me

---

[11] Whether matter and energy do have this capacity is another matter that is discussed in the books noted at the end of this appendix.

[12] Dawkins, *Growing Up in the Universe* (study guide), 21.

[13] Crick, *Astonishing Hypothesis*, 3.

to be quite as fundamental as anything we could measure in the laboratory. A worldview that does not take them adequately into account is woefully incomplete.[14]

The most devastating criticism of ontological reductionism is that it is self-destructive. Polkinghorne describes its programme as ultimately suicidal:

> For, not only does it relegate our experiences of beauty, moral obligation, and religious encounter to the epiphenomenal scrapheap. It also destroys rationality. Thought is replaced by electrochemical neural events. Two such events cannot confront each other in rational discourse. They are neither right nor wrong. They simply happen. . . . The very assertions of the reductionist himself are nothing but blips in the neural network of his brain. The world of rational discourse dissolves into the absurd chatter of firing synapses. Quite frankly, that cannot be right and none of us believes it to be so.[15]

BASIC OPERATIONAL PRESUPPOSITIONS

So far we have been concentrating on the scientific method and have seen that this is a much more complex (and, for that reason, a much more interesting) topic than may first appear. As promised earlier, we must now consider the implications of the fact that scientists, being human like the rest of us, do not come to any situation with their mind completely clear of preconceived ideas. The widespread idea that any scientist, if only he or she tries to be impartial, can be a completely dispassionate observer in any but the most trivial of situations, is a fallacy, as has been pointed out repeatedly by philosophers of science and by scientists themselves. At the very least scientists must already

> The widespread idea that any scientist, if only he or she tries to be impartial, can be a completely dispassionate observer in any but the most trivial of situations, is a fallacy.

---

[14] Polkinghorne, *One World*, 72–3.
[15] Polkinghorne, *One World*, 92–3.

have formed some idea or theory about the nature of what they are about to study.

Observation is dependent on theory

It is simply not possible to make observations and do experiments without any presuppositions. Consider, for example, the fact that science, by its very nature, has to be selective. It would clearly be impossible to take every aspect of any given object of study into account. Scientists must therefore choose what variables are likely to be important and what are not. For example, physicists do not think of taking into account the colour of billiard balls when they are conducting a laboratory investigation of the application of Newton's laws to motion: but the shape of the balls is very important—cubical balls would not be much use! In making such choices, scientists are inevitably guided by already formed ideas and theories about what the important factors are likely to be. The problem is that such ideas may sometimes be wrong and cause scientists to miss vital aspects of a problem to such an extent that they draw false conclusions. A famous story about the physicist Heinrich Hertz illustrates this.

Maxwell's electromagnetic theory predicted that radio and light waves would be propagated with the same velocity. Hertz designed an experiment to check this and found that the velocities were different. His mistake, only discovered after his death, was that he did not think that the shape of his laboratory could have any influence on the results of his experiment. Unfortunately for him, it did. Radio waves were reflected from the walls and distorted his results.

The validity of his observations depended on the (preconceived) theory that the shape of the laboratory was irrelevant to his experiment. The fact that this preconception was false invalidated his conclusions.

This story also points up another difficulty. How does one decide in this kind of situation whether it is the theory or the experiment that is at fault, whether one should trust the results of the experiment and abandon the theory and look for a better one, or whether one should keep on having faith in the theory and try to discover what was wrong with the experiment? There is no easy answer to this question. A great deal will depend on the experience and judgment of the scientists involved, and, inevitably, mistakes can and will be made.

Knowledge cannot be gained without making certain assumptions to start with

Scientists not only inevitably have preconceived ideas about particular situations, as illustrated by the story about Hertz, but their science is done within a framework of general assumptions about science as such. World-famous Harvard geneticist Richard Lewontin writes: 'Scientists, like other intellectuals, come to their work with a world view, a set of preconceptions that provides the framework for their analysis of the world.'[16]

And those preconceptions can significantly affect scientists' research methods as well as their results and interpretations of those results, as we shall see.

We would emphasise, however, that the fact that scientists have presuppositions is not to be deprecated. That would, in fact be a nonsensical attitude to adopt. For the voice of logic reminds us that we cannot get to know anything if we are not prepared to presuppose something. Let's unpack this idea by thinking about a common attitude. 'I am not prepared to take anything for granted', says someone, 'I will only accept something if you prove it to me.' Sounds reasonable—but it isn't. For if this is your view then you will never accept or know anything! For suppose I want you to accept some proposition A. You will only accept it if I prove it to you. But I shall have to prove it to you on the basis of some other proposition B. You will only accept B if I prove it to you. I shall have to prove B to you on the basis of C. And so it will go on forever in what is called an infinite regress—that is, if you insist on taking nothing for granted in the first place!

We must all start somewhere with things we take as self-evident, basic assumptions that are not proved on the basis of something else. They are often called *axioms*.[17] Whatever axioms we adopt, we then proceed to try to make sense of the world by building on those

---

[16] Lewontin, *Dialectical Biologist*, 267.

[17] It should be borne in mind, however, that the axioms which appear in various branches of pure mathematics, for example, the theory of numbers or the theory of groups, do not appear out of nowhere. They usually arise from the attempt to encapsulate and formalise years, sometimes centuries, of mathematical research, into a so-called 'axiomatic system'.

axioms. This is true, not only at the worldview level but also in all of our individual disciplines. We retain those axioms that prove useful in the sense that they lead to theories which show a better 'fit' with nature and experience, and we abandon or modify those which do not fit so well. One thing is absolutely clear: none of us can avoid starting with assumptions.

Gaining knowledge involves trusting our senses and other people

There are essentially two sources from which we accumulate knowledge:

1. directly by our own 'hands-on' experience, for example, by accidentally putting our finger in boiling water, we learn that boiling water scalds;
2. we learn all kinds of things from sources external to ourselves, for example, teachers, books, parents, the media, etc.

In doing so we all constantly exercise faith. We intuitively trust our senses, even though we know they deceive us on times. For example, in extremely cold weather, if we put our hand on a metal handrail outside, the rail may feel hot to our touch.

We have faith, too, in our minds to interpret our senses, though here again we know that our minds can be deceived.

We also normally believe what other people tell us—teachers, parents, friends, etc. Sometimes we check what we learn from them because, without insulting them, we realise that even friends can be mistaken, and other people may set out to deceive us. However, much more often than not, we accept things on authority—if only because no one has time to check everything! In technical matters we trust our textbooks. We have faith in what (other) scientists have done. And it is, of course, reasonable so to do, though those experts themselves would teach us to be critical and not just to accept everything on their say-so. They would remind us also that the fact that a statement appears in print in a book, does not make it automatically true!

Gaining scientific knowledge involves belief in the rational intelligibility of the universe

We all take so much for granted the fact that we can use human reason as a probe to investigate the universe that we can fail to see that this is really something to be wondered at. For once we begin to think about the intelligibility of the universe, our minds demand an explanation. But where can we find one? Science cannot give it to us, for the very simple reason that science has to assume the rational intelligibility of the universe in order to get started. Einstein himself, in the same article we quoted earlier, makes this very clear in saying that the scientist's belief in the rational intelligibility of the universe goes beyond science and is in its very nature essentially religious:

> Science can only be created by those who are thoroughly imbued with the aspiration toward truth and understanding. This source of feeling, however, springs from the sphere of religion. To this there also belongs the faith in the possibility that the regulations valid for the world of existence are rational, that is, comprehensible to reason. I cannot conceive of a genuine scientist without that profound faith.[18]

Einstein saw no reason to be embarrassed by the fact that science involves at its root belief in something that science itself cannot justify.

Allied to belief in the rational intelligibility of the universe is the belief that patterns and law-like behaviour are to be expected in nature. The Greeks expressed this by using the word *cosmos* which means 'ordered'. It is this underlying expectation of order that lies behind the confidence with which scientists use the inductive method. Scientists speak of their belief in the uniformity of nature—the idea that the order in nature and the laws that describe it are valid at all times and in all parts of the universe.

Many theists from the Jewish, Islamic or Christian tradition would want to modify this concept of the uniformity of nature by adding their conviction that God the Creator has built regularities

---

[18] Einstein, *Out of My Later Years*, 26.

FIGURE Ap.3. Milky Way Galaxy.

The Milky Way galaxy is visible from earth on clear nights away from urban areas. Appearing as a cloud in the night sky, our galaxy's spiral bands of dust and glowing nebulae consist of billions of stars as seen from the inside.

into the working of the universe so that in general we can speak of uniformity—the norms to which nature normally operates. But because God is the Creator, he is not a prisoner of those regularities but can vary them by causing things to happen that do not fit into the regular pattern.

Here, again, commitment to the uniformity of nature is a matter of belief. Science cannot prove to us that nature is uniform, since we must assume the uniformity of nature in order to do science. Otherwise we would have no confidence that, if we repeat an experiment under the same conditions as it was done before, we shall get the same result. Were it so, our school textbooks would be useless. But surely, we might say, the uniformity of nature is highly probable since assuming it has led to such stunning scientific advance. However, as C. S. Lewis has observed: 'Can we say that Uniformity is at any rate very probable? Unfortunately not. We have just seen that all probabilities depend on *it*. Unless Nature is uniform, nothing is either probable or improbable.'[19]

---

[19] Lewis, *Miracles*, 163.

Operating within the reigning paradigms

Thomas Kuhn in his famous book *The Structure of Scientific Revolutions* (1962) pictured science as preceding through the following stages: pre-science, normal science, crisis revolution, new normal science, new crisis, and so on. Pre-science is the diverse and disorganised activity characterised by much disagreement that precedes the emergence of a new science that gradually becomes structured when a scientific community adheres to a paradigm. The paradigm is a web of assumptions and theories that are more or less agreed upon and are like the steelwork around which the scientific edifice is erected. Well-known examples are the paradigms of Copernican astronomy, Newtonian mechanics and evolutionary biology.

Normal science is then practised within the paradigm. It sets the standards for legitimate research. The normal scientist uses the paradigm to probe nature. He or she does not (often) look critically at the paradigm itself, because it commands so much agreement, much as we look down the light of a torch to illuminate an object, rather than look critically at the light of the torch itself. For this reason the paradigm will be very resistant to attempts to demonstrate that it is false. When anomalies, difficulties and apparent falsifications turn up, the normal scientists will hope to be able to accommodate them preferably within the paradigm or by making fine adjustments to the paradigm. However, if the difficulties can no longer be resolved and keep on piling up, a crisis situation develops, which leads to a scientific revolution involving the emergence of a new paradigm that then gains the ground to such an extent that the older paradigm is eventually completely abandoned. The essence of such a paradigm shift is the replacing of an old paradigm by a new one, not the refining of the old one by the new. The best known example of a major paradigm shift is the transition from Aristotelian geocentric (earth-centred) astronomy to Copernican heliocentric (sun-centred) astronomy in the sixteenth century.

Although Kuhn's work is open to criticism at various points, he has certainly made scientists aware of a number of issues that are important for our understanding of how science works:

1. the central role that metaphysical ideas play in the development of scientific theories;
2. the high resistance that paradigms show to attempts to prove them false;
3. the fact that science is subject to human frailty.

The second of these points has both a positive and a negative outworking. It means that a good paradigm will not be overturned automatically by the first experimental result or observation that appears to speak against it. On the other hand, it means that a paradigm which eventually proves to be inadequate or false, may take a long time to die and impede scientific progress by constraining scientists within its mesh and not giving them the freedom they need to explore radically new ideas that would yield real scientific advance.

It is important to realise that paradigms themselves are often influenced at a very deep level by worldview considerations. We saw earlier that there are essentially two fundamental worldviews, the materialistic and the theistic. It seems to be the case in science that there is sometimes a tacit understanding that only paradigms which are based on materialism are admissible as scientific. Richard Dawkins, for example, says, 'the kind of explanation we come up with must not contradict the laws of physics. Indeed it will make use of the laws of physics, and nothing more than the laws of physics.'[20] It is the words 'nothing more than' that show that Dawkins is only prepared to accept reductionist, materialistic explanations.

Further reading

Books by John Lennox:

Can Science Explain Everything? (Good Book Company, 2019)

God and Stephen Hawking: Whose Design Is It Anyway? (Lion, 2011)

God's Undertaker: Has Science Buried God? (Lion, 2009)

Gunning for God: A Critique of the New Atheism (Lion, 2011)

Miracles: Is Belief in the Supernatural Irrational? VeriTalks Vol. 2. (The Veritas Forum, 2013)

Seven Days That Divide the World (Zondervan, 2011)

---

[20] Dawkins, *Blind Watchmaker*, 24.

SERIES BIBLIOGRAPHY

See also reading list on p. 179.

BOOKS

A

Abbott, Edwin. *Flatland: A Romance of Many Dimensions*. London, 1884. Repr. Oxford: Oxford University Press, 2006.

Ambrose, E. J. *The Nature and Origin of the Biological World*. New York: Halsted Press, 1982.

Ammon, Otto. *Die Gesellschaftsordnung und ihre natürlichen Grundlagen*. Jena: Gustav Fisher, 1895.

Anderson, J. N. D. (Norman). *Christianity: The Witness of History*. London: Tyndale Press, 1969.

Anderson, J. N. D. (Norman). *The Evidence for the Resurrection*. 1950. Leicester: InterVarsity Press, 1990.

Anderson, J. N. D. (Norman). *Islam in the Modern World*. Leicester: Apollos, 1990.

Andreyev, G. L. *What Kind of Morality Does Religion Teach?* Moscow: 'Znaniye', 1959.

Aristotle. *Metaphysics*. Tr. W. D. Ross, *Aristotle's Metaphysics: A Revised Text with Introduction and Commentary*. Vol. 2. Oxford: Clarendon Press, 1924.

Aristotle. *Nicomachean Ethics*. Tr. W. D. Ross. Oxford: Clarendon Press, 1925. Repr. Kitchener, Ont.: Batoche Books, 1999. Also tr. David Ross. Oxford: Oxford University Press, 1980.

Arnold, Thomas. *Christian Life, Its Hopes, Its Fears, and Its Close: Sermons preached mostly in the chapel of Rugby School, 1841–1842*. 1842. New edn, London: Longmans, 1878.

Ashman, Keith M. and Philip S. Baringer, eds. *After the Science Wars*. London: Routledge, 2001.

Atkins, Peter. *Creation Revisited*. Harmondsworth: Penguin, 1994.

Augustine of Hippo. *Confessions*. AD 397–400. Tr. Henry Chadwick, *The Confessions*. Oxford, 1991. Repr. Oxford World's Classics. Oxford: Oxford University Press, 2008.

Avise, John C. *The Genetic Gods, Evolution and Belief in Human Affairs*. Cambridge, Mass.: Harvard University Press, 1998.

Ayer, A. J., ed. *The Humanist Outlook*. London: Pemberton, 1968.

B

Bacon, Francis. *Advancement of Learning.* 1605. Ed. G. W. Kitchin, 1915. Repr. London: Dent, 1930. Online at http://archive.org/details/ advancementlearn00bacouoft (facsimile of 1915 edn).

Bādarāyana, Śankarācārya and George Thibaut. *The Vedānta Sūtras of Bādarāyana.* Vol. 34 of *Sacred books of the East.* Oxford: Clarendon Press, 1890.

Baier, Kurt. *The Moral Point of View: A Rational Basis of Ethics.* Ithaca, N.Y.: Cornell University Press, 1958.

Behe, Michael J. *Darwin's Black Box: The Biochemical Challenge to Evolution.* 1988. 10th ann. edn with new Afterword, New York: Simon & Schuster, 2006.

Bentham, Jeremy. *An Introduction to the Principles of Morals and Legislation.* 1780, 1789. Dover Philosophical Classics. Repr. of Bentham's 1823 rev. edn, Mineola, N.Y.: Dover Publications, 2007.

Berdyaev, N. A. *The Beginning and The End.* Tr. R. M. French. London: Geoffrey Bles, 1952.

Berlinski, David. *The Deniable Darwin and Other Essays.* Seattle, Wash.: Discovery Institute, 2009.

Bickerton, Derek. *Language and Species.* 1990. Repr. Chicago: University of Chicago Press, 1992.

Biddiss, M. D. *Father of Racist Ideology: The Social and Political Thought of Count Gobineau.* New York: Weybright & Talley, 1970.

Bouquet, A. C. *Comparative Religion.* Harmondsworth: Penguin (Pelican), 1962.

Breck, John. *The Sacred Gift of Life: Orthodox Christianity and Bioethics.* Crestwood, N.Y.: St. Vladimir's Seminary Press, 1998.

Bronowski, Jacob. *The Identity of Man.* Harmondsworth: Penguin, 1967.

Brow, Robert. *Religion, Origins and Ideas.* London: Tyndale Press, 1966.

Bruce, F. F. *1 and 2 Corinthians.* New Century Bible Commentary. London: Oliphants, 1971.

Bruce, F. F. *The New Testament Documents: Are They Reliable?* 1943. 6th edn, Nottingham: Inter-Varsity Press, 2000.

Butterfield, Herbert. *Christianity and History.* London: Bell, 1949. Repr. London: Fontana, 1958.

C

Cairns-Smith, A. G. *The Life Puzzle.* Edinburgh: Oliver & Boyd, 1971.

Caputo, John D., ed. *Deconstruction in a Nutshell: A Conversation with Jacques Derrida.* Perspectives in Continental Philosophy No. 1. 1997. Repr. New York: Fordham University Press, 2004.

Cary, M. and T. J. Haarhoff. *Life and Thought in the Greek and Roman World.* 5th edn, London: Methuen, 1951.

Chalmers, David J. *The Conscious Mind: In Search of a Fundamental Theory.* Oxford: Oxford University Press, 1996.

Chamberlain, Paul. *Can We Be Good Without God?: A Conversation about Truth, Morality, Culture and a Few Other Things That Matter*. Downers Grove, Ill.: InterVarsity Press, 1996.

Chomsky, Noam. *Knowledge of Language: Its Nature, Origin and Use*. New York: Praeger, 1986.

Chomsky, Noam. *Language and Mind*. 1972. 3rd edn, Cambridge: Cambridge University Press, 2006.

Chomsky, Noam. *Syntactic Structures*. The Hague: Mouton, 1957.

Cicero, Marcus Tullius. *Cicero, Selected Political Speeches*. Tr. Michael Grant. Harmondsworth: Penguin Books, 1969.

Cicero, Marcus Tullius. *De Natura Deorum*. Tr. H. Rackham, Loeb Classical Library, No. 268. Cambridge, Mass.: Harvard University Press, 1933.

Cicero, Marcus Tullius. *The Nature of the Gods*. Tr. H. C. P. McGregor. London: Penguin, 1972.

Cicero, Marcus Tullius. *Pro Rabirio*.

Clement of Alexandria. *Stromata* [or, Miscellanies]. In Kirk, G. S., J. E. Raven and M. Schofield. *The Presocratic Philosophers: A Critical History with a Selection of Texts*. 1957. Rev. edn, Cambridge: Cambridge University Press, 1983. Online at http://www.ccel.org/ccel/schaff/anf02.vi.iv.html, accessed 29 Sept. 2015.

Cornford, F. M. *Before and After Socrates*. 1932. Repr. Cambridge: Cambridge University Press, 1999. doi: 10.1017/CBO9780511570308, accessed 29 Sept. 2015.

Craig, Edward, gen. ed. *Concise Routledge Encyclopaedia of Philosophy*. London: Routledge, 2000.

Craig, William Lane. *Reasonable Faith: Christian Truth and Apologetics*. 1994. 3rd edn, Wheaton, Ill.: Crossway, 2008.

Crane, Stephen. *War Is Kind*. New York: Frederick A. Stokes, 1899. Online at http://www.gutenberg.org/ebooks/9870, accessed 11 Sept. 2015.

Cranfield, C. E. B. *A Critical and Exegetical Commentary on the Epistle to the Romans*. Vol. 1. The International Critical Commentary. Edinburgh: T&T Clark, 1975.

Crick, Francis. *The Astonishing Hypothesis: The Scientific Search for the Soul*. New York: Scribner, 1994.

Crick, Francis. *Life Itself: Its Origin and Nature*. New York: Simon & Schuster, 1981.

Crick, Francis. *Of Molecules and Men*. 1966 Jessie and John Danz Lectures. Seattle, Wash.: University of Washington Press, 1966.

Cudakov. A. *Komsomol'skaja Pravda* (11 Oct. 1988).

Culler, Jonathan. *On Deconstruction: Theory and Criticism after Structuralism*. 1982. 25th ann. edn, Ithaca, N.Y.: Cornell University Press, 2007.

D

Darwin, Charles. *The Descent of Man, and Selection in Relation to Sex*. 1871. 2nd edn, New York: A. L. Burt, 1874. Ed. James Moore and Adrian Desmond, Penguin Classics, London: Penguin Books, 2004.

Darwin, Charles. *On the Origin of Species.* 1859. Repr. World's Classics Edition, Oxford: Oxford University Press, 2008. Also cited is the 6th edn (1872) reprinted by New York University Press, 1988. Citations to one or the other edition are indicated as such.

Darwin, Francis. *The Life and Letters of Charles Darwin.* London: John Murray, 1887. doi: 10.5962/bhl.title.1416, accessed 29 June 2015.

Davies, Paul. *The Cosmic Blueprint: New Discoveries in Nature's Creative Ability to Order the Universe.* 1988. Repr. West Conshohocken, Pa.: Templeton Foundation Press, 2004.

Davies, Paul. *The Fifth Miracle: The Search for the Origin and Meaning of Life.* 1999. Repr. New York: Touchstone, 2000.

Davies, Paul. *God and the New Physics.* London: J. M. Dent, 1983. Repr. London: Penguin Books, 1990.

Davies, Paul. *The Mind of God: Science and the Search for Ultimate Meaning.* 1992. Repr. London: Simon & Schuster, 2005.

Davies, Paul and John Gribbin. *The Matter Myth: Dramatic Discoveries that Challenge Our Understanding of Physical Reality.* London, 1991. Repr. London: Simon & Schuster, 2007.

Davis, Percival and Dean H. Kenyon. *Of Pandas and People: The Central Question of Biological Origins.* 1989. 2nd edn, Dallas, Tex.: Haughton Publishing, 1993.

Dawkins, Richard. *The Blind Watchmaker.* 1986. Rev. edn, 2006. Repr. London: Penguin, 2013.

Dawkins, Richard. *Climbing Mount Improbable.* New York: Norton, 1996.

Dawkins, Richard. *Growing Up in the Universe.* The Royal Institution Christmas Lectures for Children, 1991. Five one-hour episodes directed by Stuart McDonald for the BBC. 2-Disc DVD set released 20 April 2007 by the Richard Dawkins Foundation. Available on the Ri Channel, http://www.rigb.org/christmas-lectures/watch/1991/growing-up-in-the-universe. Study Guide with the same title. London: BBC Education, 1991.

Dawkins, Richard. *River Out of Eden: A Darwinian View of Life.* 1995. Repr. London: Phoenix, 2004.

Dawkins, Richard. *The Selfish Gene.* 1976. Repr. 30th ann. edn, Oxford: Oxford University Press, 2006.

Dawkins, Richard. *Unweaving the Rainbow: Science, Delusion and the Appetite for Wonder.* 1998. Repr. London: Penguin Books, 2006.

Dawkins, Richard and John Lennox. 'The God Delusion Debate', hosted by Fixed Point Foundation, University of Alabama at Birmingham, filmed and broadcast live 3 October 2007, online at http://fixed-point.org/video/richard-dawkins-vs-john-lennox-the-god-delusion-debate/. Transcript provided courtesy of ProTorah.com, http://www.protorah.com/god-delusion-debate-dawkins-lennox-transcript/.

Deacon, Terrence. *The Symbolic Species: The Co-Evolution of Language and the Human Brain.* London: Allen Lane, 1997.

Dembski, William A. *Being as Communion: A Metaphysics of Information.* Ashgate Science and Religion. Farnham, Surrey: Ashgate, 2014.

Dembski, William A. *The Design Inference: Eliminating Chance through Small Probabilities*. Cambridge Studies in Probability, Induction and Decision Theory. Cambridge: Cambridge University Press, 1998.

Dembski, William A., ed. *Uncommon Dissent: Intellectuals Who Find Darwinism Unconvincing*. Wilmington, Del.: Intercollegiate Studies Institute, 2004.

Dennett, Daniel. *Darwin's Dangerous Idea: Evolution and the Meanings of Life*. 1995; London: Penguin, 1996.

Denton, Michael. *Evolution: A Theory in Crisis*. 1986. 3rd rev. edn, Bethesda, Md.: Adler & Adler, 1986.

Derrida, Jacques. *Of Grammatology*. 1967 (French). Tr. G. C. Spivak, 1974. Repr. Baltimore, Md.: Johns Hopkins University Press, 1997.

Derrida, Jacques. *Positions*. 1972 (French). Tr. and ed. Alan Bass, 1981. 2nd edn 2002. Repr. London: Continuum, 2010.

Derrida, Jacques. *Writing and Difference*. 1967 (French). Tr. Alan Bass, Chicago, 1978. Repr. London: Routledge Classics, 2001.

Descartes, René. *Discourse on the Method of Rightly Conducting Reason and Reaching the Truth in the Sciences*. 1637. Online at https://www.gutenberg.org/files/59/59-h/59-h.htm, accessed 11 Sept. 2015.

Descartes, René. *Meditations on First Philosophy*. Paris, 1641.

Deutsch, David. *The Fabric of Reality*. London: Penguin, 1997.

Dewey, John. *A Common Faith*. New Haven: Yale University Press, 1934.

Dostoevsky, F. *The Collected Works of Dostoevsky*. Tr. Rodion Raskolnikoff [German]. Munich: Piper, 1866.

Dostoevsky, Fyodor. *The Karamazov Brothers*. 1880 (Russian). Tr. and ed. David McDuff, Penguin Classics, 1993. Rev. edn, London: Penguin Books, 2003.

E

Eastwood, C. Cyril. *Life and Thought in the Ancient World*. Derby: Peter Smith, 1964.

Easwaran, Eknath. *The Bhagavad Gita*. 1985. Berkeley, Calif.: Nilgiri Press, 2007.

Easwaran, Eknath. *The Upanishads*. 1987. Berkeley, Calif.: Nilgiri Press, 2007.

Eccles, John C. *Evolution of the Brain, Creation of the Self*. 1989. Repr. London: Routledge, 2005.

Einstein, A. *Letters to Solovine: 1906–1955*. New York: Philosophical Library, 1987.

Einstein, A. *Out of My Later Years: The Scientist, Philosopher, and Man Portrayed Through His Own Words*. 1956. Secaucus, N.J.: Carol Publishing, 1995.

Eldredge, Niles. *Reinventing Darwin: The Great Debate at the High Table of Evolutionary Theory*. New York: Wiley, 1995.

Eldredge, Niles. *Time Frames: The Evolution of Punctuated Equilibria*. 1985. Corr. edn, Princeton, N.J.: Princeton University Press, 1989.

Ellis, John M. *Against Deconstruction*. Princeton, N.J.: Princeton University Press, 1989.

The Encyclopedia Britannica. 15th edn (*Britannica 3*), ed. Warren E. Preece and Philip W. Goetz. Chicago: Encyclopaedia Britannica, 1974–2012.

Engels, Friedrich. *Ludwig Feuerbach and the End of Classical German Philosophy.* German original first published in 1886, in *Die Neue Zeit.* Moscow: Progress Publishers, 1946.

Erbrich, Paul. *Zufall: Eine Naturwissenschaftlich-Philosophische Untersuchung.* Stuttgart: Kohlhammer, 1988.

Euripides. *The Bacchae.* Tr. James Morwood, *Bacchae and Other Plays.* Oxford World's Classics. 1999. Repr. Oxford: Oxford University Press, 2008.

Evans-Pritchard, E. E. *Nuer Religion.* 1956. 2nd edn, London: Oxford University Press, 1971.

F

Feuerbach, Ludwig. *The Essence of Christianity.* 1841. Ed. and tr. George Eliot (Mary Ann Evans). New York: Harper Torchbooks, 1957.

Feynman, Richard. *Six Easy Pieces.* 1963. Repr. London: Penguin Books, 1995.

Fischer, Ernst. *Marx in His Own Words.* Tr. Anna Bostock. London: Penguin Books, 1973.

Fish, Stanley. *Is There a Text in This Class? The Authority of Interpretive Communities.* Cambridge, Mass.: Harvard University Press, 1980.

Fish, Stanley. *There's No Such Thing as Free Speech, and It's a Good Thing Too.* New York: Oxford University Press, 1994.

Flew, Antony with Roy Abraham Varghese. *There Is a God: How the World's Most Notorious Atheist Changed His Mind.* London: HarperCollins, 2007.

Fox, S. W., ed. *The Origins of Prebiological Systems and of Their Molecular Matrices.* New York: Academic Press, 1965.

Frazer, J. G. *The Golden Bough.* 1890, 1900, 1906–15, 1937.

Fromm, Erich. *You Shall be as Gods: A Radical Interpretation of the Old Testament and its Tradition.* New York: Holt, Rinehart & Winston, 1966.

G

Gates, Bill. *The Road Ahead.* 1995. Rev. edn, Harmondsworth: Penguin, 1996.

Geisler, Norman L., and William E. Nix, *A General Introduction to the Bible* (Chicago: Moody Press, 1986), 475. Gerson, Lloyd P. *Plotinus.* London: Routledge, 1994.

Gilligan, Carol. *In a Different Voice: Psychological Theory and Women's Development.* Cambridge, Mass.: Harvard University Press, 1982.

Goldschmidt, Richard. *The Material Basis of Evolution.* The Silliman Memorial Lectures Series. 1940. Repr. Yale University Press, 1982.

Gooding, David W. and John C. Lennox. *The Human Quest for Significance: Forming a Worldview* [in Russian]. Minsk: Myrtlefield Trust, 1999.

Gould, Stephen Jay. *The Lying Stones of Marrakech: Penultimate Reflections in Natural History.* 2000. Repr. Cambridge, Mass.: Harvard University Press, 2011.

Gould, Stephen Jay. *Wonderful Life: The Burgess Shale and the Nature of History.* 1989. Repr. London: Vintage, 2000.

Grant, Michael. *Jesus: An Historian's Review of the Gospels*. New York: Scribner, 1977.

Grene, Marjorie. *A Portrait of Aristotle*. London: Faber & Faber, 1963.

Groothuis, Douglas. *Truth Decay: Defending Christianity against the Challenges of Postmodernism*. Leicester: Inter-Varsity Press, 2000.

Guthrie, W. K. C. *The Greek Philosophers from Thales to Aristotle*. 1950. Repr. London: Methuen, 2013.

Guthrie, W. K. C. *Plato: the man and his dialogues, earlier period*. Vol. 4 of *A History of Greek Philosophy*. 1875. Repr. Cambridge: Cambridge University Press, 2000.

H

Haldane, J. B. S. *Possible Worlds*. 1927. London: Chatto & Windus, 1945.

Harrison, E. *Masks of the Universe*. 1985. 2nd edn, New York: Macmillan, 2003. Citations are to the first Macmillan edition.

Harvey, William. *On the Motion of the Heart and the Blood of Animals*. 1628. Online at https://ebooks.adelaide.edu.au/h/harvey/william/motion/complete.html, accessed 4 Sept. 2018.

Hawking, Stephen. *A Brief History of Time*. 1988. Updated and expanded 10th ann. edn, London: Bantam Press, 1998.

Hawking, Stephen and Leonard Mlodinow. *The Grand Design*. New York: Bantam Books, 2010.

Hegel, G. W. F. *Hegel's Logic*. Being Part One of the Encyclopaedia of the Philosophical Sciences (1830). Tr. William Wallace, 1892. Repr. Oxford: Clarendon Press, 1984–87.

Hegel, G. W. F. *The Phenomenology of the Mind* (Spirit). 1807. 2nd edn 1841. Tr. J. B. Baillie, London, 1910. Repr. Dover Philosophical Classics, New York: Dover Publications, 2003.

Hegel, G. W. F. *The Philosophy of History*. 1861. Tr. J. Sibree, 1857. Repr. New York: Dover Publications, 1956. Repr. Kitchener, Ont.: Batoche Books, 2001. Online at Internet Archive: https://archive.org/details/lecturesonphilos00hegerich/, accessed 19 Oct. 2018.

Hegel, G. W. F. *Wissenschaft der Logik* [The Science of Logic]. Nurnberg, 1812–16.

Hemer, Colin. *The Book of Acts in the Setting of Hellenistic History*. Tübingen: J. C. B. Mohr, Paul Siebeck, 1989.

Hengel, Martin. *Judaism and Hellenism: Studies in their Encounter in Palestine during the Early Hellenistic Period*. Tr. John Bowden. London: SCM Press, 1974. Repr. Eugene, Oreg.: Wipf & Stock, 2003.

Hengel, Martin. *Studies in Early Christology*. Tr. Rollin Kearns. Edinburgh: T&T Clark, 1995.

Herodotus. *The Histories*. Tr. Robin Waterfield, 1998, Oxford World's Classics. Repr. New York: Oxford University Press, 2008.

Herzen, Alexander Ivanovich. *Byloe i dumy*. London, 1853. Tr. C. Garnett, *My Past and Thoughts, The Memoirs of Alexander Herzen*. Revised by H. Higgens, introduced by I. Berlin, 1968. Repr. London: Chatto and Windus, 2008.

Hesiod. *Theogony*. In Charles Abraham Elton, tr. *The remains of Hesiod*. London: Lackington, Allen, 1812. Also in Dorothea Wender, tr. *Hesiod and Theognis*. Harmondsworth: Penguin, 1973.

Hippolytus, *Refutation of all Heresies*. In Kirk, G. S., J. E. Raven and M. Schofield. *The Presocratic Philosophers: A Critical History with a Selection of Texts*. 1957. Rev. edn, Cambridge: Cambridge University Press, 1983.

Holmes, Arthur F. *Ethics*. Downers Grove, Ill.: InterVarsity Press, 1984; 2nd edn, 2007.

Honderich, Ted, ed. *The Oxford Companion to Philosophy*. Oxford, 1995. 2nd edn, Oxford: Oxford University Press, 2005.

Hooper, Judith. *Of Moths and Men*. New York: Norton, 2002.

Hooykaas, R. *Religion and the Rise of Modern Science*. 1972. Repr. Edinbugh: Scottish Academic Press, 2000.

Hospers, John. *An Introduction to Philosophical Analysis*. 1953. 4th edn, Abingdon: Routledge, 1997.

Houghton, John. *The Search for God—Can Science Help?* Oxford: Lion Publishing, 1995.

Hoyle, Fred. *The Intelligent Universe*. London: Joseph, 1983.

Hoyle, Fred and Chandra Wickramasinghe. *Cosmic Life-Force, the Power of Life Across the Universe*. London: Dent, 1988.

Hoyle, Fred and Chandra Wickramasinghe. *Evolution from Space: A Theory of Cosmic Creationism*. New York: Simon & Schuster, 1984.

Hume, David. *David Hume: A Treatise of Human Nature*. 1739–40. Ed. Lewis Amherst Selby-Bigge and P. H. Nidditch. Oxford: Clarendon Press, 1888. Repr. 1978. Repr. Oxford: Oxford University Press, 2014. doi: 10.1093/actrade/9780198245872.book.1, accessed 11 Sept. 2015; also online at https://davidhume.org/texts/t/, accessed 4 Sept.2018.

Hume, David. *Dialogues Concerning Natural Religion*. 1779. Repr. ed. J. C. A. Gaskin, *Dialogues Concerning Natural Religion, and The Natural History of Religion*. Oxford World's Classics. Oxford: Oxford University Press, 2008. Online at https://davidhume.org/texts/d/, accessed 2 Aug. 2017. (Abbreviated as DNR.)

Hume, David. *An Enquiry Concerning Human Understanding*. London: A. Millar, 1748. Repr. Dover Philosophical Classics, Mineola, N.Y.: Dover Publications, 2012. Online at http://www.davidhume.org/texts/e, accessed 2 Aug. 2017. (Abbreviated as EHU.)

Hume, David. *Treatise of Human Nature*. 1739–40. Eds. David Norton and Mary J. Norton, *David Hume: A Treatise of Human Nature: A critical edition*. Vol. 1 of The Clarendon Edition of The Works Of David Hume. Oxford: Oxford University Press, 2007. Online at http://www.davidhume.org/texts/t/, accessed 2 Aug. 2017. (Abbreviated as THN.)

Hunt, R. N. Carew. *The Theory and Practice of Communism*. Baltimore: Penguin Books, 1966.

Hurley, Thomas. *Method and Results: Collected Essays*. Vol. I. London: Macmillan, 1898.

Husserl, Edmund. *Ideas: General Introduction to Pure Phenomenology.* Ger. orig. *Ideen zu einer reinen Phänomenologie und phänomenologischen Philosophie. Erstes Buch: Allgemeine Einführung in die reine Phänomenologie* (1913). Tr. W. R. Boyce Gibson. London: Macmillan, 1931.

Huxley, Julian. *Essays of a Humanist.* 1964. Repr. Harmondsworth: Penguin Books, 1969.

Huxley, Julian. *Religion Without Revelation.* New York: Mentor, 1957.

I

Isherwood, Christopher, ed. *Vedanta for Modern Man.* 1951. Repr. New York: New American Library, 1972.

J

Jacob, François. *Chance and Necessity: An Essay on the Natural Philosophy of Modern Biology.* Tr. Austryn Wainhouse. New York: Alfred A. Knopf, 1971.

Jacob, François. *The Logic of Life: A History of Heredity.* Tr. Betty E. Spillman. New York: Pantheon Books, 1973.

Jaeger, Werner. *The Theology of the Early Greek Philosophers.* The Gifford Lectures, 1936. Oxford: Oxford University Press, 1967.

James, E. O. *Christianity and Other Religions.* London: Hodder & Stoughton, 1968.

Jaroszwski, T. M. and P. A. Ignatovsky, eds. *Socialism as a Social System.* Moscow: Progress Publishers, 1981.

Jeremias, J. *New Testament Theology: The Proclamation of Jesus.* Tr. John Bowden. New York: Scribner, 1971.

Joad, C. E. M. *The Book of Joad: A Belligerent Autobiography* [= *Under the Fifth Rib*]. London: Faber & Faber, 1944.

Johnson, Phillip E. *Objections Sustained: Subversive Essays on Evolution, Law and Culture.* Downers Grove, Ill.: InterVarsity Press, 1998.

Jones, Steve. *In the Blood: God, Genes and Destiny.* London: Harper Collins, 1996.

Josephus, Flavius. *Antiquities of the Jews.* Tr. William Whiston, *The Works of Flavius Josephus.* 1737. Repr. Grand Rapids: Kregel, 1974. Repr. Peabody, Mass.: Hendrickson, 1995.

K

Kant, Immanuel. *Critique of Practical Reason.* 1788. Tr. and ed. Mary Gregor. Cambridge Texts in the History of Philosophy. 1997. Repr. Cambridge: Cambridge University Press, 2003.

Kant, Immanuel. *Critique of Pure Reason.* 1781. 2nd edn, 1787. Tr. Norman Kemp Smith. London: Macmillan, 1929. Repr. Blunt Press, 2007. Also Paul Guyer and Allen Wood, eds., Cambridge: Cambridge University Press, 1999.

Kant, Immanuel. *Groundwork of the Metaphysics of Morals.* 1785. In H. J. Paton, tr. *The Moral Law.* London: Hutchinson, 1972.

Kant, Immanuel. *The Metaphysics of Morals*. 1797. Tr. and ed. Mary J. Gregor. Cambridge Texts in the History of Philosophy. Cambridge: Cambridge University Press, 1996.

Kant, Immanuel. *Prolegomena to Any Future Metaphysics*. 1783. Tr. and ed. Gary Hatfield, *Prolegomena to Any Future Metaphysics with Selections from the Critique of Pure Reason*. Cambridge Texts in the History of Philosophy. 1997. Rev. edn, Cambridge: Cambridge University Press, 2004.

Kantikar, V. P. (Hemant) and W. Owen. *Hinduism—An Introduction: Teach Yourself*. 1995. Repr. London: Hodder Headline, 2010.

Kaye, Howard L. *The Social Meaning of Modern Biology, From Social Darwinism to Sociobiology*. 1986. Repr. with a new epilogue, New Brunswick, N.J.: Transaction Publishers, 1997.

Kenny, Anthony. *An Illustrated Brief History of Western Philosophy*. Oxford: Blackwell, 2006. First published as *A Brief History of Western Philosophy*, 1998.

Kenyon, D. H. and G. Steinman. *Biochemical Predestination*. New York: McGraw-Hill, 1969.

Kenyon, Frederic. *Our Bible and the Ancient Manuscripts*. 1895. 4th edn, 1938. Repr. Eugene, Oreg.: Wipf & Stock, 2011.

Kilner, J. F., C. C. Hook and D. B. Uustal, eds. *Cutting-Edge Bioethics: A Christian Exploration of Technologies and Trends*. Grand Rapids: Eerdmans, 2002.

Kirk, G. S., J. E. Raven and M. Schofield. *The Presocratic Philosophers: A Critical History with a Selection of Texts*. 1957. Rev. edn, Cambridge: Cambridge University Press, 1983.

Kirk, M. and H. Madsen. *After the Ball*. New York: Plume Books, 1989.

Knott, Kim. *Hinduism: A Very Short Introduction*. Oxford: Oxford University Press, 1998.

Koertge, Noretta, ed. *A House Built on Sand: Exposing Postmodernist Myths About Science*. Oxford: Oxford University Press, 1998.

Kolbanovskiy, V. N. *Communist Morality*. Moscow, 1951.

Krikorian, Yervant H., ed. *Naturalism and the Human Spirit*. 1944. Repr. New York: Columbia University Press, 1969.

Kuhn, Thomas. *The Structure of Scientific Revolutions*. 1962. 3rd edn, Chicago: University of Chicago Press, 1996.

Kurtz, Paul. *The Fullness of Life*. New York: Horizon Press, 1974.

Kurtz, Paul. *The Humanist Alternative*. Buffalo, N.Y.: Prometheus, 1973.

Kurtz, Paul, ed. *Humanist Manifestos I & II*. Buffalo, N.Y.: Prometheus, 1980.

Kurtz, Paul, ed. *Humanist Manifesto II*. Buffalo, N.Y.: Prometheus Books, 1980. Online at https://americanhumanist.org/what-is-humanism/manifesto2/, accessed 11 Sept. 2105.

L

Lamont, Corliss. *A Lifetime of Dissent*. Buffalo, N.Y.: Prometheus Books, 1988.

Lamont, Corliss. *The Philosophy of Humanism*. 1947. 8th edn, Emherst, N.Y.: Humanist Press, 1997.

Lapouge, G. Vacher de. *Les Sélections Sociales*. Paris: Fontemoing, 1899.

Leakey, Richard. *The Origin of Humankind*. London: Weidenfeld & Nicolson, 1994.

Leitch, Vincent B. *Deconstructive Criticism: An Advanced Introduction*. New York: Columbia University Press, 1982.

Lenin, V. I. *Complete Collected Works*. Tr. Andrew Rothstein. 4th Eng. edn, Moscow: Progress Publishers, 1960–78. Online at http://www.marx2mao.com/Lenin/Index.html (facsimile), accessed 11 Sept. 2015. Repr. Moscow: Progress Publishers, 1982.

Lenin, V. I. *Materialism and Empirico-Criticism*. New York: International Publishers, 1927.

Lennox, John C. *Can Science Explain Everything?* Epsom, UK: Good Book Company, 2019.

Lennox, John C. *Determined to Believe: The Sovereignty of God, Freedom, Faith and Human*. Oxford: Monarch Books, 2017.

Lennox, John C. *God and Stephen Hawking: Whose Design is it Anyway?* Oxford: Lion, 2010.

Lennox, John C. *God's Undertaker: Has Science Buried God?* Oxford, Lion Books, 2007, 2009.

Leslie, John. *Universes*. London: Routledge, 1989.

Levinskaya, Irina. *The Book of Acts in its First Century Setting*. Vol. 5. Diaspora Setting. Grand Rapids: Eerdmans, 1996.

Lewis, C. S. *The Abolition of Man*. London, 1945. Repr. London: Collins, Fount, 1978.

Lewis, C. S. *Christian Reflections*. London, 1967. Repr. New York: HarperCollins, 1998.

Lewis, C. S. *God in the Dock*. London, 1979. Repr. Grand Rapids: Eerdmans, 2014.

Lewis, C. S. *Mere Christianity*. London, 1952. Rev. edn with new introduction and foreword by Kathleen Norris, New York: HarperCollins, 2001.

Lewis, C. S. *Miracles*. 1947. Repr. London: Collins, 2012.

Lewis, C. S. *The Problem of Pain*. 1940. Repr. London: Collins, 2009.

Lewis, C. S. *Transposition and other Addresses*. London: Geoffrey Bles, 1949.

Lewontin, Richard. *The Dialectical Biologist*. Cambridge, Mass.: Harvard University Press, 1987.

Locke, John. *An Essay Concerning Human Understanding*. London, 1689. Ed. Peter H. Nidditch, Oxford: Oxford University Press, 1975.

Long, A. A. *Hellenistic Philosophy*. 1974. 2nd edn, Berkeley, Calif.: University of California Press, 1986.

Lossky, N. O. *History of Russian Philosophy*. London: Allen & Unwin, 1952.

Lucretius (Titus Lucretius Carus). *De Rerum Natura*. 50 BC. Tr. A. E. Stallings as *The Nature of Things*. London: Penguin, 2007. Also tr. and ed. William Ellery Leonard. 1916. Online at: http://www.perseus.tufts.edu/hopper/text?doc=Lucr or http://classics.mit.edu/Carus/nature_things.html.

Lumsden, Charles J. and Edward O. Wilson. *Promethean Fire: Reflections on the Origin of Mind*. Cambridge, Mass.: Harvard University Press, 1983.

M

Mabbott, J. D. *An Introduction to Ethics*. Hutchinson University Library. London: Hutchinson, 1966.

McKay, Donald. *The Clockwork Image: A Christian Perspective on Science*. London: Inter-Varsity Press, 1974.

Majerus, Michael. *Melanism: Evolution in Action*. Oxford: Oxford University Press, 1998.

Margenau, Henry and Roy Abraham Varghese, eds. *Cosmos, Bios, and Theos: Scientists Reflect on Science, God, and the Origins of the Universe, Life, and Homo Sapiens*. La Salle, Ill.: Open Court, 1992.

Marx, Karl. *Marx's Theses on Feuerbach*. 1845.

Mascall, E. L. *Words and Images, a study in the Possibility of Religious Discourse*. London: Longmans, 1957.

Mascarō, Juan, tr. *The Upanishads*. Harmondsworth: Penguin, 1965.

Maslow, Abraham. *Towards a Psychology of Being*. New York: Van Nostrand Reinhold, 1968.

Masterson, Patrick. *Atheism and Alienation*. Harmondsworth: Pelican Books, 1972.

May, Rollo. *Psychology and the Human Dilemma*. Princeton, N.J., 1967. Repr. New York: Norton, 1996.

Medawar, Peter. *Advice to a Young Scientist*. New York: Harper & Row, 1979.

Medawar, Peter. *The Limits of Science*. Oxford: Oxford University Press, 1985.

Medawar, Peter and Jean Medawar. *The Life Science*. London: Wildwood House, 1977.

Metzger, Bruce. *The Text of the New Testament, its Transmission, Corruption and Restoration*. 1964. 3rd edn, Oxford: Oxford University Press, 1992.

Mill, John Stuart. *Utilitarianism*. 1861, 1863. Repr. Mineola, N.Y.: Dover Publications, 2007.

Millard, Alan. *Reading and Writing in the Time of Jesus*. Sheffield: Sheffield Academic Press, 2000.

Miller, David, Janet Coleman, William Connolly, and Alan Ryan, eds. *The Blackwell Encyclopaedia of Political Thought*. 1987. Repr. Oxford: Blackwell, 1991.

Monod, Jacques. *Chance and Necessity: An Essay on the Natural Philosophy of Modern Biology*. 1970 (French). Tr. Austryn Wainhouse, 1971. Repr. London: Penguin Books, 1997. Citations are from Vintage Books 1972 edn.

Monod, Jacques. *From Biology to Ethics*. San Diego: Salk Institute for Biological Studies, 1969.

Morris, Simon Conway. *The Crucible of Creation: The Burgess Shale and the Rise of Animals*. 1998. New edn, Oxford: Oxford University Press, 1999.

Mossner, Ernest C., ed. *David Hume, A Treatise of Human Nature*. London: Penguin Classics, 1985.

Moule, C. F. D. *The Phenomenon of the New Testament: An Inquiry into the Implications of Certain Features of the New Testament*. London: SCM, 1967.

Murphy, John P. *Pragmatism: From Peirce to Davidson*. Boulder, Colo.: Westview Press, 1990.

N

Nagel, Thomas. *The Last Word*. Oxford: Oxford University Press, 1997.

Nagel, Thomas. *Mortal Questions*. Cambridge: Cambridge University Press. 1979.

Nahem, Joseph. *Psychology and Psychiatry Today: A Marxist View*. New York: International Publishers, 1981.

Nasr, Seyyed Hossein, and Oliver Leaman, eds. *History of Islamic Philosophy*. Part 1, Vol. 1 of *Routledge History of World Philosophies*. 1996. Repr. London: Routledge, 2001.

Nettleship, R. L. *Lectures on the Republic of Plato*. London: Macmillan, 1922.

Newton, Isaac. *Principia Mathematica*. London, 1687.

Nietzsche, Friedrich. *Beyond Good and Evil: Prelude to a Philosophy of the Future*. Leipzig, 1886. 1973. Repr. tr. R. J. Hollingdale, Harmondsworth: Penguin, 1975.

Noddings, Nel. *Caring: A Feminine Approach to Ethics and Moral Education*. 1984. Repr. Berkeley, Calif.: University of California Press, 2013.

Norris, Christopher. *Deconstruction: Theory and Practice*. 1982. 3rd edn, London: Methuen, 2002.

O

Olivelle, Patrick. *The Early Upanishads: Annotated Text and Translation*. 1996. Repr. Oxford: Oxford University Press, 1998.

O'Meara, Dominic J. *Plotinus: An Introduction to the Enneads*. Oxford: Clarendon Press, 1993.

P

Paley, William. *Natural Theology on Evidence and Attributes of Deity*. 1802. Repr. Oxford: Oxford University Press, 2006.

Patterson, Colin. *Evolution*. 1978. 2nd edn, Ithaca, N.Y.: Cornstock Publishing Associates, 1999.

Peacocke, Arthur. *The Experiment of Life*. Toronto: University of Toronto Press, 1983.

Pearsall, Judy and Bill Trumble, eds. *The Oxford English Reference Dictionary*. 2nd edn, Oxford: Oxford University Press, 1996.

Pearse, E. K. Victor. *Evidence for Truth: Science*. Guildford: Eagle, 1998.

Penfield, Wilder. *The Mystery of the Mind*. Princeton, N.J.: Princeton University Press, 1975.

Penrose, Roger. *The Emperor's New Mind*. 1986. Repr. with new preface, Oxford: Oxford University Press, 1999.

Penrose, Roger. *The Road to Reality: A Complete Guide to the Laws of the Universe*. London: Jonathan Cape, 2004.

Peterson, Houston, ed. *Essays in Philosophy*. New York: Pocket Library, 1959.

Pinker, Steven. *The Language Instinct: How the Mind Creates Language*. New York: Morrow, 1994.

Plantinga, Alvin. *Warranted Christian Belief.* Oxford: Oxford University Press, 2000.

Plato. *Apology.* Tr. Hugh Tredennick, 1954. Repr. Harmondsworth: Penguin Books, 1976. Also in *The Collected Dialogues of Plato including the letters.* 1961. Repr. with corrections, Princeton, N.J.: Princeton University Press, 1973.

Plato. *The Euthyphro.*

Plato. *The Last Days of Socrates.* Tr. Hugh Tredennick. Harmondsworth: Penguin Books, 1969.

Plato. *Phaedo.*

Plato. *Republic.* Tr. Desmond Lee. 2nd edn, Harmondsworth: Penguin, 1974. Also tr. Paul Shorey, Loeb Classical Library. Cambridge, Mass.: Harvard University Press, 1930. Also in *The Collected Dialogues of Plato including the letters,* 1961. Repr. with corrections, Princeton, N.J.: Princeton University Press, 1973.

Plato. *Timaeus.*

Pliny the Younger. *Letters.* Tr. Betty Radice as *The Letters of the Younger Pliny.* Harmondsworth: Penguin Books, 1963.

Plotinus. *Enneads.* Tr. Stephen MacKenna, 1917–30. Repr. London: Penguin, 2005.

Polanyi, Michael. *The Tacit Dimension.* New York: Doubleday, 1966.

Polkinghorne, John. *One World: The Interaction of Science and Theology.* London: SPCK, 1986.

Polkinghorne, John. *Reason and Reality: The Relationship between Science and Theology.* 1991. Repr. London: SPCK, 2011.

Polkinghorne, John. *Science and Creation: The Search for Understanding.* 1988. Rev. edn, West Conshohocken, Pa.: Templeton Foundation Press, 2009.

Polkinghorne, John. *Science and Providence: God's Interaction with the World.* 1989. Repr. West Conshohocken, Pa.: Templeton Foundation Press, 2011.

Popper, Karl R. *The World of Parmenides.* London: Routledge, 1998.

Popper, Karl R. and John C. Eccles. *The Self and Its Brain: An Argument for Interactionism.* 1977. Repr. Springer Berlin Heidelberg, 2012.

Pospisil, Leopold J. *Kapauku Papuans and their Law.* Yale University Publications in Anthropology 54. New Haven, 1958.

Pospisil, Leopold J. *The Kapauku Papuans of West New Guinea.* Case Studies in Cultural Anthropology. 1963. 2nd edn, New York: Holt, Rinehart and Winston, 1978.

Powers, B. Ward. *The Progressive Publication of Matthew.* Nashville: B&H Academic, 2010.

Poythress, Vern S. *Inerrancy and the Gospels: A God-Centered Approach to the Challenges of Harmonization.* Wheaton, Ill.: Crossway, 2012.

Pritchard, J. B., ed. *Ancient Near Eastern Texts Relating to the Old Testament.* Princeton, 1950. 3rd edn, Princeton, N.J.: Princeton University Press, 1969.

Putnam, Hilary. *Reason, Truth and History.* Cambridge: Cambridge University Press, 1981.

R

Rachels, James. *Elements of Moral Philosophy*. New York: McGraw-Hill, 1986.

Ragg, Lonsdale and Laura Ragg, eds. *The Gospel of Barnabas*. Oxford: Clarendon Press, 1907.

Ramsay, William. *St. Paul the Traveller and the Roman Citizen*. London: Hodder & Stoughton, 1895.

Randall, John H. *Cosmos*. New York: Random House, 1980.

Raphael, D. D. *Moral Philosophy*. 1981. 2nd edn, Oxford: Oxford University Press, 1994.

Rawls, John. *A Theory of Justice*. Cambridge, Mass.: Harvard University Press, 1971.

Redford, Donald B., ed. *The Oxford Encyclopaedia of Ancient Egypt*. Oxford: Oxford University Press, 2001. doi: 10.1093/acref/9780195102345.001.0001.

Reid, Thomas. *An Enquiry Concerning Human Understanding*. Oxford: Clarendon Press, 1777.

Reid, Thomas. *An Inquiry into the Human Mind on the Principles of Common Sense*. 1764. Repr. Cambridge: Cambridge University Press, 2011.

Renfrew, Colin. *Archaeology and Language: The Puzzle of Indo-European Origins*. 1987. Repr. Cambridge: Cambridge University Press, 1999.

Ricoeur, Paul. *Hermeneutics and the Human Sciences*. 1981. Ed. and tr. J. B. Thompson. Repr. Cambridge: Cambridge University Press, 1998.

Ricoeur, Paul. *Interpretation Theory: Discourse and the Surplus of Meaning*. Fort Worth, Tex.: Texas Christian University Press, 1976.

Ridley, Mark. *The Problems of Evolution*. Oxford: Oxford University Press, 1985.

Rodwell, J. M., tr. *The Koran*. Ed. Alan Jones. London: Phoenix, 2011.

Rorty, Richard. *Consequences of Pragmatism: Essays, 1972–1980*. Minneapolis, Minn.: University of Minnesota Press, 1982.

Rose, Steven. *Lifelines: Biology, Freedom, Determinism*. 1998. Repr. New York: Oxford University Press, 2003.

Ross, Hugh. *The Creator and the Cosmos*. Colorado Springs: NavPress, 1995.

Ross, W. D. *The Right and the Good*. Oxford: Clarendon Press, 1930. Repr. 2002.

Rousseau, Jean Jacques. *The Social Contract*. 1762.

Russell, Bertrand. *The Autobiography of Bertrand Russell*. 1967–69. Repr. London: Routledge, 1998.

Russell, Bertrand. *History of Western Philosophy*. 1946. New edn, London: Routledge, 2004.

Russell, Bertrand. *Human Society in Ethics and Politics*. New York: Mentor, 1962.

Russell, Bertrand. *The Problems of Philosophy*. 1912. Repr. New York: Cosimo Classics, 2010.

Russell, Bertrand. *Religion and Science*. Oxford: Oxford University Press, 1970.

Russell, Bertrand. *Understanding History*. 1943. New York: Philosophical Library, 1957.

Russell, Bertrand. *Why I Am Not a Christian and Other Essays on Religion and Related Subjects*. New York: Simon & Schuster, 1957.

Russell, L. O. and G. A. Adebiyi. *Classical Thermodynamics*. Oxford: Oxford University Press, 1993.

Ryle, Gilbert. *The Concept of Mind*. London, 1949. Repr. London: Routledge, 2009.

S

Sagan, Carl. *The Cosmic Connection: An Extraterrestrial Perspective*. New York: Anchor Press, 1973.

Sagan, Carl. *Cosmos: The Story of Cosmic Evolution, Science and Civilisation*. 1980. Repr. London: Abacus, 2003.

Sagan, Carl. *The Demon-Haunted World: Science as a Candle in the Dark*. London: Headline, 1996.

Sandbach, F. H. *The Stoics*. 1975. Rev. edn, London: Bloomsbury, 2013.

Sartre, Jean-Paul. *Being and Nothingness: An Essay on Phenomenological Ontology*. 1943. Tr. Hazel E. Barnes. 1956. Repr. New York: Pocket Books, 1984.

Sartre, Jean-Paul. *Existentialism and Human Emotions*. Tr. Bernard Frechtman. New York: Philosophical Library, 1957.

Sartre, Jean-Paul. *Existentialism and Humanism*. Tr. and ed. P. Mairet. London: Methuen, 1948.

Sartre, Jean-Paul. *The Flies*. 1943 (French). Tr. Stuart Gilbert. New York: Knopf, 1947.

Schaff, Adam. *A Philosophy of Man*. London: Lawrence and Wishart, 1963.

Scherer, Siegfried. *Evolution. Ein kritisches Lehrbuch*. Weyel Biologie, Giessen: Weyel Lehrmittelverlag, 1998.

Schmidt, W. *The Origin and Growth of Religion*. Tr. J. Rose. London: Methuen, 1931.

Scruton, Roger. *Modern Philosophy*. 1994; London: Arrow Books, 1996.

Searle, John R. *The Construction of Social Reality*. London: Penguin, 1995.

Searle, John R. *Minds, Brains and Science*. 1984 Reith Lectures. London: British Broadcasting Corporation, 1984.

Selsam, Howard. *Socialism and Ethics*. New York: International Publishers, 1943.

Sen, Amartya and Bernard Williams, eds. *Utilitarianism and Beyond*. Cambridge: Cambridge University Press, 1982. 8th repr. in association with La Maison Des Sciences De L'Homme, Paris, 1999.

Shakespeare, William. *As You Like It*.

Sherrington, Charles S. *The Integrative Action of the Nervous System*. 1906. Repr. with new preface, Cambridge: Cambridge University Press, 1947.

Sherwin-White, A. N. *Roman Society and Roman Law in the New Testament*. The Sarum Lectures 1960–61. Oxford: Clarendon Press, 1963. Repr. Eugene, Oreg.: Wipf & Stock, 2004.

Simplicius. *Commentary on Aristotle's Physics* [or, Miscellanies]. In Kirk, G. S., J. E. Raven, and M. Schofield. *The Presocratic Philosophers: A Critical History with a Selection of Texts*. 1957. Rev. edn, Cambridge: Cambridge University Press, 1983.

Simpson, George Gaylord. *The Meaning of Evolution: A Study of the History of Life and of Its Significance for Man.* The Terry Lectures Series. 1949. Rev. edn, New Haven, Conn.: Yale University Press, 1967.

Singer, Peter. *Practical Ethics.* 1979. 2nd edn, Cambridge: Cambridge University Press, 1993.

Singer, Peter. *Rethinking Life and Death: The Collapse of Our Traditional Ethics.* Oxford: Oxford University Press, 1994.

Singer, Peter and Helga Kuhse. *Should the Baby Live?: The Problem of Handicapped Infants* (Studies in Bioethics). Oxford: Oxford University Press, 1985.

Sire, James. *The Universe Next Door.* Downers Grove, Ill.: InterVarsity Press, 1988.

Skinner, B. F. *Beyond Freedom and Dignity.* 1971; Harmondsworth: Penguin, 1974.

Skinner, B. F. *Lectures on Conditioned Reflexes.* New York: International Publishers, 1963.

Skinner, B. F. *Science and Human Behaviour.* New York: Macmillan, 1953.

Sleeper, Raymond S. *A Lexicon of Marxist-Leninist Semantics.* Alexandria, Va.: Western Goals, 1983.

Smart, J. J. C. and Bernard Williams. *Utilitarianism For and Against.* 1973. Repr. Cambridge: Cambridge University Press, 1998.

Smith, Adam. *An Enquiry into the Nature and Causes of the Wealth of Nations.* 1776. With introduction by Mark G. Spencer, Ware, UK: Wordsworth Editions, 2012.

Smith, John Maynard and Eörs Szathmary. *The Major Transitions in Evolution.* 1995. Repr. Oxford: Oxford University Press, 2010.

Smith, Wilbur. *Therefore Stand.* Grand Rapids: Baker, 1965.

Sober, E. *Philosophy of Biology.* 1993. Rev. 2nd edn, Boulder, Colo.: Westview Press, 2000.

Social Exclusion Unit. *Teenage Pregnancy.* Cmnd 4342. London: The Stationery Office, 1999.

Sophocles. *Antigone.* Tr. F. H. Storr, *Sophocles* Vol. 1. London: Heinemann, 1912.

Spencer, Herbert. *Social Statics.* New York: D. Appleton, 1851.

Stalin, Joseph. *J. Stalin Works.* Moscow: Foreign Languages Publishing House, 1953.

Stam, James H. *Inquiries into the Origin of Language: The Fate of a Question.* New York: Harper & Row, 1976.

Starkey, Mike. *God, Sex, and the Search for Lost Wonder: For Those Looking for Something to Believe In.* 1997. 2nd edn, Downers Grove, Ill.: InterVarsity Press, 1998.

Stauber, Ethelbert. *Jesus—Gestalt und Geschichte.* Bern: Francke Verlag, 1957.

Storer, Morris B., ed. *Humanist Ethics: Dialogue on Basics.* Buffalo, N.Y.: Prometheus Books, 1980.

Stott, John R. W. *The Message of Romans.* Leicester: Inter-Varsity Press, 1994.

Strabo. *Geography.* Tr. with introduction Duane W. Roller as *The Geography of Strabo*, Cambridge: Cambridge University Press, 2014. Tr. H. C. Hamilton and W. Falconer, London, 1903. Online at Perseus, Tufts University, http://www.

perseus.tufts.edu/hopper/text?doc=Perseus%3Atext%3A1999.01.0239, accessed 11 Sept. 2015.

Strickberger, Monroe. *Evolution*. 1990. 3rd edn, London: Jones and Bartlett, 2000.

Strobel, Lee. *The Case for Christ: A Journalist's Personal Investigation of the Evidence for Jesus*. Grand Rapids: Zondervan, 1998.

Suetonius. *Lives of the Caesars*. Tr. Catharine Edwards. 2000. Repr. Oxford World's Classics. Oxford: Oxford University Press, 2008.

Sunderland, Luther D. *Darwin's Enigma*. Green Forest, Ark.: Master Books, 1998.

Swinburne, Richard. *The Existence of God*. 1979. Repr. Oxford: Oxford University Press, 2004.

Swinburne, Richard. *Faith and Reason*. 1981. Repr. Oxford: Clarendon Press, 2002.

Swinburne, Richard. *Is There a God?* Oxford: Oxford University Press, 1996.

Swinburne, Richard. *Providence and the Problem of Evil*. Oxford: Oxford University Press, 1998.

T

Tacitus, Cornelius. *Annals*. Tr. Alfred John Church and William Jackson Brodribb as *Complete Works of Tacitus*. New York: Random House, 1872. Repr. 1942. Online at Sara Byrant, ed., Perseus Digital Library, Tufts University, Medford, MA: http://www.perseus.tufts.edu/hopper/text?doc=Perseus:text:1999.02.0078, accessed 2 Aug. 2017.

Tada, Joni Eareckson and Steven Estes. *When God Weeps: Why Our Sufferings Matter to the Almighty*. Grand Rapids: Zondervan, 1997.

Tax, Sol and Charles Callender, eds. *Issues in Evolution*. Chicago: University of Chicago Press, 1960.

Thaxton, Charles B., Walter L. Bradley and Roger L. Olsen. *The Mystery of Life's Origin*. Dallas: Lewis & Stanley, 1992.

Thibaut, George, tr. *The Vedānta Sūtras of Bādarāyana* with the Commentary by Śankara, 2 Parts. New York: Dover, 1962.

Torrance, T. F. *The Ground and Grammar of Theology*. Belfast: Christian Journals Limited, 1980; and Charlottesville: The University Press of Virginia, 1980. Repr. with new preface, Edinburgh: T&T Clark, 2001.

Torrance, T. F. *Theological Science*. Oxford: Oxford University Press, 1978.

U

Unamuno, Don Miguel de. *The Tragic Sense of Life*. Tr. J. E. Crawford. 1921. Repr. Charleston, S.C.: BiblioBazaar, 2007.

V

Von Neumann, John. *Theory of Self-Reproducing Automata*. Ed. and completed by Arthur W. Burks, Urbana: University of Illinois Press, 1966.

W

Waddington, C. H., ed. *Science and Ethics: An Essay.* London: Allen & Unwin, 1942.

Wallis, R. T. *Neoplatonism.* 1972. Repr. London: Duckworth, 1985.

Ward, Keith. *God, Chance and Necessity.* 1996. Repr. Oxford: Oneworld Publications, 2001.

Warner, Richard, and Tadeusz Szubka. *The Mind-Body Problem.* Oxford: Blackwell, 1994.

Weiner, Jonathan. *The Beak of the Finch.* London: Cape, 1994.

Welch, I. David, George A. Tate and Fred Richards, eds. *Humanistic Psychology.* Buffalo, N.Y.: Prometheus Books, 1978.

Wenham, John. *Easter Enigma—Do the Resurrection Stories Contradict One Another?* Exeter: Paternoster Press, 1984. Repr. as *Easter Enigma: Are the Resurrection Accounts in Conflict?*, Eugene, Oreg.: Wipf & Stock, 2005.

Wesson, Paul. *Beyond Natural Selection.* 1991. Repr. Cambridge, Mass.: Massachusetts Institute of Technology Press, 1997.

Westminster Shorter Catechism. 1647. [Widely available in print and online.]

Wetter, Gustav A. *Dialectical Materialism.* Westport, Conn.: Greenwood Press, 1977.

Whitehead, Alfred North. *Process and Reality.* Gifford Lectures 1927–28. London: Macmillan, 1929. Repr. New York: The Free Press, 1978.

Wilson, Edward O. *Consilience.* London: Little, Brown, 1998.

Wilson, Edward O. *Genes, Mind and Culture.* Cambridge, Mass.: Harvard University Press, 1981.

Wilson, Edward O. *On Human Nature.* Cambridge, Mass.: Harvard University Press, 1978.

Wilson, Edward O. *Sociobiology: The New Synthesis.* Cambridge, Mass.: Harvard University Press, 1975.

Wimsatt, William K. and Monroe Beardsley. *The Verbal Icon: Studies in the Meaning of Poetry.* 1954. Repr. Lexington, Ky.: University of Kentucky Press, 1982.

Wippel, John F., ed. *Studies in Medieval Philosophy.* Vol. 17 of *Studies in Philosophy and the History of Philosophy.* Washington D.C.: Catholic University of America Press, 1987.

Wittgenstein, L. *On Certainty.* Ed. G. E. M. Anscombe and G. H. von Wright; tr. Denis Paul and G. E. M. Anscombe. Oxford, 1969. Repr. New York: Harper & Row, 1972.

Wolpert, Lewis. *The Unnatural Nature of Science.* London: Faber & Faber, 1992.

Wolstenholme, Gordon, ed. *Man and His Future.* A Ciba Foundation Volume. London: J. & A. Churchill, 1963.

Wolters, Clifton, tr. *The Cloud of Unknowing.* 1961. Repr. London: Penguin, 1978.

Wolterstorff, Nicholas. *Divine Discourse: Philosophical Reflections on the Claim that God Speaks.* 1995. Repr. Cambridge: Cambridge University Press, 2000.

X

Xenophon. *Memorabilia*. Tr. E. C. Marchant. *Memorabilia. Oeconomicus. Symposium. Apology*. Vol. 4. Loeb Classical Library, Vol. 168. 1923. Repr. Cambridge, Mass.: Harvard University Press, 1997.

Y

Yancey, Philip. *Soul Survivor: How my Faith Survived the Church*. London: Hodder & Stoughton, 2001.

Yockey, Hubert. *Information Theory and Biology*. Cambridge: Cambridge University Press, 1992.

Z

Zacharias, Ravi. *Jesus Among Other Gods: The Absolute Claims of the Christian Message*. Nashville, Tenn.: Thomas Nelson, 2000.

Zacharias, Ravi. *The Real Face of Atheism*. Grand Rapids: Baker, 2004.

Zaehner, Z. C., ed. *The Concise Encyclopedia of Living Faiths*. 1959. 2nd edn, 1971. Repr. London: Hutchinson, 1982.

ARTICLES, PAPERS, CHAPTERS AND LECTURES

A

Adams, R. M. 'Religious Ethics in a Pluralistic Society.' In G. Outka and J. P. Reeder, Jr., eds. *Prospects for a Common Morality*. Princeton, N.J.: Princeton University Press, 1993.

Alberts, Bruce. 'The Cell as a Collection of Protein Machines: Preparing the Next Generation of Molecular Biologists.' *Cell* 92/3 (6 Feb. 1998), 291–4. doi: 10.1016/S0092-8674(00)80922-8.

Almond, Brenda. 'Liberty or Community? Defining the Post-Marxist Agenda.' In Brenda Almond, ed. *Introducing Applied Ethics*. Oxford: Wiley Blackwell, 1995.

Alpher, R. A., H. Bethe and G. Gamow. 'The Origin of Chemical Elements.' *Physical Review* 73/7 (Apr. 1948), 803–4. doi: 10.1103/PhysRev.73.803.

Anscombe, G. E. M. 'Modern Moral Philosophy.' *Philosophy* 33 (1958), 1–19.

Asimov, Isaac (interview by Paul Kurtz). 'An Interview with Isaac Asimov on Science and the Bible.' *Free Enquiry* 2/2 (Spring 1982), 6–10.

Auer, J. A. C. F. 'Religion as the Integration of Human Life.' *The Humanist* (Spring 1947).

Austin, J. L., P. F. Strawson and D. R. Cousin. 'Truth.' *Proceedings of the Aristotelian Society, Supplementary Volumes, Vol. 24, Physical Research, Ethics and Logic* (1950), 111–72. Online at http://www.jstor.org/stable/4106745. Repr. in Paul Horwich, ed. *Theories of Truth*. Aldershot: Dartmouth Publishing, 1994.

B

Bada, Jeffrey L. 'Stanley Miller's 70th Birthday.' *Origins of Life and Evolution of Biospheres* 30/2 (2000), 107–12. doi: 10.1023/A:1006746205180.

Baier, Kurt E. M. 'Egoism.' In P. Singer, ed. *A Companion to Ethics*. Oxford: Blackwell, 1991. Repr. 2000, 197–204.

Baier, Kurt E. M. 'Freedom, Obligation, and Responsibility.' In Morris B. Storer, ed. *Humanist Ethics: Dialogue on Basics*. Buffalo, N.Y.: Prometheus Books, 1980, 75–92.

Baier, Kurt E. M. 'The Meaning of Life.' 1947. In Peter Angeles, ed. *Critiques of God*, Buffalo, N.Y.: Prometheus Books, 1976. Repr. in E. D. Klemke, ed. *The Meaning of Life*. New York: Oxford University Press, 1981, 81–117.

Baker, S. W. 'Albert Nyanza, Account of the Discovery of the Second Great Lake of the Nile.' *Journal of the Royal Geographical Society* 36 (1866). Also in *Proceedings of the Royal Geographical Society of London* 10 (13 Nov. 1856), 6–27.

Bates, Elizabeth, Donna Thal and Virginia Marchman. 'Symbols and Syntax: A Darwinian Approach to Language Development.' In Norman A. Krasnegor, Duane M. Rumbaugh, Richard L. Schiefelbusch and Michael Studdert-Kennedy, eds. *Biological and Behavioural Determinants of Language Development*. 1991. Repr. New York: Psychology Press, 2014, 29–65.

Behe, Michael J. 'Reply to My Critics: A Response to Reviews of *Darwin's Black Box: The Biochemical Challenge to Evolution*.' *Biology and Philosophy* 16 (2001), 685–709.

Berenbaum, Michael. 'T4 Program' In *Encyclopaedia Britannica*. Online at https://www.britannica.com/event/T4-Program, accessed 2 Nov. 2017.

Berlinski, David. 'The Deniable Darwin.' *Commentary* (June 1996), 19–29.

Bernal, J. D. 'The Unity of Ethics.' In C. H. Waddington, ed. *Science and Ethics: An Essay*. London: Allen & Unwin, 1942.

Black, Deborah L. 'Al-Kindi.' In Seyyed Hossein Nasr and Oliver Leaman, eds. *History of Islamic Philosophy*. Part 1, Vol. 1 of *Routledge History of World Philosophies*. 1996. Repr. London: Routledge, 2001, 178–97.

Boghossian, Paul A. 'What the Sokal hoax ought to teach us: The pernicious consequences and internal contradictions of "postmodernist" relativism.' *Times Literary Supplement*, Commentary (13 Dec. 1996), 14–15. Reprinted in Noretta Koertge, ed. *A House Built on Sand: Exposing Postmodernist Myths about Science*. Oxford: Oxford University Press, 1998, 23–31.

Briggs, Arthur E. 'The Third Annual Humanist Convention.' *The Humanist* (Spring 1945).

Bristol, Evelyn. 'Turn of a Century: Modernism, 1895–1925.' Ch. 8 in C. A. Moser, ed. *The Cambridge History of Russian Literature*. 1989. Rev. edn, 1992. Repr. 1996, Cambridge: Cambridge University Press, 387–457.

C

Caputo, John D. 'The End of Ethics.' In Hugh LaFollette, ed. *The Blackwell Guide to Ethical Theory*. Oxford: Blackwell, 1999, 111–28.

Cartmill, Matt. 'Oppressed by Evolution.' *Discover* Magazine 19/3 (Mar. 1998), 78–83. Reprinted in L. Polnac, ed. *Purpose, Pattern, and Process*. 6th edn, Dubuque: Kendall-Hunt, 2002, 389–97.

Cavalier-Smith, T. 'The Blind Biochemist.' *Trends in Ecology and Evolution* 12 (1997), 162–3.

Chaitin, Gregory J. 'Randomness in Arithmetic and the Decline and Fall of Reductionism in Pure Mathematics.' Ch. 3 in John Cornwell, ed. *Nature's Imagination: The Frontiers of Scientific Vision*. Oxford: Oxford University Press, 1995, 27–44.

Chomsky, Noam. 'Review of B. F. Skinner.' *Verbal Behavior*. *Language* 35/1 (1959), 26–58.

Chomsky, Noam. 'Science, Mind, and Limits of Understanding.' Transcript of talk given at the Science and Faith Foundation (STOQ), The Vatican (Jan. 2014). No pages. Online at https://chomsky.info/201401__/, accessed 3 Aug. 2017.

Coghlan, Andy. 'Selling the family secrets.' *New Scientist* 160/2163 (5 Dec. 1998), 20–1.

Collins, Harry. 'Introduction: Stages in the Empirical Programme of Relativism.' *Social Studies of Science* 11/1 (Feb. 1981), 3–10. Online at http://www.jstor.org/stable/284733, accessed 11 Sept. 2015.

Collins, R. 'A Physician's View of College Sex.' *Journal of the American Medical Association* 232 (1975), 392.

Cook, Sidney. 'Solzhenitsyn and Secular Humanism: A Response.' *The Humanist* (Nov./Dec. 1978), 6.

Cookson, Clive. 'Scientist Who Glimpsed God.' *Financial Times* (29 Apr. 1995), 20.

Cottingham, John. 'Descartes, René.' In Ted Honderich, ed. *The Oxford Companion to Philosophy*. Oxford, 1995. 2nd edn, Oxford: Oxford University Press, 2005.

Crick, Francis. 'Lessons from Biology.' *Natural History* 97 (Nov. 1988), 32–9.

Crosman, Robert. 'Do Readers Make Meaning?' In Susan R. Suleiman and Inge Crosman, eds. *The Reader in the Text: Essays on Audience and Interpretation*. Princeton, N.J.: Princeton University Press, 1980.

D

Davies, Paul. 'Bit before It?' *New Scientist* 2171 (30 Jan. 1999), 3.

Dawkins, Richard. 'Put Your Money on Evolution.' Review of Maitland A. Edey and Donald C. Johanson. *Blueprint: Solving the Mystery of Evolution*. Penguin, 1989. *The New York Times Review of Books* (9 Apr. 1989), sec. 7, 34–5.

Dembski, William. 'Intelligent Design as a Theory of Information.' *Perspectives on Science and Christian Faith* 49/3 (Sept. 1997), 180–90.

Derrida, Jacques. 'Force of Law: The "Mystical Foundation of Authority".' In Drucilla Cornell, Michel Rosenfeld and David Gray Carlson, eds. *Deconstruction and the Possibility of Justice*. 1992. Repr. Abingdon: Routledge, 2008.

Dirac, P. A. M. 'The Evolution of the Physicist's Picture of Nature.' *Scientific American* 208/5 (1963), 45–53. doi: 10.1038/scientificamerican0563-45.

Dobzhansky, Theodosius. 'Chance and Creativity in Evolution.' Ch. 18 in Francisco J. Ayala and Theodosius Dobzhansky, eds. *Studies in the Philosophy of Biology: Reduction and Related Problems*. Berkeley, Calif.: University of California Press, 1974, 307–36.

Dobzhansky, Theodosius. Discussion of paper by Gerhard Schramm, 'Synthesis of Nucleosides and Polynucleotide with Metaphosphate Esters.' In Sidney W. Fox, ed. *The Origins of Prebiological Systems and of Their Molecular Matrices*, 299–315. Proceedings of a Conference Conducted at Wakulla Springs, Florida, on 20–30 October 1963 under the auspices of the Institute for Space Biosciences, the Florida State University and the National Aeronautics and Space Administration. New York: Academic Press, 1965.

Dobzhansky, Theodosius. 'Evolutionary Roots of Family Ethics and Group Ethics.' In *The Centrality of Science and Absolute Values*, Vol. I of *Proceedings of the Fourth International Conference on the Unity of the Sciences*. New York: International Cultural Foundation, 1975.

Documents of the 22nd Congress of the Communist Party of the Soviet Union. 2 vols. Documents of Current History, nos. 18–19. New York: Crosscurrents Press, 1961.

Dose, Klaus. 'The Origin of Life: More Questions Than Answers.' *Interdisciplinary Science Reviews* 13 (Dec. 1988), 348–56.

Druart, Th.-A. 'Al-Fārābī and Emanationism.' In J. F. Wippel, ed. *Studies in Medieval Philosophy*. Vol. 17 of Studies in Philosophy and the History of Philosophy. Washington D.C.: Catholic University of America Press, 1987, 23–43.

Dyson, Freeman. 'Energy in the Universe.' *Scientific American* 225/3 (1971), 50–9.

E

Eddington, Arthur. 'The End of the World: From the Standpoint of Mathematical Physics.' *Nature* 127 (21 Mar. 1931), 447–53. doi: 10.1038/127447a0.

Edwards, William. 'On the Physical Death of Jesus Christ.' *Journal of the American Medical Association* 255/11 (21 Mar. 1986), 1455–63.

Eigen, Manfred, Christof K. Biebricher, Michael Gebinoga and William C. Gardiner. 'The Hypercycle: Coupling of RNA and Protein Biosynthesis in the Infection Cycle of an RNA Bacteriophage.' *Biochemistry* 30/46 (1991), 11005–18. doi: 10.1021/bi00110a001.

Einstein, Albert. 'Physics and Reality.' 1936. In Sonja Bargmann, tr. *Ideas and Opinions*. New York: Bonanza, 1954.

Einstein, Albert. 'Science and Religion.' 1941. Published in *Science, Philosophy and Religion, A Symposium*. New York: The Conference on Science, Philosophy and Religion in Their Relation to the Democratic Way of Life, 1941. Repr. in *Out of My Later Years*, 1950, 1956. Repr. New York: Open Road Media, 2011.

Eysenck, H. J. 'A Reason with Compassion.' In Paul Kurtz, ed. *The Humanist Alternative*. Buffalo, N.Y.: Prometheus Books, 1973.

F

Feynman, Richard P. 'Cargo Cult Science.' Repr. in *Engineering and Science* 37/7 (1974), 10–13. Online at http://calteches.library.caltech.edu/51/2/CargoCult.pdf (facsimile), accessed 11 Sept. 2015. (Originally delivered as Caltech's 1974 commencement address in Pasadena, Calif.)

Fletcher, J. 'Comment by Joseph Fletcher on Nielsen Article.' In Morris B. Storer, ed. *Humanist Ethics: Dialogue on Basics*. Buffalo, N.Y.: Prometheus Books, 1980, 70.

Flew, Anthony. 'Miracles.' In Paul Edwards, ed. *The Encyclopedia of Philosophy*. New York: Macmillan, 1967, 5:346–53.

Flew, Anthony. 'Neo-Humean Arguments about the Miraculous.' In R. D. Geivett and G. R. Habermas, eds. *In Defence of Miracles*. Leicester: Apollos, 1997, 45–57.

Flieger, Jerry Aline. 'The Art of Being Taken by Surprise.' *Destructive Criticism: Directions. SCE Reports* 8 (Fall 1980), 54–67.

Fodor, J. A. 'Fixation of Belief and Concept Acquisition.' In M. Piattelli-Palmarini, ed., *Language and Learning: The Debate Between Jean Piaget and Noam Chomsky*. Cambridge, Mass.: Harvard University Press, 1980, 143–9.

Fotion, Nicholas G. 'Logical Positivism.' In Ted Honderich, ed. *The Oxford Companion to Philosophy*. 2nd edn, Oxford: Oxford University Press, 2005.

Frank, Lawrence K. 'Potentialities of Human Nature.' *The Humanist* (Apr. 1951).

Frankena, William K. 'Is morality logically dependent on religion?' In G. Outka and J. P. Reeder, Jr., eds. *Religion and Morality*. Garden City, N.Y.: Anchor, 1973.

G

Genequand, Charles. 'Metaphysics.' Ch. 47 in Seyyed Nossein Nasr and Oliver Leaman, eds. *History of Islamic Philosophy*. Vol. 1 of *Routledge History of World Philosophies*. London: Routledge, 1996, 783–801.

Genné, William H. 'Our Moral Responsibility.' *Journal of the American College Health Association* 15/Suppl (May 1967), 55–60.

Gilbert, Scott F., John Opitz and Rudolf A Raff. 'Resynthesizing Evolutionary and Developmental Biology.' *Developmental Biology* 173/2 (1996), 357–72.

Ginsburg, V. L. *Poisk* 29–30 (1998).

Gould, Stephen Jay. 'Evolution as Fact and Theory.' In Ashley Montagu, ed. *Science and Creationism*. Oxford: Oxford University Press, 1984.

Gould, Stephen Jay. 'Evolution's Erratic Pace.' *Natural History* 86/5 (May 1977), 12–16.

Gould, Stephen Jay. 'Evolutionary Considerations.' Paper presented at the McDonnell Foundation Conference, 'Selection vs. Instruction'. Venice, May 1989.

Gould, Stephen Jay. 'In Praise of Charles Darwin.' Paper presented at the Nobel Conference XVIII, Gustavus Adolphus College, St. Peter, Minn. Repr. in Charles L. Hamrum, ed. *Darwin's Legacy*. San Francisco: Harper & Row, 1983.

Gould, Stephen Jay. 'The Paradox of the Visibly Irrelevant.' *Annals of the New York Academy of Sciences* 879 (June 1999), 87–97. doi: 10.1111/j.1749-6632.1999 .tb10407.x. Repr. in *The Lying Stones of Marrakech: Penultimate Reflections in Natural History*. 2000. Repr. Cambridge, Mass.: Harvard University Press, 2011.

Gribbin, John. 'Oscillating Universe Bounces Back.' *Nature* 259 (1 Jan. 1976), 15–16. doi: 10.1038/259015c0.

Grigg, Russell. 'Could Monkeys Type the 23rd Psalm?' *Interchange* 50 (1993), 25–31.

Guth, A. H. 'Inflationary Universe: A Possible Solution to the Horizon and Flatness Problems.' *Physical Review D* 23/2 (1981), 347–56.

Guttmacher Institute. 'Induced Abortion in the United States', Fact Sheet. New York: Guttmacher Institute, Jan. 2018. Online at https://www.guttmacher.org/ fact-sheet/induced-abortion-united-states, accessed 1 Feb. 2018.

H

Haldane, J. B. S. 'When I am Dead.' In *Possible Worlds*. [1927] London: Chatto & Windus, 1945, 204–11.

Hansen, Michèle; Jennifer J. Kurinczuk, Carol Bower and Sandra Webb. 'The Risk of Major Birth Defects after Intracytoplasmic Sperm Injection and in Vitro Fertilization.' *New England Journal of Medicine* 346 (2002), 725–30. doi: 10.1056/NEJMoa010035.

Hardwig, John. 'Dying at the Right Time: Reflections on (Un)Assisted Suicide.' In Hugh LaFollette, ed. *Ethics In Practice*. Blackwell Philosophy Anthologies. 2nd edn, Oxford: Blackwell, 1997, 101–11.

Hawking, S. W. 'The Edge of Spacetime: Does the universe have an edge and time a beginning, as Einstein's general relativity predicts, or is spacetime finite without boundary, as quantum mechanics suggests?' *American Scientist* 72/4 (1984), 355–9. Online at http://www.jstor.org/stable/27852759, accessed 15 Sept. 2015.

Hawking, S. W. Letters to the Editors. Reply to letter by J. J. Tanner relating to article 'The Edge of Spacetime'. *American Scientist* 73/1 (1985), 12. Online at http://www.jstor.org/stable/27853056, accessed 15 Sept. 2015.

Hawking, S. W. and R. Penrose. 'The Singularities of Gravitational Collapse and Cosmology.' *Proceedings of the Royal Society London A* 314/1519 (1970), 529–48. doi: 10.1098/rspa.1970.0021.

Hocutt, Max. 'Does Humanism Have an Ethic of Responsibility?' In Morris B. Storer, ed. *Humanist Ethic: Dialogue on Basics.* Buffalo, N.Y.: Prometheus Books, 1980, 11–24.

Hocutt, Max. 'Toward an Ethic of Mutual Accommodation.' In Morris B. Storer, ed. *Humanist Ethics: Dialogue on Basics.* Buffalo, N.Y.: Prometheus Books, 1980, 137–46.

Hookway, C. J. 'Scepticism.' In Ted Honderich, ed. *The Oxford Companion to Philosophy.* Oxford, 1995. 2nd edn, Oxford: Oxford University Press, 2005.

Hoyle, Fred. 'The Universe: Past and Present Reflections.' *Annual Reviews of Astronomy and Astrophysics* 20 (1982), 1–35. doi: 10.1146/annurev.aa.20.090182 .000245.

Hursthouse, Rosalind. 'Virtue theory and abortion.' *Philosophy and Public Affairs* 20, 1991, 223–46.

Huxley, Julian. 'The Emergence of Darwinism.' In Sol Tax, ed. *The Evolution of Life: Its Origins, History, and Future.* Vol. 1 of *Evolution after Darwin.* Chicago: University of Chicago Press, 1960, 1–21.

Huxley, Julian. 'The Evolutionary Vision: The Convocation Address.' In Sol Tax and Charles Callender, eds. *Issues in Evolution.* Vol. 3 of *Evolution after Darwin.* Chicago: University of Chicago Press, 1960, 249–61.

I

Inwood, M. J. 'Feuerbach, Ludwig Andreas.' In Ted Honderich, ed. *The Oxford Companion to Philosophy.* Oxford, 1995. 2nd edn, Oxford: Oxford University Press, 2005.

J

Jeeves, Malcolm. 'Brain, Mind, and Behaviour.' In Warren S. Brown, Nancey Murphy and H. Newton Malony, eds. *Whatever Happened to the Soul: Scientific and Theological Portraits of Human Nature.* Minneapolis: Fortress Press, 1998.

Johnson, Barbara. 'Nothing Fails Like Success.' *Deconstructive Criticism: Directions. SCE Reports* 8 (Fall 1980), 7–16.

Josephson, Brian. Letters to the Editor. *The Independent* (12 Jan. 1997), London.

K

Kant, Immanuel. 'Beantwortung der Frage: Was ist Aufklärung?' *Berlinische Monatsschrift* 4 (Dec. 1784), 481–94. Repr. in *Kant's Gesammelte Schriften.* Berlin: Akademie Ausgabe, 1923, 8:33–42.

Khrushchev, Nikita. *Ukrainian Bulletin* (1–15 Aug. 1960), 12.

Klein-Franke, Felix. 'Al-Kindi.' In Seyyed Hossein Nasr and Oliver Leaman, eds. *History of Islamic Philosophy.* Vol. 1, Part 1 of *Routledge History of World Philosophies.* 1996. Repr. London: Routledge, 2001, 165–77.

Kurtz, Paul. 'A Declaration of Interdependence: A New Global Ethics.' *Free Inquiry* 8/4 (Fall 1988), 4–7. Also published in Vern L. Ballough and Timothy J. Madigan, ed. *Toward a New Enlightenment: The Philosophy of Paul Kurtz*. New Brunswick, N.J.: Transaction Publishers, 1994 (ch. 3, 'The Twenty-First Century and Beyond: The Need for a New Global Ethic and a Declaration of Interdependence').

Kurtz, Paul. 'Does Humanism Have an Ethic of Responsibility?' In Morris B. Storer, ed. *Humanist Ethics: Dialogue on Basics*. Buffalo, N.Y.: Prometheus Books, 1980, 11–24.

Kurtz, Paul. 'Is Everyone a Humanist?' In Paul Kurtz, ed. *The Humanist Alternative*. Buffalo, N.Y.: Prometheus Books, 1973.

L

Lamont, Corliss. 'The Ethics of Humanism.' In Frederick C. Dommeyer, ed. *In Quest of Value: Readings in Philosophy and Personal Values*. San Francisco: Chandler, 1963, 46–59. Repr. from ch. 6 of Corliss Lamont. *Humanism as a Philosophy*. Philosophical Library, 273–97.

Larson, Erik. 'Looking for the Mind.' (Review of David J. Chalmers. *The Conscious Mind: In Search of a Fundamental Theory*.) *Origins & Design* 18/1(34) (Winter 1997), Colorado Springs: Access Research Network, 28–9.

Leitch, Vincent B. 'The Book of Deconstructive Criticism.' *Studies in the Literary Imagination* 12/1 (Spring 1979), 19–39.

Lewis, C. S. 'The Funeral of a Great Myth.' In Walter Hooper, ed. *Christian Reflections*. Grand Rapids: Eerdmans, 1967, 102–116.

Lewis, C. S. 'The Weight of Glory.' In *Transposition and other Addresses*. London: Geoffrey Bles, 1949. Repr. in *The Weight of Glory and Other Addresses*. HarperOne, 2001.

Lewontin, Richard C. 'Billions and Billions of Demons.' *The New York Review of Books* 44/1 (9 Jan. 1997).

Lewontin, Richard C. 'Evolution/Creation Debate: A Time for Truth.' *BioScience* 31/8 (Sept. 1981), 559. Reprinted in J. Peter Zetterberg, ed. *Evolution versus Creationism*. Phoenix, Ariz.: Oryx Press, 1983. doi: 10.1093/bioscience/31.8.559, accessed 15 Sept. 2015.

Lieberman, Philip and E. S. Crelin. 'On the Speech of Neanderthal Man.' *Linguistic Inquiry* 2/2 (Mar. 1971), 203–22.

Louden, Robert. 'On Some Vices of Virtue Ethics.' Ch. 10 in R. Crisp and M. Slote, eds. *Virtue Ethics*. Oxford: Oxford University Press, 1997.

M

Mackie, J. L. 'Evil and Omnipotence.' *Mind* 64/254 (Apr. 1955), 200–12.

McNaughton, David and Piers Rawling. 'Intuitionism.' Ch. 13 in Hugh LaFollette, ed. *The Blackwell Guide to Ethical Theory*. Oxford: Blackwell, 2000, 268–87. Ch. 14 in 2nd edn, Wiley Blackwell, 2013, 287–310.

Maddox, John. 'Down with the Big Bang.' *Nature* 340 (1989), 425. doi: 10.1038/340425a0.

Marx, Karl. 'The Difference between the Natural Philosophy of Democritus and the Natural Philosophy of Epicurus.' In *K. Marx and F. Engels on Religion*. Moscow: Foreign Languages Publishing House, 1955.

Marx, Karl. 'Economic and Philosophical Manuscripts.' In T. B. Bottomore, tr. and ed. *Karl Marx: Early Writings*. London: Watts, 1963.

Marx, Karl. 'Theses on Feuerback.' In Frederick Engels, *Ludwig Feuerback*. New York: International Publishers, 1941.

May, Rollo. 'The Problem of Evil: An Open Letter to Carl Rogers.' *Journal of Humanistic Psychology* (Summer 1982).

Merezhkovsky, Dmitry. 'On the Reasons for the Decline and on the New Currents in Contemporary Russian Literature.' 1892 lecture. In Dmitry Merezhkovsky. *On the reasons for the decline and on the new currents in contemporary Russian literature*. Petersburg, 1893.

Meyer, Stephen C. 'The Explanatory Power of Design: DNA and the Origin of Information.' In William A. Dembski, ed. *Mere Creation: Science, Faith and Intelligent Design*. Downers Grove, Ill.: InterVarsity Press, 1998, 114–47.

Meyer, Stephen C. 'The Methodological Equivalence of Design and Descent.' In J. P. Moreland, ed. *The Creation Hypothesis*. Downers Grove, Ill.: InterVarsity Press, 1994, 67–112.

Meyer, Stephen C. 'Qualified Agreement: Modern Science and the Return of the "God Hypothesis".' In Richard F. Carlson, ed. *Science and Christianity: Four Views*. Downers Grove, Ill.: InterVarsity Press, 2000, 129–75.

Meyer, Stephen C. 'The Return of the God Hypothesis.' *Journal of Interdisciplinary Studies* 11/1&2 (Jan. 1999), 1–38. Online at http://www.discovery.org/a/642, accessed 3 Aug. 2017. Citations are to the archived version, which is repaginated, and online at http://www.discovery.org/scripts/viewDB/filesDB-download. php?command=download&id=12006, accessed 3 Aug. 2017.

Miller, J. Hillis. 'Deconstructing the Deconstructors.' Review of Joseph N. Riddel. *The Inverted Bell: Modernism and the Counterpoetics of William Carlos Williams*. *Diacritics* 5/2 (Summer 1975), 24–31. Online at http://www.jstor.org/ stable/464639, accessed 3 Aug. 2017. doi: 10.2307/464639.

Monod, Jacques. 'On the Logical Relationship between Knowledge and Values.' In Watson Fuller, ed. *The Biological Revolution*. Garden City, N.Y.: Doubleday, 1972.

N

Nagel, Ernest. 'Naturalism Reconsidered.' 1954. In Houston Peterson, ed. *Essays in Philosophy*. New York: Pocket Books, 1959. Repr. New York: Pocket Books, 1974.

Nagel, Thomas. 'Rawls, John.' In Ted Honderich, ed. *The Oxford Companion to Philosophy*. 1995. 2nd edn, Oxford: Oxford University Press, 2005.

Nagler, Michael N. 'Reading the Upanishads.' In Eknath Easwaran. *The Upanishads*. 1987. Repr. Berkeley, Calif.: Nilgiri Press, 2007.

Neill, Stephen. 'The Wrath of God and the Peace of God.' In Max Warren, *Interpreting the Cross*. London: SCM Press, 1966.

Newing, Edward G. 'Religions of pre-literary societies.' In Sir Norman Anderson, ed. *The World's Religions*. 4th edn, London: Inter-Varsity Press, 1975.

Nielsen, Kai. 'Religiosity and Powerlessness: Part III of "The Resurgence of Fundamentalism".' *The Humanist* 37/3 (May/June 1977), 46–8.

O

The Oxford Reference Encyclopaedia. Oxford: Oxford University Press, 1998.

P

Palmer, Alasdair. 'Must Knowledge Gained Mean Paradise Lost?' *Sunday Telegraph.* London (6 Apr. 1997).

Penzias, Arno. 'Creation is Supported by all the Data So Far.' In Henry Margenau and Roy Abraham Varghese, eds. *Cosmos, Bios, Theos: Scientists Reflect on Science, God, and the Origins of the Universe, Life, and Homo Sapiens.* La Salle, Ill.: Open Court, 1992.

Pinker, Steven, and Paul Bloom. 'Natural Language and Natural Selection.' *Behavioral and Brain Sciences* 13/4 (Dec. 1990), 707–27. doi: 10.1017/ S0140525X00081061.

Polanyi, Michael. 'Life's Irreducible Structure. Live mechanisms and information in DNA are boundary conditions with a sequence of boundaries above them.' *Science* 160/3834 (1968), 1308–12. Online at http://www.jstor.org/stable/1724152, accessed 3 Aug. 2017.

Poole, Michael. 'A Critique of Aspects of the Philosophy and Theology of Richard Dawkins.' *Christians and Science* 6/1 (1994), 41–59. Online at http://www.scienceandchristianbelief.org/serve_pdf_free.php?filename=SCB+6-1+Poole.pdf, accessed 3 Aug. 2017.

Popper, Karl. 'Scientific Reduction and the Essential Incompleteness of All Science.' In F. J. Ayala and T. Dobzhansky, ed. *Studies in the Philosophy of Biology, Reduction and Related Problems.* London: MacMillan, 1974.

Premack, David. '"Gavagai!" or The Future History of the Animal Controversy.' *Cognition* 19/3 (1985), 207–96. doi: 10.1016/0010-0277(85)90036-8.

Provine, William B. 'Evolution and the Foundation of Ethics.' *Marine Biological Laboratory Science* 3 (1988), 27–8.

Provine, William B. 'Scientists, Face it! Science and Religion are Incompatible.' *The Scientist* (5 Sept. 1988), 10–11.

R

Rachels, James. 'Naturalism.' In Hugh LaFollette, ed. *The Blackwell Guide to Ethical Theory.* Oxford: Blackwell, 2000, 74–91.

Randall, John H. 'The Nature of Naturalism.' In Yervant H. Krikorian, ed. *Naturalism*, 354–82.

Raup, David. 'Conflicts between Darwin and Palaeontology.' *Field Museum of Natural History Bulletin* 50/1 (Jan. 1979), 22–9.

Reidhaar-Olson, John F. and Robert T. Sauer. 'Functionally Acceptable Substitutions in Two α-helical Regions of λ Repressor.' *Proteins: Structure, Function, and Genetics* 7/4 (1990), 306–16. doi: 10.1002/prot.340070403.

Rescher, Nicholas. 'Idealism.' In Jonathan Dancy and Ernest Sosa, eds. *A Companion to Epistemology*. 1992. Repr. Oxford: Blackwell, 2000.

Ridley, Mark. 'Who Doubts Evolution?' *New Scientist* 90 (25 June 1981), 830–2.

Rogers, Carl. 'Notes on Rollo May.' *Journal of Humanistic Psychology* 22/3 (Summer 1982), 8–9. doi: 10.1177/0022167882223002.

Rorty, Richard. 'Untruth and Consequences.' *The New Republic* (31 July 1995), 32–6.

Ruse, Michael. 'Is Rape Wrong on Andromeda?' In E. Regis Jr., ed. *Extraterrestrials*. Cambridge: Cambridge University Press, 1985.

Ruse, Michael. 'Transcript: Speech by Professor Michael Ruse,' Symposium, 'The New Antievolutionism', 1993 Annual Meeting of the American Association for the Advancement of Science, 13 Feb. 1993. Online at http://www.arn.org/docs/orpages/or151/mr93tran.htm, accessed 3 Aug. 2017.

Ruse, Michael and Edward O. Wilson. 'The Evolution of Ethics.' *New Scientist* 108/1478 (17 Oct. 1985), 50–2.

Russell, Bertrand. 'A Free Man's Worship.' 1903. In *Why I Am Not a Christian*. New York: Simon & Schuster, 1957. Also in *Mysticism and Logic Including A Free Man's Worship*. London: Unwin, 1986.

Russell, Colin. 'The Conflict Metaphor and its Social Origins.' *Science and Christian Belief* 1/1 (1989), 3–26.

S

Sanders, Blanche. *The Humanist* 5 (1945).

Sanders, Peter. 'Eutychus.' *Triple Helix* (Summer 2002), 17.

Sayre-McCord, Geoffrey. 'Contractarianism.' In Hugh LaFollette, ed. *The Blackwell Guide to Ethical Theory*. Oxford: Blackwell, 2000, 247–67. 2nd edn, Wiley Blackwell, 2013, 332–53.

Scruton, Roger. *The Times* (Dec. 1997), London.

Searle, John. 'Minds, Brains and Programs.' In John Haugeland, ed. *Mind Design*. Cambridge, Mass.: Cambridge University Press, 1981.

Sedgh, Gilda, et al., 'Abortion incidence between 1990 and 2014: global, regional, and subregional levels and trends.' *The Lancet* 388/10041 (16 July 2016), 258–67. doi: 10.1016/S0140-6736(16)30380-4.

Shapiro, James A. 'In the Details . . . What?' *National Review* (16 Sept. 1996), 62–5.

Simpson, George Gaylord. 'The Biological Nature of Man.' *Science* 152/3721 (22 Apr. 1966), 472–8.

Singer, Peter. 'Hegel, Georg Wilhelm Friedrich.' In Ted Honderich, ed. *The Oxford Companion to Philosophy*. Oxford, 1995. 2nd edn, Oxford: Oxford University Press, 2005.

Skorupski, John. 'Mill, John Stuart.' In Ted Honderich, ed. *The Oxford Companion to Philosophy*. Oxford, 1995. 2nd edn, Oxford: Oxford University Press, 2005.

Slote, Michael. 'Utilitarianism.' In Ted Honderich, ed. *The Oxford Companion to Philosophy*. Oxford, 1995. 2nd edn, Oxford: Oxford University Press, 2005.

Slote, Michael. 'Virtue Ethics.' In Hugh LaFollette, ed. *The Blackwell Guide to Ethical Theory*. Oxford: Blackwell, 2000, 325–47.

Sokal, Alan D. 'Transgressing the boundaries: towards a transformative hermeneutic of Quantum Gravity.' *Social Text* (Spring/Summer 1996), 217–52.

Sokal, Alan D. 'What the Social Text Affair Does and Does Not Prove.' In Noretta Koertge, ed. *A House Built on Sand: Exposing Postmodernist Myths About Science*. Oxford: Oxford University Press, 1998, 9–22.

Solzhenitsyn, Alexander. 'Alexandr Solzhenitsyn—Nobel Lecture.' *Nobelprize.org*. Nobel Media AB 2014. Online at https://www.nobelprize.org/nobel_prizes/literature/laureates/1970/solzhenitsyn-lecture.html, accessed 15 Aug. 2017.

Spetner, L. M. 'Natural selection: An information-transmission mechanism for evolution.' *Journal of Theoretical Biology* 7/3 (Nov. 1964), 412–29.

Stalin, Joseph. Speech delivered 24 April 1924. New York, International Publishers, 1934.

Stolzenberg, Gabriel. 'Reading and relativism: an introduction to the science wars.' In Keith M. Ashman and Philip S. Baringer, eds. *After the Science Wars*. London: Routledge, 2001, 33–63.

T

Tarkunde, V. M. 'Comment by V. M. Tarkunde on Hocutt Article.' In Morris B. Storer, ed. *Humanist Ethics: Dialogue on Basics*. Buffalo, N.Y.: Prometheus Books, 1980, 147–8.

Taylor, Robert. 'Evolution is Dead.' *New Scientist* 160/2154 (3 Oct. 1998), 25–9.

W

Walicki, Andrzej. 'Hegelianism, Russian.' In Edward Craig, gen. ed. *Concise Routledge Encyclopedia of Philosophy*. London: Routledge, 2000.

Wallace, Daniel, "The Majority Text and the Original Text: Are They Identical?," *Bibliotheca Sacra*, April-June, 1991, 157-8.

Walton, J. C. 'Organization and the Origin of Life.' *Origins* 4 (1977), 16–35.

Warren, Mary Ann. 'On the Moral and Legal Status of Abortion.' Ch. 11 in Hugh LaFollette, ed. *Ethics in Practice: An Anthology*, 1997, 72–82. 4th edn, Oxford: Blackwell, 2014, 132–40.

Watters, Wendell W. 'Christianity and Mental Health.' *The Humanist* 37 (Nov./Dec. 1987).

Weatherford, Roy C. 'Freedom and Determinism.' In Ted Honderich, ed. *The Oxford Companion to Philosophy*. Oxford, 1995. 2nd edn, Oxford: Oxford University Press, 2005.

Wheeler, John A. 'Information, Physics, Quantum: The Search for Links.' In Wojciech Hubert Zurek. *Complexity, Entropy, and the Physics of Information*. The Proceedings of the 1988 Workshop on Complexity, Entropy, and the Physics of Information, held May–June, 1989, in Santa Fe, N. Mex. Redwood City, Calif.: Addison-Wesley, 1990.

Wigner, Eugene. 'The Unreasonable Effectiveness of Mathematics in the Natural Sciences', Richard Courant Lecture in Mathematical Sciences, delivered at New York University, 11 May 1959. *Communications in Pure and Applied Mathematics*, 13/1 (Feb. 1960), 1–14. Repr. in E. Wiger. *Symmetries and Reflections.* Bloomingon, Ind., 1967. Repr. Woodbridge, Conn.: Ox Bow Press, 1979, 222–37.

Wilford, John Noble. 'Sizing Up the Cosmos: An Astronomer's Quest.' *New York Times* (12 Mar. 1991), B9.

Wilkinson, David. 'Found in space?' Interview with Paul Davies. *Third Way* 22:6 (July 1999), 17–21.

Wilson, Edward O. 'The Ethical Implications of Human Sociobiology.' *Hastings Center Report* 10:6 (Dec. 1980), 27–9. doi: 10.2307/3560296.

Y

Yockey, Hubert. 'A Calculation of the Probability of Spontaneous Biogenesis by Information Theory.' *Journal of Theoretical Biology* 67 (1977), 377–98.

Yockey, Hubert. 'Self-Organisation Origin of Life Scenarios and Information Theory.' *Journal of Theoretical Biology* 91 (1981), 13–31.

STUDY QUESTIONS FOR TEACHERS AND STUDENTS

CHAPTER 1. INDIAN PANTHEISTIC MONISM

Historical introduction

1.1   When would you say Indian civilisation began?

1.2   What is meant by saying that Sanskrit is a member of the Indo-European family of languages? Can you name any other members of this family? Is your language among them?

1.3   What basic beliefs would an orthodox Hindu be expected to hold?

1.4   What is the difference in meaning between 'Brahman' and 'Brahmā'?

1.5   What is the meaning of the terms 'Atman', 'Samsara' and 'Moksha'?

1.6   What is the difference between what Hinduism teaches about the Creator and what Judaism, Christianity and Islam teach?

1.7   What are the Vedas and the Upanishads? Why are they referred to as Shrutī?

1.8   Why is Shankara's philosophical system known as 'Advaita Vedantism'?

Shankara's Advaita Vedanta philosophy

1.9   What, according to Shankara, is Ultimate Reality? What is it like? How are we related to it?

1.10 What are the different implications of these two claims:

   (*a*)   the universe and all that is in it are emanations out of God himself;

   (*b*)   the universe and all that is in it were created by God out of nothing.

1.11 The existence of evil is an insoluble problem for pantheism. Why is that?

1.12 Common sense tells us that the individuality of our friends is real and valuable. Why does Shankara say that their individuality is an illusion? And what does he mean by it?

1.13 What is meant by the famous Hindu phrases: 'Atman is Brahman' and 'THOU ART THAT'?

1.14 According to Shankara what undesirable penalty is imposed on those who continue to imagine they are distinct individuals?

1.15 'What a thing is and what its function is, is much more important than what it is made of.' Comment, and illustrate your answer with examples.

1.16 Is it likely, do you think, that the Creator is less complex than we are?

CHAPTER 2. GREEK PHILOSOPHY AND MYSTICISM

The chief significance of Greek philosophy and precautionary observations

2.1   What was new in the approach of the Ionian philosophers to the understanding of the universe?

2.2   What was Socrates' special interest? How did he propose to decide moral questions such as what is life for, and how should we behave?

2.3   The Ionian philosophers in their attempt to understand the universe set aside the old mythologies of the gods. Does that mean they were all atheists?

2.4   What do you understand to be the difference between the terms 'emanation' and 'creation'?

2.5   What is meant by saying that the Greek gods are stationed *inside* the world, not *outside* it as in Jewish, Christian and Islamic theology?

The search for what the world is made of and for how it works

2.6   What according to Thales, Anaximander, Anaximenes and Empedocles was the primal stuff of the universe?

2.7   What would you say was Anaximander's most brilliant conjecture?

2.8   What was Heraclitus trying to illustrate by using the analogy of a bow and bowstring?

2.9   Empedocles' use of the terms 'love' and 'hate' to describe physical forces at work in the universe may seem crude to us. Do they bear any resemblance to the way physical forces are described nowadays?

2.10   How many centuries passed by after Empedocles before Newton was able to describe the force of gravity mathematically?

2.11   What was remarkably new about Anaxagoras' theory?

2.12   Can you spot the fallacies in Parmenides' arguments?

2.13   Describe some of the differences between the atomic theory of Leucippus and Democritus and modern atomic theory.

2.14   What is the main point of Cornford's critique of Leucippus and Democritus' atomic theory? Is it fair?

The search for humanity's purpose and goal

2.15   What was the new emphasis that Socrates brought into ancient Greek philosophy?

2.16   Why was Socrates disappointed with Anaxagoras' theory? And why did he hold that theories like that of Anaxagoras' could never adequately explain why Socrates remained sitting in prison and did not attempt to escape?

2.17   Do you agree with Socrates that there is a purpose behind human existence? What would you say is humanity's chief function?

2.18   State in your own words the difference between a description of a thing and a definition of that thing.

2.19   Why is it important to be able to define what justice is?

2.20   Would you agree with Socrates that there are some things in life more important than life itself?

2.21   The sophists said that there was no Mind behind the universe. Plato argued that there must be Mind behind the universe. What would you say?

2.22   What do you think justice is? And how should we decide what it is? Is it:

  (*a*)   a standard that each one of us decides for himself or herself?

  (*b*)   a standard that is set by the majority of the people in a nation?

  (*c*)   a standard that should be set by some international body like the United Nations?

  (*d*)   a standard that exists independently of what individuals or nations think, but to which the whole world should submit?

2.23   Is there one Chief Good that we should all seek in life? If so, what is it? Aristotle said it was happiness. Epicureans said it was pleasure. Stoics said it was 'to live according to reason'. Christians say it is to serve God and to enjoy him forever. What do you say?

2.24   List and explain the meaning of Aristotle's Four Causes.

2.25   Consider a telescope:

  If the Material Cause is the material(s) it is made of;

  If the Efficient Cause is the manufacturer;

  If the Formal Cause is its design, shape and the arrangement of its lenses,

  What is its Final Cause?

2.26   Is it true that the Final Cause had to be in the mind of the maker before the telescope began to be made? Would that be true of the universe as well?

2.27   Explain the meaning of the terms 'potential' and 'actual' in Aristotle's philosophy.

2.28   Is a human embryo already a human being? And ought it to be treated as such?

2.29   Socrates, Plato and Aristotle all considered that there must be a Mind behind the universe. Were they right?

2.30   What criticisms have been made of Aristotle's concept of God? Are they fair?

Neoplatonic mysticism

2.31   What is meant by describing Plotinus' philosophy as 'negative theology'?

2.32   What, according to Plotinus, is the attitude of the One to human beings?

2.33   Why is reason, by itself, inadequate to discover what God is like?

2.34   In what respects is Plotinus' philosophy similar to Hinduism?

2.35   Plotinus gained no knowledge of what God is like by his mysticism. Discuss.

2.36   What are the moral implications of Plotinus' doctrine of reincarnation?

CHAPTER 3. NATURALISM AND ATHEISM

Materialistic naturalism: 'Ultimate Reality is inanimate mindless matter'

3.1   What does the term 'Nature' mean to you? How much would you include in it?

3.2   How would you define naturalism?

3.3   What is the difference between evidence that suggests that something may be true and proof that something is true?

3.4   Would you agree that materialistic naturalism is an article of faith? Or do you think that it can be proved that there is no supernatural realm? And if so, how?

3.5   If mindless matter is the Ultimate Reality, how, do you think, did human reason come to be? Do you think that your mind is composed of nothing but mindless matter?

3.6   In a class or group study setting, debate the propositions set out against materialistic naturalism on page 111.

3.7   What does Prof. Davies mean by 'information theory' and 'complexity theory'?

3.8   Where do you think the basic laws of physics come from originally? It has taken great intelligence to discover and understand them; and it takes highly sophisticated mathematics to express them. Do you agree with Prof. Davies that they must have come from some intelligent source? Or do you find it easier to suppose that they simply exist apart from reason?

Reactions to materialistic naturalism

3.9   Who were the Stoics? What attitude did they take to the atomic theory of Leucippus and Democritus, and why?

3.10   What are some of the meanings of the Greek word *logos*?

3.11   What was the Stoic concept of God?

3.12   What does the New Testament mean by calling Jesus the *Logos* (John 1:1–3)? How is this different from what the Stoics meant by *logos*?

3.13   The Stoic ideal was that human beings should live 'according to Nature'. What did they mean by that?

3.14   What moral difficulty is entailed in the Stoic idea that God is in everything?

3.15   'For Carl Sagan the Cosmos is a surrogate god': What does this mean? Do you agree?

3.16   What makes Prof. Davies describe life as a stupendously improbable accident?

3.17   What is it about God that Prof. Davies doesn't like? And why? What kind of a God does he believe in?

3.18   Mathematical laws can help us to understand how the world works. Why is it difficult to think that they could have created the world?

3.19   When it comes to whether we believe in God or not, to what extent are we influenced by our personal likes and dislikes?

CHAPTER 4. CHRISTIAN THEISM

God is the Ultimate Reality and he can be known

4.1   When the Bible says, 'In the beginning was the Word', what is meant by 'the Word'?

4.2   Did the Word ever have a beginning?

4.3 According to the Bible, by what means was the universe made, and by what means is it maintained?

4.4 What is meant by saying 'In him was life, and the life was the light of men' (John 1:4)?

4.5 In what various ways did God speak to the human race before the coming of Christ?

4.6 Read from the Old Testament Isaiah 53. Discover when it was written. How accurately, in your opinion, did it predict what happened to Jesus?

4.7 What evidence do the Old and New Testaments give that God is personal?

4.8 Do Christians believe in three Gods?

4.9 Jesus was certainly a man. Did he himself claim to be God as well?

4.10 What does the New Testament say is the significance of Christ's death on the cross?

4.11 According to the Bible, why do we need the Holy Spirit? What does he do for us?

How we are related to Ultimate Reality

4.12 What is different between the Bible's view of creation, and the other views that we have covered in this section?

4.13 What is the Bible's attitude to matter and to the human body?

4.14 What does the Bible mean by saying that man and woman were made in the image of God? How should that affect our attitude to people?

4.15 What are the implications of saying that human beings are emanations from God?

4.16 Sum up in your own words what Colossians 1:16–17 says about the relation of the Son of God to creation.

4.17 Which two commandments did Christ describe as the greatest of all?

4.18 What is meant by saying that we are not robots? Is it true?

4.19 Most people consider themselves to be rational human beings. How then would you account for the tragic mess that the world is in?

4.20 Do you think that everything in the universe is determined? Or would you agree that it has a large degree of freedom and openness? Do you feel that you are free to choose? If so, is that feeling true to the fact?

4.21 'Life is worth living.' Discuss.

APPENDIX: THE SCIENTIFIC ENDEAVOUR

Scientific method

A.1 In what different ways have you heard the word 'science' used? How would you define it?

A.2 How is induction understood as part of our everyday experience and also of the scientific endeavour?

A.3 In what ways does deduction differ from induction, and what role does each play in scientific experiments?

A.4   Do you find the idea of 'falsifiability' appealing, or unsatisfactory? Why?

A.5   How does abduction differ from both induction and deduction, and what is the relationship among the three?

Explaining explanations

A.6   How many levels of explanation can you think of to explain a cake, in terms of how was it made, what was it made from, and why was it made? What can scientists tell us? What can 'Aunt Olga' tell us?

A.7   In what ways is reductionism helpful in scientific research, and in what ways could it be limiting, or even detrimental, to scientific research?

A.8   How do you react to physicist and theologian John Polkinghorne's statement that reductionism relegates 'our experiences of beauty, moral obligation, and religious encounter to the epiphenomenal scrapheap. It also destroys rationality'?

The basic operational presuppositions of the scientific endeavour

A.9   What is meant by the statement 'Observation is dependent on theory'?

A.10   What are some of the axioms upon which your thinking about scientific knowledge rests?

A.11   What does trust have to do with gaining knowledge?

A.12   What does belief have to do with gaining knowledge?

A.13   According to physicist and philosopher of science Thomas Kuhn, how do new scientific paradigms emerge?

SCRIPTURE INDEX

GENERAL INDEX

ABOUT THE AUTHORS

David W. Gooding is Professor Emeritus of Old Testament Greek at Queen's University Belfast and a Member of the Royal Irish Academy. He has taught the Bible internationally and lectured on both its authenticity and its relevance to philosophy, world religions and daily life. He has published scholarly articles on the Septuagint and Old Testament narratives, as well as expositions of Luke, John, Acts, Hebrews, the New Testament's use of the Old Testament, and several books addressing arguments against the Bible and the Christian faith. His analysis of the Bible and our world continues to shape the thinking of scholars, teachers and students alike.

John C. Lennox is Professor Emeritus of Mathematics at the University of Oxford and Emeritus Fellow in Mathematics and the Philosophy of Science at Green Templeton College. He is also an Associate Fellow of the Saïd Business School. In addition, he is an Adjunct Lecturer at the Oxford Centre for Christian Apologetics, as well as being a Senior Fellow of the Trinity Forum. In addition to academic works, he has published on the relationship between science and Christianity, the books of Genesis and Daniel, and the doctrine of divine sovereignty and human free will. He has lectured internationally and participated in a number of televised debates with some of the world's leading atheist thinkers.

David W. Gooding (right)
and John C. Lennox (left)

Photo credit: Barbara Hamilton.

The Quest for Reality and Significance

Being Truly Human: *The Limits of our Worth, Power, Freedom and Destiny*
In Book 1, Gooding and Lennox address issues surrounding the value of humans. They consider the nature and basis of morality, compare what morality means in different systems, and assess the dangerous way freedom is often devalued. What should guide our use of power? What should limit our choices? And to what extent can our choices keep us from fulfilling our potential?

Finding Ultimate Reality: *In Search of the Best Answers to the Biggest Questions*
In Book 2, they remind us that the authority behind ethics cannot be separated from the truth about ultimate reality. Is there a Creator who stands behind his moral law? Are we the product of amoral forces, left to create moral consensus? Gooding and Lennox compare ultimate reality as understood in: Indian Pantheistic Monism, Greek Philosophy and Mysticism, Naturalism and Atheism, and Christian Theism.

Questioning Our Knowledge: *Can we Know What we Need to Know?*
In Book 3, Gooding and Lennox discuss how we could know whether any of these competing worldviews are true. What is truth anyway, and is it absolute? How would we recognize truth if we encountered it? Beneath these questions lies another that affects science, philosophy, ethics, literature and our everyday lives: how do we know anything at all?

The Quest for Reality and Significance

Doing What's Right: *Whose System of Ethics is Good Enough?*

In Book 4, Gooding and Lennox present particular ethical theories that claim to hold the basic principles everyone should follow. They compare the insights and potential weaknesses of each system by asking: what is its authority, its supreme goal, its specific rules, and its guidance for daily life? They then evaluate why even the best theories have proven to be impossible to follow consistently.

Claiming to Answer: *How One Person Became the Response to our Deepest Questions*

In Book 5, they argue it is not enough to have an ethical theory telling us what standards we ought to live by, because we often fail in our duties and do what we know is wrong. How can we overcome this universal weakness? Many religions claim to be able to help, but is the hope they offer true? Gooding and Lennox state why they think the claims of Jesus Christ are valid and the help he offers is real.

Suffering Life's Pain: *Facing the Problems of Moral and Natural Evil*

In Book 6, they acknowledge the problem with believing in a wise, loving and just God who does not stop natural disasters or human cruelty. Why does he permit congenital diseases, human trafficking and genocide? Is he unable to do anything? Or does he not care? Gooding and Lennox offer answers based on the Creator's purpose for the human race, and his entry into his own creation.

Myrtlefield Encounters

Key Bible Concepts
How can one book be so widely appreciated and so contested? Millions revere it and many ridicule it, but the Bible is often not allowed to speak for itself. Key Bible Concepts explores and clarifies the central terms of the Christian gospel. Gooding and Lennox provide succinct explanations of the basic vocabulary of Christian thought to unlock the Bible's meaning and its significance for today.

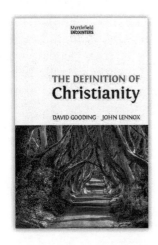

The Definition of Christianity
Who gets to determine what Christianity means? Is it possible to understand its original message after centuries of tradition and conflicting ideas? Gooding and Lennox throw fresh light on these questions by tracing the Book of Acts' historical account of the message that proved so effective in the time of Christ's apostles. Luke's record of its confrontations with competing philosophical and religious systems reveals Christianity's own original and lasting definition.

Myrtlefield Encounters

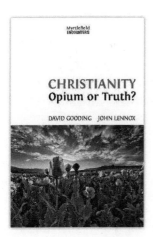

Christianity: Opium or Truth

Is Christianity just a belief that dulls the pain of our existence with dreams that are beautiful but false? Or is it an accurate account of reality, our own condition and God's attitude toward us? Gooding and Lennox address crucial issues that can make it difficult for thoughtful people to accept the Christian message. They answer those questions and show that clear thinking is not in conflict with personal faith in Jesus Christ.

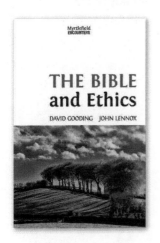

The Bible and Ethics

Why should we tell the truth or value a human life? Why should we not treat others in any way we like? Some say the Bible is the last place to find answers to such questions, but even its critics recognize the magnificence of Jesus' ethical teaching. To understand the ethics of Jesus we need to understand the values and beliefs on which they are based. Gooding and Lennox take us on a journey through the Bible and give us a concise survey of its leading events and people, ideas, poetry, moral values and ethics to bring into focus the ultimate significance of what Jesus taught about right and wrong.

Myrtlefield Expositions

Myrtlefield Expositions provide insights into the thought–flow and meaning of the biblical writings, motivated by devotion to the Lord who reveals himself in the Scriptures. Scholarly, engaging, and accessible, each book addresses the reader's mind and heart to increase faith in God and to encourage obedience to his Word. Teachers, preachers and all students of the Bible will find the approach to Scripture adopted in these volumes both instructive and enriching.

- The Riches of Divine Wisdom: *The New Testament's Use of the Old Testament*
- According to Luke: *The Third Gospel's Ordered Historical Narrative*
- True to the Faith: *The Acts of the Apostles: Defining and Defending the Gospel*
- In the School of Christ: *Lessons on Holiness in John 13–17*
- An Unshakeable Kingdom: *The Letter to the Hebrews for Today*

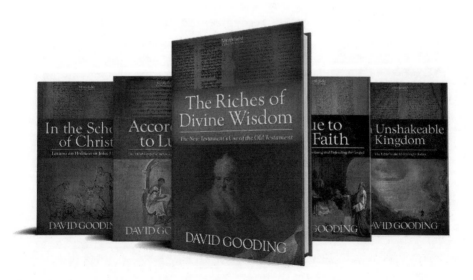

www.myrtlefieldhouse.com

Our website, www.myrtlefieldhouse.com, contains hundreds of resources in a variety of formats. You can read, listen or watch David Gooding's teaching on over 35 Bible books and 14 topics.

You can also view the full catalogue of Myrtlefield House publications and download e-book editions of the *Myrtlefield Expositions*, *Encounters* and *Discoveries* series.

The website is optimized for both computer and mobile viewing, making it easy for you to access the resources at home or on the go.

For more information about any of our publications or resources contact us at: info@myrtlefieldhouse.com

Clear, simple, fresh and highly practical—this David Gooding/John Lennox series is a goldmine for anyone who desires to live Socrates' 'examined life'.

Above all, the books are comprehensive and foundational, so they form an invaluable handbook for negotiating the crazy chaos of today's modern world.

Os Guinness, author of *Last Call for Liberty*

These six volumes, totalling almost 2000 pages, were written by two outstanding scholars who combine careers of research and teaching at the highest levels. David Gooding and John Lennox cover well the fields of Scripture, science, and philosophy, integrating them with one voice. The result is a set of texts that work systematically through a potpourri of major topics, like being human, discovering ultimate reality, knowing truth, ethically evaluating life's choices, answering our deepest questions, plus the problems of pain and suffering. To get all this wisdom together in this set was an enormous undertaking! Highly recommended!

Gary R. Habermas, Distinguished Research Professor & Chair, Dept. of Philosophy, Liberty University & Theological Seminary

David Gooding and John Lennox are exemplary guides to the deepest questions of life in this comprehensive series. It will equip thinking Christians with an intellectual roadmap to the fundamental conflict between Christianity and secular humanism. For thinking seekers it will be a provocation to consider which worldview makes best sense of our deepest convictions about life.

Justin Brierley, host of the *Unbelievable?* radio show and podcast

I would recommend these books to anyone searching to answer the big questions of life. Both Gooding and Lennox are premier scholars and faithful biblicists—a rare combination.

Alexander Strauch, author of *Biblical Eldership*